Battle at Ball's Bluff

by Kim Bernard Holien

©1985 by Kim Bernard Holien, Box 22485, Alexandria, VA 22304

All rights reserved under international and Pan-American Copyright Conventions. No part of this work may be used or reproduced in any manner whatsoever without written permission except in the case of brief quotations embodied in critical articles and reviews. Contact the author above or Publisher's Press, Inc., Drawer 631, Orange, VA 22960.

Originally designed by Moss Publications. Additional designs for revised edition by Nancy Dearing Rossbacher, Fit To Print Desktop Publishing Services.

First printing 1985, Moss Publications. Second printing 1989, Rapidan Press.
Revised third printing with addendum 1995, Publisher's Press, Inc.

LIBRARY OF CONGRESS CATALOGING-IN-PUBLICATION DATA

Holien, Kim Bernard.
    Battle at Ball's Bluff. — 3rd ed.
    Includes index.
1. United States—History—Civil War, 1861-1865—Pictorial works. I. Holien, Kim Bernard. II. Title.

85-061550

ISBN 0-943522-10-2

Publisher's Press, Inc.

*This book is dedicated to the memory of my father,
Lieutenant Colonel Maurice J. Holien, Sr., who taught me
the meaning of Duty, Honor, Country.*

Maurice J. Holien, Sr.
1914-1984

Introduction

In the field of Civil War historiography the Battle of Ball's Bluff and its political aftermath are somewhat of a mystery. Only two books have been published (note, not written) on the subject. The first was an 1880's cut-and-paste version of the hearings before the Joint Committee on the Conduct of the War. The second was a 1950's cut-and-paste version of the reports in the *Official Records of the War of the Rebellion*. (This second volume was published to prevent the U.S. Army from eliminating the small National Cemetery as an economy move during the 1950's. In that sense the book was successful.) In addition, regimental records were not preserved by all of the regiments that fought at Ball's Bluff. This is especially true of the Confederate units. Also, unlike most other Civil War sites there is no visitor's center or sign-marked battlefield tour route to aid the visitor in reconstructing the action of October 21, 1861.

It is imperative to understand the events surrounding the battle in order to judge the charge of treason leveled at General Stone. It should be noted that the hearings before the Joint Committee were held in secret. Therefore, the only primary source of information regarding these hearings was published by the U.S. Government in 1863.

In the interest of history, I have attempted to gather all relevant books, pamphlets, and articles concerning Ball's Bluff and the personalities involved. Information such as the 262 pages of testimony before the Joint Committee has been studied and summarized. In addition, I have spent countless hours tracing the footsteps of the Union and Confederate soldiers who fought the battle.

This then is the first comprehensive account and analysis of the campaign and its political consequences. From the events preceding the battle, to the action itself, to the sordid political aftermath the story can now, at long last, be told of the battle at Ball's Bluff.

Kim B. Holien
April, 1985

Acknowledgments

There are two gentlemen without whose assistance this book could not have been written. They are Mr. John Divine of Leesburg, Virginia and Mr. Josh Billings of Georgetown, Washington, DC.

John is the epitome of a Virginia gentleman and *the* Civil War authority on Loudoun County. There is not an old roadway or personality of the Civil War era in Loundoun County that John does not have intimate knowledge of. Many hours walking Ball's Bluff with John have given me invaluable insights into the epic struggle that took place there.

Mr. Eden E. "Josh" Billings of the District of Columbia/Alexandria Civil War Round Tables is also a true gentleman and *the* Civil War bibliographical expert in the country. His private library of books, pamphlets and clippings proved to be a treasure house of information.

In addition I would like to especially thank Mr. Ted Ballard of Manassas, Virginia, who turned my original maps into works of art; Mr Chuck Cooney of Falls Church, Virginia, who did outstanding research that was exceptionally helpful; Mr. R. Gary Evans of Jacksonville, Florida, who was of great assistance regarding his ancestor, General Shanks Evans; and Lieutenant Colonel Joe Whitehorne, United States Army, who shared his original discoveries on Ball's Bluff.

The help of the following individuals and organizations is deeply appreciated.

Alexandria (VA) Civil War Round Table
Mr. Bob Armstrong, Alexandria, Virginia
Mr. Walter Ball, Chevy Chase, Maryland
Mr. Gary Baker, Columbia, South Carolina
Mr. Christopher Bliss, Heber Springs, Arkansas
C&O Canal, Great Falls Visitor Center Staff
Mr. Robert Campbell, Beverly, Massachusetts
Mr. Tom Clemons, Smithsburg, Maryland
Mr. Jim Clifford, Ft. Myers, Florida
Mr. Robert Corrette, Fitzwilliams, New Hampshire
   Council on America's Military Past
Mr. Howard Crouch, Falls Church, Virginia
Mr. Jim Davidson, Yorktown, Virginia
Mr. Henry Deeks, Cambridge, Massachusetts
District of Columbia Civil War Round Table
Mr. Tom Evans, Vienna, Virginia
Fort Ward Museum Staff, Alexandria, Virginia
Mr. Mickey Gall, Annandale, Virginia
Dr. Martin Gordon, Columbia, Maryland
Hagerstown (MD) Civil War Round Table
Mr. Dick Hammond, Herndon, Virginia
Mr. Hugh Harmon, Economic Development Office,
   Loudoun County, Virginia
Harpers Ferry Civil War Round Table
Mr. Doug Harvey, Curator, Manassas Museum,
   Manassas, Virginia
Jonathan Heller, National Archives, Washington, DC
Mr. John Hennessy, Manassas National Battlefield Park
Mr. Chris Ivy, Annandale, Virginia
Mr. Charles Jacobs, Montgomery County Civil War Round Table
Mr. V.C. "Pat" Jones, Centreville, Virginia
Mr. G.L. Kackley, Oak Hill Cemetery,
   Georgetown, Washington, DC
Mrs. Jeanne Klitgaard, Loudoun County, Virginia
Mr. Lewis Leigh, Mt. Gilead, Centreville, Virginia
Dr. Francis A. Lord, Columbia, South Carolina

Loudoun County Museum, Inc., Leesburg, Virginia
Mr. Blake Magner, Westmont, New Jersey
Manassas National Battlefield Park Staff
Mr. George McNamara, Philadelphia, Pennsylvania,
   Military Images Magazine
Montgomery County Historical Society
Mr. Rick Murdock, Bluemont, Virginia
Mr. Dick Murry, Fairfax, Virginia
Mr. Jim Musser, 35th Virginia Cavalry (reactivated)
Mr. Weldon Nash, Dallas, Texas
Dr. Peter Nicholas, Westminster, Maryland
North South Trader's Civil War Magazine
Northern Virginia Relic Hunters Association
Mr. Jerome Orton, Sons of Union Veterans, Candor, New York
Mr. Chip Paciulli, Fairfax, Virginia
Mr. Robert Pierce, West Newton, Massachusetts
Mr. William Prince, East Lansing, Michigan
Mr. Brian Pohanka, Alexandria, Virginia
Mrs. Jasper Richard, Lovettsville, Virginia
Ms. Nancy Dearing Rossbacher, Orange, Virginia
Mr. Richard Sauers, Pennsylvania Flag Preservation Office,
   Smithsonian Institution (Associates Program)
Mr. Dale Snair, Virginia State Library, Richmond, Virginia
Sons of the American Revolution, Fairfax Resolves Chapter
Mr. Kurt Stein, Springfield, Pennsylvania
Theme Prints, Ltd., Bayside, New York
Chuck and Kathy Thompson, Manassas, Virginia
Mr. Dean Thomas, Arendtsville, Pennsylvania
Mr. Richard Thompson, Gainesville, Virginia
Mr. Lloyd Wagner, Hood College, Frederick, Maryland
Mr. Fred Weaver, Ellicott City, Maryland
Mrs. Sandra Webb, Veterans Administration, Washington, DC
Mr. James Wexler, State Historical Society of Wisconsin,
   Madison, Wisconsin
Mike Winey

Mistakes made are the fault of the author alone and not of any of the good people or fine organizations listed above. The views expressed are also those of the author alone and do not represent the Center of Military History, Department of the Army or the Department of Defense.

Table of Contents

I	*First Soldier of the Republic*	6
II	*A Slight Demonstration*	18
III	*The Battle for the Bluff*	42
IV	*Panic on the Heights*	72
V	*Congressional Investigation*	90
VI	*Imprisonment and Release*	104
VII	*Captains and Kings Depart*	122

Postwar

Regiments Meet Again	136
Battlefield Chronicle	138
Tour Guide	146

Endnotes

Bibliography	154
Footnotes	159
Index	165

Addendum

I	Changes and Additions at the Battlefield	171
II	Pictorial Supplement	176

I

First Soldier of the Republic

The origin of the battle of Ball's Bluff begins on the plains of Manassas, Virginia, on 21 July 1861, with the defeat and stampede of the Union Army. A green Union Army of 36,000 men, under General Irvin McDowell, was turned into a rabble seeking safety in Washington City and on the banks of the Potomac River.[1] Upon the defeat of the Union Army, a telegram had been sent, from the Adjutant General in Washington, to General George Brinton McClellan in the hills of western Virginia. It read as follows: "Circumstances make your presence here necessary. Charge General Rosecrans or some other officer with your command and come hither without delay."[2]

As General McClellan stated in his memoirs, the situation was truly a desperate one.

"All was chaos, and the streets, hotels, and barrooms were filled with drunken officers and men absent from their regiments without leave—a perfect pandemonium."[3]

He continued:

> The condition of things on the Virginia side was not much better than on the other. The troops were on the river banks or on the high ground immediately overlooking them. Few were in a condition to fight and but little had been done in the way of entrenching the approaches.[4]

The condition of affairs which thus presented itself to me upon assuming command was one of extreme difficulty and fraught with great danger. The defeated army of McDowell could not properly be called an army—it was only a collection of undisciplined, ill-officered and uninstructed men, who were, as a rule, much demoralized by defeat and ready to run at the first shot. Positions from which the city could be commanded by the enemy's guns were open for their occupation. The period of service of many regiments had expired or would do so in a few days. There was so little discipline that officers and men left their camps at their own will, and, as I have already stated, the city was full of drunken men in uniform. The Executive was demoralized; and attack by the enemy was expected from hour to hour; material of war did not exist in anything like sufficient quantities; and lastly, I was not supreme and unhampered but often thwarted by the lieutenant general.[5]

The rest of the newly forming Army of the Potomac consisted of raw regiments raised by the northern states and sent to Washington. These green troops, along with the defeated regiments which had re-enlisted for the duration of the war, were first brigaded together, by General McClellan, for the purpose of training both the officers and men as to their duties. The men had to learn how to be soldiers, and the line officers had to learn how to command men.

In addition, the newly promoted general officers and staff officers had to adjust to no longer commanding small detachments of regulars but large bodies of green recruits. To this end, General McClellan established an army with twelve brigades on 4 August 1861.[6] One of these brigades was given to Brigadier General Charles P. Stone to command.[7]

Charles Pomeroy Stone came from an old Puritan family of Massachusetts.[8] Born in 1824, he entered the United States Military Academy in 1841 graduating in the class of 1845.[9] During the Mexican War of 1846-48 he participated as an officer in General Scott's army in its victorious campaign from Vera Cruz to Mexico City. His battle credits include the seige of Vera Cruz, the battles of Contreras, Molino del Ray, and Chapultapec, and the assault and capture of Mexico City. He was twice brevetted

Crowds gather in front of the unfinished Capitol building awaiting Lincoln's first inauguration on March 4, 1861. Colonel Stone was responsible for the President's security. Photo, National Archives.

"for gallant meritorious conduct" in the battles of Molino del Ray and Chapultapec. Following his excellent service in the Mexican War, Charles Stone continued his army career at a variety of state side posts and a fact-finding trip to Europe. He resigned his commission in November of 1856.[10] He then was employed by the Mexican government in surveying their province of Sonora.[11]

As the storm clouds of civil war gathered force in late 1860, with the election of Lincoln and secession of South Carolina, Charles P. Stone found himself once again in the uniform of the United States Army. He was recalled to active duty in December of 1860 by his old commander Lieutenant General Winfield Scott.[12] Charles Pomeroy Stone thus became the first citizen of the United States called to active duty to face the threat of civil war.[13]

Upon assuming command of the defense of the District of Columbia, Colonel Stone found himself confronted with many ardent secessionist sympathizers in the District of Columbia militia.[14] Stone disarmed these men, expelled them from the D. C. militia, and thus prevented a military "fifth column" from further developing within the D. C. militia system and Washington, D. C. itself.[15] He next set about planning the various defenses for the Federal Capital, reporting his procedures every morning and every evening with Lieutenant General Scott.[16] By early February, Colonel Stone could

Button worn by the National Rifles, a militia unit that hailed from Washington, D. C. In April, 1861, Colonel Stone federalized the District militia and expelled those members with secessionist sympathies. Found on the Bull Run battlefield by Joe Grey of Manassas, Va.
Demoralized Yankees, below, retreat from disaster at Bull Run in this famous sketch by Rufus Zogbaum.
Courtesy Battles and Leaders.

report that he had equipped, uniformed and trained 925 District militia to defend the Federal Capital.[17]

In addition to defending the Federal Capital, Colonel Stone had the additional important duty of making certain that President-elect Lincoln arrived safely in Washington, D. C. in late February for his inauguration in early March.[18] Because of this responsibility Colonel Stone became deeply involved in preventing the potential assassination of Lincoln in his passage through Baltimore to Washington, D. C. Due to the efforts of Colonel Stone, and other government officials and various civilians, Abraham Lincoln arrived safely in Washington.[19] However Lincoln never knew of Stone's efforts to stop the Baltimore assassination plot!

General Winfield Scott, commander of the Union forces at the war's outset. Scott selected Colonel Stone to protect Lincoln and the nation's capital. Photo, National Archives.
Below: Washington, D. C. as it appeared from the signal station on Georgetown heights. Courtesy Battles and Leaders.

Abraham Lincoln stands with one of his generals and detective Pinkerton during a visit to the Union Army. Lincoln was anxious for the security of Washington until reenforcements arrived in May, 1861. Photos, National Archives.

Following Lincoln's arrival in Washington, D. C., Colonel Stone found himself continuously busy in preparations for the security of Lincoln's inauguration on 4 March 1861.[20] Stone reported his preparations and activities during that period as follows:

> On the afternoon of the 3d of March, General Scott held a conference at his headquarters, there being present his staff, General Sumner, and myself, and then was arranged the programme of the procession. President Buchanan was to drive to Willard's hotel, and call upon the President-elect. The two were to ride in the same carriage, between double files of a squadron of the District of Columbia cavalry. The company of sappers and miners were to march in front of the presidential carriage, and the infantry and riflemen of the District of Columbia were to follow it. Riflemen in squads were to be placed on the roofs of certain commanding houses which I had selected, along Pennsylvania Avenue, with orders to watch the windows on the opposite side and to fire upon them in case any attempt should be made to fire from those windows on the presidential carriage. The small force of regular cavalry which had arrived was to guard the side-street crossings of Pennsylvania Avenue, and to move from one to another during the passage of the procession. A battalion of District of Columbia troops were to be placed near the steps of the Capitol, and riflemen in the windows of the wings of the Capitol. On the arrival of the presidential party at the Capitol, the troops were to be stationed so as to return in the same order after the ceremony.

During the night of the 3d of March, notice was brought me that an attempt would be made to blow up the platform on which the President would stand to take the oath of office. I immediately placed men under the steps, and at daybreak a trusted battalion of District troops formed in a semicircle at the foot of the great stairway, and prevented all entrance from without. When the crowd began to assemble in front of the portico, a large number of policemen in plain clothes were scattered through the mass to observe closely, to place themselves near any person who might act suspiciously, and to strike down any hand which might raise a weapon.

At the appointed hour, Mr. Buchanan was escorted to Willard's hotel, which he entered. There I found a number of mounted "marshals of the day," and posted them around the carriage, within the cavalry guard. The two Presidents were saluted by the troops as they came out of the hotel and took

Charles Pomeroy Stone, West Point graduate, Mexican War hero, and defender of Washington during the critical months between December, 1860 and May, 1861. Photo, National Archives.

Fort Washington on the Maryland shore of the Potomac River several miles below Washington. Colonel Stone closed the river to small maritime traffic to prevent information from passing to the Virginia secessionists. Photo, National Archives.

A telegraph operator sends a message out over the wires; the fastest means of communication in 1861. In one of his first wartime decisions, Colonel Stone seized control of the telegraph office in downtown Washington, D. C. Photo, National Archives.
Below: Union troops under Colonel Stone advance into Alexandria, Va. on May 24, 1861. Photo, National Archives.

Chain Bridge across the Potomac River connecting Washington with Virginia. Photo, National Archives.

their places in the carriage. The procession started. During the march to the Capitol I rode near the carriage, and by an apparently clumsy use of my spurs managed to keep the horses of the cavalry in an uneasy state, so that it would have been very difficult for even a good marksman to get an aim at one of the inmates of the carriage between the prancing horses.[21]

Even after Lincoln's inauguration the dangers for the safety of the Capitol of the Union continued. Events of the Border states continued to undermine the power of the Federal Government in Washington.[22] Because of these events, the open expression of secessionist sympathizers in Washington, and the potential for an open rebellion in the city that continued to exist,[23] Colonel Stone finally received permission to Federalize the militia of the District of Columbia on 10 April.[24] Following this action Colonel Stone seized the flour at the Georgetown Wharves (in order that Washington would have food to eat), seized the river vessels plying between Washington and Virginia (to prevent secessionist sympathizers from traveling in and out of Washington), took control of the telegraph office on Pennsylvania Avenue (to prevent the newspapermen from sending military information to their newspapers in New York City which would be read by secessionists), and seized control of the Baltimore and Ohio Railroad terminal and engines in Washington (thus keeping open to Washington the lifelines for supplies and reinforcements).[25]

The desperation felt in Washington in late April of 1861 is best described by Margaret Leech in her Pulitzer Prize history of Washington during the Civil War:

The motif on this patriotic envelope depicts the untimely death of Colonel Ellsworth moments after removing a Rebel flag from the roof of Alexandria's Marshall Hotel. Courtesy Doug Bast.

The President's placid manner concealed the strain he suffered. His nerves played tricks on him, as the suspense was prolonged almost beyond endurance. One day he heard a sound like the boom of cannon. None of the White House attendants had noticed anything, and Mr. Lincoln walked out to see for himself. He walked on and on to the south, until at last he stood before the Arsenal. The gunfire had been a phantom sound, but the open doors of the Arsenal were real. Mr. Lincoln saw that there were no guards on duty. Anyone could have helped himself to the arms.

The same trancelike mood which had sent the President wandering the whole desolate length of the Island was expressed in the words he spoke to some of the wounded of the Sixth Massachusetts, who came with their officers to visit him on Wednesday. "I don't believe there is any North. The

Colonel Ellsworth's bloodstained uniform and the shotgun used to kill him were displayed in the North. Courtesy National Archives.

The first city in Virginia occupied by the Federal authorities was Alexandria, above. This wartime image looks east over a military encampment and down King Street toward the Potomac River. Photo, National Archives.

Members of the elite 7th New York Regiment in their Washington camp during the early days of the war. These soldiers were hailed as the saviors of the capital city when they first arrived in April, 1861. Photo, National Archives.

Zouaves of the 4th Michigan Regt. in camp near Washington, D. C. Photo, National Archives. The Potomac River above Washington has numerous crossing sites which required a sizeable garrison to protect. Stone was given this responsibility in August, 1861, when appointed general in charge of a division under the new Federal commander, George B. McClellan. Photo M. O'Donnell.

Seventh Regiment is a myth. Rhode Island is not known in our geography any longer. You are the only Northern realities." There was an unusual irony, too, in Mr. Lincoln's tone. Since midnight on Saturday, reinforcements had been only forty miles from Washington.

Next day, the spell was broken. The sight of a train, filled and covered with soldiers, set the militia at the depot cheering. At the Capitol, the Sixth Massachusetts raised a shout. Crowds came running, and housetops, windows and balconies swarmed with people. Reviving at the sight of its deliverers, the Federal City warmed its chill faith at the fires of the North. For six days at the very outset of hostilities, it had shivered at its fate—a border town, divided within itself, and nakedly exposed to danger in a time of great rebellion.

The deliverance of Washinton was effected in style. It was relieved by the Seventh New York, the kid-glove militia corps of the North.[26]

In looking back upon his service in the capital of the Union since December of 1860, Colonel Stone could be well pleased with his efforts. Because of his tireless work, Washington, D. C. remained the capital of the Union.

The new Lincoln Administration recognized Colonel Stone's efforts by placing him in command of the Federal advance into Virginia and subsequent capture of Alexandria on 24 May 1861.[27] Stone next assumed command of the Rockville Expedition leading a Union column from Washington through Rockville to skirmishes on the Potomac River at Edwards Ferry, Conrads Ferry, and Harpers Ferry.[28] During the Bull Run campaign Stone was given command of the 1st Brigade of General Patterson's command in the Shenandoah Valley.[29] In early August Stone found himself posted to duty, as a Brigade Commander, with the newly christened Army of the Potomac.[30] On 6 August, Colonel Stone was promoted to the rank of Brigadier General, United States Volunteers.[31]

Pickets of Gen. Stone's Corps of Observation keep a wary eye on their Rebel counterparts across the river in Virginia. From Harper's Weekly, *Nov. 2, 1861.*

II

A Slight Demonstration

Upon receiving his commission as Brigadier General of Volunteers, Stone proceeded to move his headquarters to Poolesville, Maryland.[1] His new brigade command consisted of the 34th New York Volunteer Infantry Regiment, the 42nd (Tammany) New York Volunteer Infantry Regiment, the 2nd New York State Militia (later redesignated the 82nd New York Volunteer Infantry Regiment) and the 1st Minnesota Volunteer Infantry Regiment.[2] A member of the 1st Minnesota wrote of his regiment's move from picket duty on the Potomac to Poolesville as follows:

> Scarcely had we become familiar with the scenery and associations around Seneca Falls before we were again ordered to move. On the 13th the Red Wing, Hastings, and Wabasha companies proceeded to Edward's Ferry and two days later the remaining companies followed them. Our march this time led by Seneca Mills up a steep hill and thence through a fine wooded country bordered on both sides with waving fields of corn and rich orchards while elegant dwellings dot the landscape. In some places, where orchards lined the sides of the narrow road, the branches (drooping under the heavy load of apples and peaches) formed natural arches of foliage and fruit. About noon we passed through Poolesville, a little village of about 150 inhabitants. Here Ricketts' Battery was reorganized after the late battle (Bull Run).[3]

Naming their new camp in honor of their brigade commander the 1st Minnesota settled into a life consisting primarily of picket duty along the Potomac and drill duty in camp. Their regimental history records this period of duty as follows:

> Here we performed picket duty along the Potomac, for some distance on each side of Edward's Ferry, and resumed drilling actively. Clothing was issued; pay-day came again; the sutler appeared with a heavy stock of supplies; the men built cook houses and ovens; and, by drawing flour at times, instead of hardtack, and purchasing meal at a neighboring mill, soon very much improved their fare; and being well fed, well cared for and well exercised, became more efficient and contented than ever before.[4]

During the months of September and October two more brigades joined Stone at Poolesville. These were the brigades of Colonel Edward Baker and Brigadier General Frederick Lander.[5] Baker's brigade consisted of the 1st, 2nd, 3rd and 4th California Regiments (later redesignated as the 71st, 69th, 72nd and 106th Pennsylvania Volunteer Infantry Regiments and known as the Philadelphia Brigade).[6] Lander's brigade consisted of the 7th Michigan Volunteer Infantry Regiment, the 19th and 20th Massachusetts Volunteer Infantry Regiments and Andrew's Company of Massachusetts Sharpshooters.[7]

With the arrival of these two additional brigades, General Stone found himself in command of a division in the Army of the Potomac. He proceeded to name his new command "The Corps of Observation."[8] The stretch of the Potomac River that General Stone was responsible for ran from Noland's Ferry upriver to Edward's Ferry just below Leesburg.[9] In addition to his three brigades of infantry, General Stone's artillery consisted of Kirby's Battery "I" - 1st United States Artillery, Vaughn's Battery "B" - 1st Rhode Island Artillery and Bunting's 6th New York State Militia Independent Battery. Stone's cavalry was the Van Alen Cavalry (3rd New York Cavalry Regiment) under the command of Colonel Van Alen.[10]

Having become a divisional commander, General Stone turned his brigade over to Brigadier

General Charles Stone, right, the luckless Federal commander who became a scapegoat for the debacle at Ball's Bluff. Photo, National Archives.

Below: General George McClellan and staff. McClellan had initiated the movement toward Leesburg which culminated in the action at Ball's Bluff. Photo, National Archives.

Harper's Weekly *printed this illustration in their August 31, 1861 edition of Mississippi troops in camp practicing with their Bowie knives. Overlaid is a Mississippi C (cavalry) tunic button excavated from a position occupied by the 17th and 18th Mississippi near Fort Evans. Courtesy Chuck Thompson.*

General Willis A. Gorman,[11] formerly colonel of the 1st Minnesota Regiment.[12] With regards to Colonel Baker's low rank in comparison to that of Lander and Gorman, it should be noted that Baker had earlier been offered a Brigadier General commission but had to turn it down. As a sitting member of the United States Senate he was forbidden by law to hold a rank higher than that of colonel. At the time of the Battle of Ball's Bluff he had been offered a commission as Major General—a position he neither accepted nor rejected.[13]

On October 15th General McClellan formally reorganized the Army of the Potomac from a brigade structured force into that of an army consisting of divisions, one of which, as previously noted, came under the command of General Charles P. Stone.[14] While General McClellan was busy making a modern army out of the rabble and new recruits that he had inherited in July, the Washington politicians were once again demanding an 'On to Richmond' drive by the Army of the Potomac.[15] Because of this tremendous political pressure—primarily by the Radical Republicans—McClellan searched for a locale in Virginia which he could advance against. His route down the Potomac was effectively blocked by the Confederate river batteries on the Virginia shoreline.[16] To advance once again overland toward Manassas Junction would mean attacking the heavy Confederate fortification system that had been erected at Centreville.[17] This left McClellan with one option—a movement on the upper Potomac with the potential for the capture of Leesburg, Virginia. There the Confederates had posted a small, isolated brigade to guard the crossroads town of Leesburg and the vital Potomac River crossings in the vicinity. In addition, Leesburg was the terminus of the Loudoun and Hampshire Railroad running from Alexandria to Leesburg.[18]

This lone Confederate brigade consisted of the 8th Virginia Volunteer Infantry Regiment, the 13th, 17th, 18th Mississippi Volunteer Infantry Regiments, a battery of the famous Richmond Howitzer artillery and a few troops of Virginia Cavalry.[19] This brigade was commanded by Colonel Nathan B. Evans of Bull Run fame. Evans was an astute combat veteran of the Indian Campaigns and the first great land battle of the war fought at Bull Run.[20]

A set of conditions now developed which seemed to be exactly what General McClellan needed to enable him to make an advance into the Virginia countryside. On October 18[21] Confederate General Joseph E. Johnston pulled his advanced outposts in northern Virginia back to the main Confederate positions at Centreville/Manassas Junction.[22] This caused McClellan on October 19 to advance McCall's Division of Pennsylvania Reserves along the Georgetown Pike toward its interdiction with the Alexandria-Leesburg Turnpike at a little village known as Dranesville. General George Gordon Meade, then a brigade commander under McCall, reported the movement of McCall's Division to his wife as follows:

Camp Pierpont, Va., October 18, 1861.

I had just seated myself to write you a nice long letter, when orders came to march tomorrow, requiring me to stir about and give the requisite directions. The enemy, it is understood, have fallen back to their old lines at Bull Run. They have had a force above us at Leesburg, which it is believed they are withdrawing. The object of our expedition is to advance some twelve or fifteen miles to the front, to reconnoiter the country, and also with the hope of cutting off some of their troops coming down from Leesburg. We go with the whole division, some twelve thousand strong, with three batteries of artillery, and if we encounter any of their troops, will have a very pretty chance for a nice little fight of our own. It is very late, and I have to be in the saddle very early. I am quite well.

Camp Pierpont, Va., October 21, 1861 - 9 p.m.

We returned this evening from our expedition, which, so far as my brigade was concerned, was very peaceful. The First Brigade, under Reynolds advanced some fifteen miles, and encountered the enemy's pickets, one of whom was killed; nobody hurt on our side. I advanced some ten miles and saw nothing of them. We remained out three days, getting an accurate knowledge of the country, and then returned to this camp. No sooner are we back than orders come to be ready at a moment's notice to go again, and all is now excitement and bustle, though it is night-time. I do not know the meaning, except that something is being done on some other part of the line and we are wanted to support the movement.[23]

Rows of tents mark a Federal campsite during the winter of 1861-1862. By this time relations between McClellan and the political leaders were severely strained. Photo, National Archives.

Personalized stationery of Colonel Harvey of McCall's Division, above. Author's collection.
General McCall, right, whose march down Leesburg Turnpike on October 19 preceded General Stone's crossing at Edward's Ferry and Ball's Bluff. Photo, National Archives.

McCall's advance forced the Confederate brigade at Leesburg to retreat south and abandon the town. This caused General Banks to send the following telegram to General McClellan:

> Darnestown, Oct. 20, 1861
> Gen. Marcy,
> Sir,
>   The signal station at Sugar Loaf telegraphs that the enemy have moved away from Leesburg. All quiet here.
>   R. M. Copeland, A.A.G.[24]

These three separate but interrelated actions—Johnston's retirement of his advance posts, McCall's advance to Dranesville, and Banks' telegram to McClellan—now led McClellan to send the following telegram to General Stone at Poolesville thus setting in motion the chain of events leading to the Battle of Ball's Bluff.

> Camp Griffin, Oct. 20, 1861
> Brig.-Gen. C. P. Stone,
> Poolesville,
>   Gen. McClellan desires me to inform you that Gen. McCall occupied Dranesville yesterday and is still there. Will send out heavy reconnaissances today in all directions from that point. The general desires that you keep a good lookout upon Leesburg, to see if this movement has the effect to drive them away. Perhaps a slight demonstration on your part would have the effect to move them.
>   A. V. Colburn,
>   Ass't.-Adj't. Gen.[25]

Upon receipt of McClellan's telegram, General Stone put into motion a plan of action which he had been developing for quite some time. As Stone understood the present situation, McCall was advancing westward along the Leesburg-Alexandria Turnpike toward Evans's brigade at Leesburg. This movement had already caused Evans to send his heavy baggage and sick to the rear at Centreville/Manassas Junction as reported to Stone via McClellan's telegram. In addition to having caused Evans to make the above movement, Stone felt that McCall's advancing column of twelve thousand infantry would hold Evans' attention while Stone crossed the Potomac River.

How did Stone intend to make such a dangerous military movement and insure his command's success? First, in direct conjunction with McCall's movement, Stone intended to feint with Gorman's Brigade at Edward's Ferry. This should cause Evans to feel threatened on his eastern front by McCall's movement and on his northern front by Gorman's movement. If these two movements by McCall and Gorman did not make Evans retreat they would at least hold him in check while Stone delivered the *coup de grace* via a flanking movement further upriver enabling him to roll-up Evans' lightly held left flank. This would in turn force Evans to give battle under strongly disadvantageous factors, be captured with his entire command and/or hastily retreat to the Centreville/Manassas Junction area thus abandoning Leesburg. By capturing Leesburg the Union forces would have, in a strategic sense, flanked the Confederate position at Centreville/Manassas Junction. This would place additional pressure on General Johnston to retreat farther back to the Rappahannock River (a

Above: U.S. army cartridge box plate, a relic of the battle, found on the route of McCall's advance. Courtesy Chuck Thompson.
Below: present view of the Dranesville Tavern where McCall halted his division on October 20, 1861. Photo, Mike O'Donnell.

movement Johnston would make in March of 1862 because of Union pressure, real or imagined).[26] The capture of Leesburg and potential Confederate evacuation of the Centreville/Manassas Junction area would be such a significant Union victory as to greatly reduce the intense political pressure for another 'On to Richmond' drive which McClellan found himself under in Washington.

For weeks prior to the battle of Ball's Bluff General Stone had been developing plans for a river crossing at the northern end of Harrison's Island. He had personally scouted the crossing site at Smart's Mill Ford and found that soldiers could ford there without the aid of boats or horses. In addition, he had staked-out artillery covering fire locations on the Virginia shoreline at Smart's Mill Ford enabling him to cross his infantry and maintain an enclave in Virginia under the protective fire of Union artillery on the Maryland shoreline. From that enclave at Smart's Mill Ford he could safely advance or retire his flanking column under the protection of his artillery.[27]

In accordance with his desire to cross the Potomac River, General Stone discussed with his subordinate commanders the feasibility of constructing a bridge across the river to facilitate the rapid movement of men and supplies. However this idea was dropped because of the loss of surprise such an endeavor would cause.[28]

Realizing that a feint at Edward's Ferry and a flanking column at Smart's Mill Ford would leave a substantial gap between his forces, General Stone decided to cover this gap via a scouting party to cross at Ball's Bluff. This location, opposite the western side of Harrison's Island on the Virginia shoreline, presented a number of advantages for such a mission. Ball's Bluff could only be reached by boat from Harrison's Island and because of the tremendous difficulties involved in moving soldiers, supplies, and artillery up the bluff, the Confederates had not stationed a regular picket post there. Instead, a company of Mississippi infantry were positioned upriver at Smart's Mill Ford, a logical and militarily feasible crossing site. General Stone knew this because he had been sending scouting missions across the Potomac River at Ball's Bluff for quite some time before the battle. These scouting missions had shown General Stone that the bluff was not regularly picketed, that it provided a path through the woods to a ridge overlooking Leesburg and its main north-south road, and that it would serve as a left (i.e. southern) flank guard for the Union flanking column crossing just 3/8 of a mile upriver at Smart's Mill Ford.[29] In conjunction with these scouting missions, for weeks prior to the battle General Stone had been stationing infantry units on Harrison's Island during the day and withdrawing them at night. This movement of soldiers back and forth provided a launching force for the scouting missions and a back-up force if they ran into any trouble. In addition by withdrawing these forces (which could be clearly seen by the Confederates from the Virginia shoreline) at the end of each day, General Stone left the distinct but false impression with the Confederates that no Union forces were moving into Virginia from Harrison's Island via Ball's Bluff.[30]

In combination with General McCall's movement at Dranesville, General Stone ordered a demonstration to be made in the early afternoon of 20 October at Edward's Ferry.[31] It was hoped that this Union troop movement, made at the request of General McClellan, would assist General McCall in scaring the Confederates out of Leesburg.[32] If it did not accomplish that it was to at least hold the Confederates' attention while the Union flanking column crossed at Smart's Mill Ford and the Union scouting party crossed at Ball's Bluff.[33] General Stone described his feint and crossing at Edward's Ferry in his official report as follows:

> I ordered General Gorman to display his forces in view of the enemy which was done without inducing any movement on their part and then ordered three flat-boats to be passed from the canal into the river, at the same time throwing shells and spherical case shot into and beyond the wood where the enemy were concealed and into all cover from which fire could be opened on boats crossing the river, to produce an impression that a crossing was to be made.
>
> The launching of the boats and shelling at Edward's Ferry caused the rapid retiring of the force which had been seen there, and I caused the embarkation of three boat loads of 35 men each from the First Minnesota Volunteers, who, under cover of the shelling, crossed and recrossed the river, the boats consuming in the passage four minutes, six minutes, and seven minutes, respectively. The spirit displayed by officers and men at the thought of passing the river was most cheering, and satisfied me they could be depended on for most gallant service whenever something more than a demonstration might be required of them.
>
> As darkness came on I ordered Gorman's brigade and the Seventh Michigan Volunteers back

MAP, opposite: the route of Captain Philbrick's scouting mission between 8 and 10 p.m. on October 20, 1861.

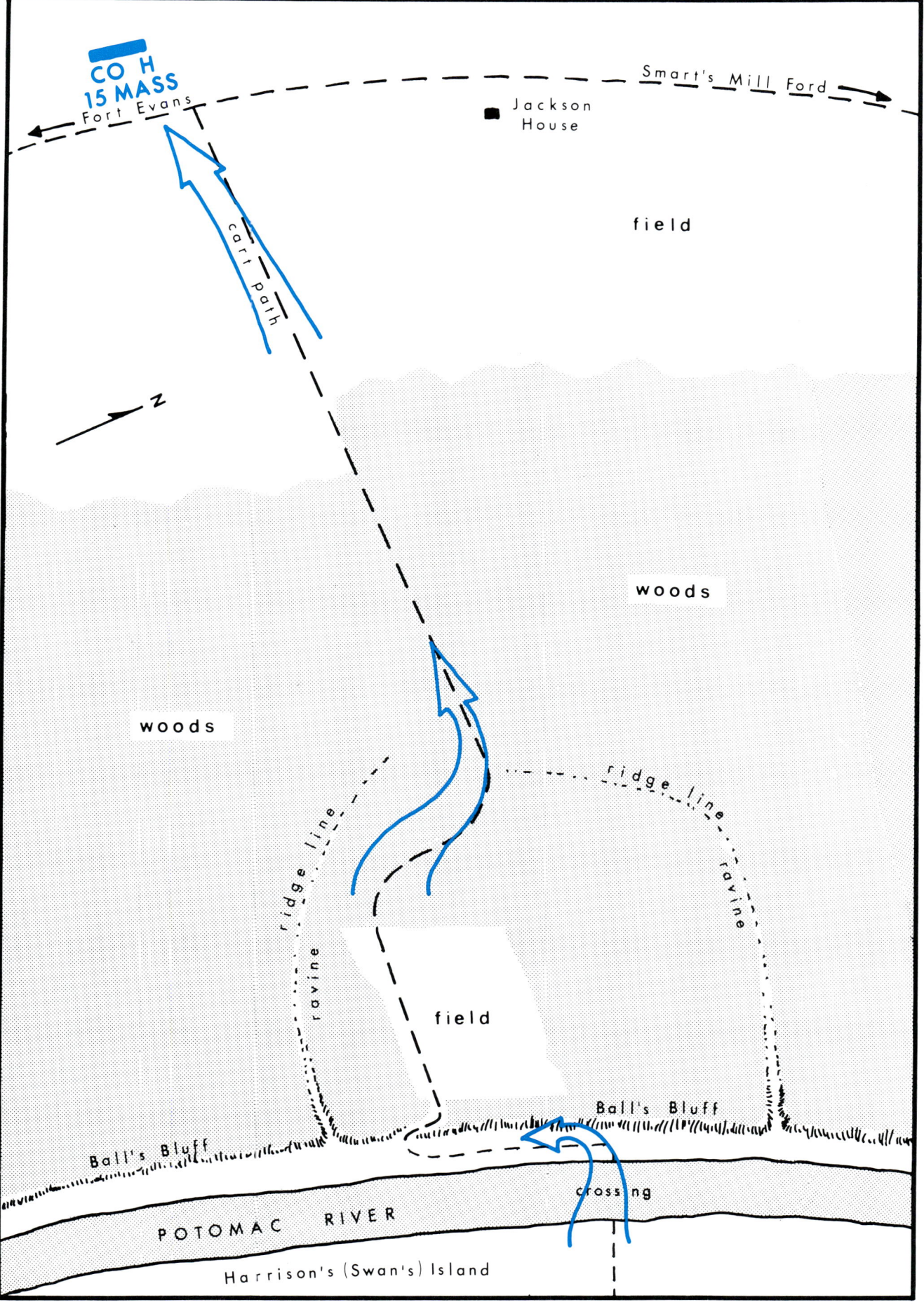

to their respective camps, but retained the Tammany Regiment, the companies of the Fifteenth Massachusetts Volunteers, and the artillery near Conrad's Ferry in their positions, awaiting the result of Captain Philbrick's scout, remaining with my staff at Edward's Ferry.[34]

At the same time General Stone was conducting his feint at Edward's Ferry he started his scouting party into Virginia, via Ball's Bluff, in preparation for his flanking column's movement at Smart's Mill Ford the next morning.[35] This scouting party consisted of twenty picked men of Company H, 15th Massachusetts Volunteer Infantry Regiment, under Captain Chase Philbrick. It proceeded to cross from Harrison's Island into Virginia via Ball's Bluff around midnight on the night of 20 October. Captain Philbrick advanced approximately one mile inland along the cart path to the edge of the woods which swept back to the river. From the edge of the woods along the brow of the ridgeline that geologically formed Ball's Bluff, Philbrick looked onto what he thought was a small Confederate encampment without any sentries. He reported this Confederate camp and the fact that he had discovered it without being detected to General Stone via Lieutenant Church Howe, Adjutant of the 15th Massachusetts. Unfortunately this major Union tactical mistake gave General Stone the false im-

Above: an artist's rendition of Captain Philbrick's night reconnaissance across the Potomac. From Harper's Weekly, *October 26, 1861.*
Below: Captain Chase Philbrick who led the scouting party of twenty men from Co. H, 15th Massachusetts on the night of October 20, 1861. One-half mile inland his patrol spied a field of "Confederate tents" which turned out to be haystacks. Courtesy U.S.A. Military History Institute.

pression that his reconnaissance party had successfully completed its mission, that the Confederates had only a small force north of Leesburg and that this force was slovenly with regard to their alertness and security. In actuality what Captain Philbrick had seen were rows of hay gathered together in the valley below the ridgeline. When seen in the moonlight with the fog that gathers in low areas during the evening hours it was a natural mistake to be made by a green officer on his first combat patrol and a night one at that.[37]

In addition to the tactical mistake made by Captain Philbrick another (also unknown to General Stone) disaster had occurred to Union forces earlier in the day. This incident happened around mid-day on 20 October along the Leesburg-Alexandria Turnpike. The Confederates had captured a Union courier bearing dispatches from General McCall to General Meade. These dispatches informed Colonel Evans as to the purpose, movement and position of McCall's division at Dranesville.[38] Thus when the feint came at Edward's Ferry and the battle developed at Ball's Bluff, Colonel Evans was able to strip his defenses at the Burnt Bridge crossing of the Leesburg-Alexandria Turnpike and move them to the actual points of danger at Edward's Ferry and Ball's Bluff.[39]

Upon receipt of Captain Philbrick's report, General Stone ordered Colonel Charles Devens (Commander of the 15th Massachusetts Infantry Regiment) to proceed from his position on Harrison's Island into Virginia via the cart path taken by Captain Philbrick and destroy the Confederate encampment. Thus, in the early morning hours of 21 October, Colonel Devens began to cross at Ball's Bluff with four of his companies (approximately 300 men) and move to the attack.[40]

As Colonel Devens moved inland he was followed by Colonel William Lee (Commander of the 20 Massachusetts Infantry Regiment) with two of his companies totaling 102 men. These two companies formed a covering/blocking force on either side of the cart path where it departed the cleared field atop Ball's Bluff and descended to the Potomac River.[41]

When Colonel Devens reached Captain Philbrick's reconnaissance position he realized the mistake that had been made by Philbrick. However, since he did not see any Confederates, Devens proceeded with a small scouting party along the wooded ridgeline toward the south. At 6:30 a.m. he

The field today where Philbrick's phantom Rebel legions were encamped. The position is approximately the same as that from which Philbrick made his observation. Photo, Mike O'Donnell.

Conrad's Ferry, site of Baker's crossing from Maryland to Harrison's Island. From Frank Leslie's Illustrated Newspaper, Nov. 16, 1861.
Lt. Col. George Ward, below, deputy commander of the 15th Mass. Ward's crossing at Ball's Bluff instead of Smart's Mill shifted the axis of battle from Stone's original plan. Photo, National Archives.

MAP, opposite: shown are the Federal troop movements from 4 to 8 a.m. on October 21, 1861. At 7 a.m. Col. Devens' scouting party collides with pickets of the 17th Miss. on the road to Smart's Mill Ford.

forwarded a report with the results of his scout to General Stone via Lieutenant Church Howe. Included in this report were Devens's statements that the 15th Massachusetts had not been detected and that he felt they could remain concealed in the woodline until reinforced.[42]

Unknown to Colonel Devens, his report to General Stone was false regarding his being undetected by the Confederates. The early morning crossing at Ball's Bluff had alerted Company K (The Magnolia Guard) of the 17th Mississippi then on picket duty at the crossing located at Smart's Mill Ford. These veterans of the Battle of Manassas were under the command of Captain William Duff who submitted the following after-action report:[43]

Camp at Carter's Mill, Va.
October 25, 1861

COLONEL:
I have the honor to submit the following report of the action near Big Spring on the morning of the 21st instant: We had, as you are aware, been on detached service since August 24, having pickets at Stuart's Mill, Conrad's Ferry, Ball's Mill and Mrs. Mason's Island. Early on the morning of the 21st our pickets ... reported the enemy crossing opposite Harrison's Island at the Big Bluff. I ordered Lieutenant Harten to report these facts to General

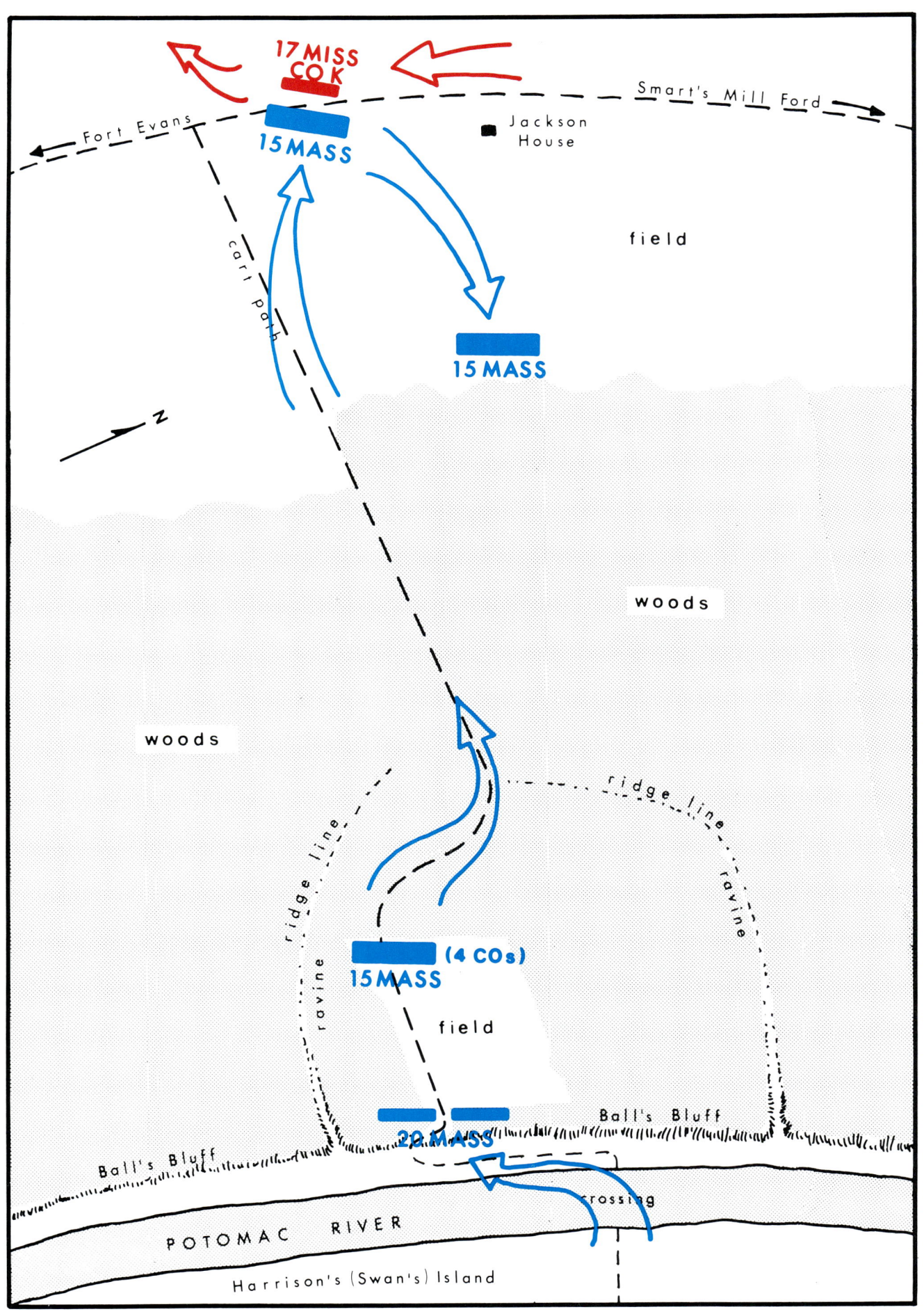

Evans and immediately formed my company and marched in the direction of Stuart's Mill where my pickets had been driven in. On reaching the mouth of the lane leading to the river, some 500 or 600 yards from the mill, I threw forward twelve skirmishers to scour a clump of woods to the front and right, ordered one of my men to bring in the rest of my pickets, filed my company to the right up a long hollow in an old field, leaving the clump of woods on my left. When we reached the top of the hill near Mrs. Stephens' house we saw the skirmishers of the enemy on the left, and in large force in Mrs. Jackson's yard, some 150 yards in front. I filed to the right, for the purpose of getting between them and Leesburg, and formed a line of battle.

The enemy threw forward a strong force in line of battle. I having but 40 men in line thought it best to draw him as far as possible from his reserve. I accordingly fell back on the foot of the hill, some 300 yards from his reserve, and in the direction of Leesburg. He advanced in line of battle in good order at a "make ready," his force amounting to at least five or six companies. I halted my company and ordered the enemy to halt five or six times. He responded each time, "Friends," but continued to advance within 60 yards, when I ordered my men to kneel and fire, which they did with deadly effect, completely breaking his line. The second time he fell back, but getting re-enforcements from the reserve he rallied, and maintained his position about twenty minutes, when the whole force fled in confusion to a thicket of woods to the right of Mrs. Jackson's house, carrying with them most of the killed and wounded.

Not knowing where our forces were, and having

General Devens, above, led the advance onto Ball's Bluff during the morning of October 21. At that time Devens was colonel of the 15th Massachusetts Regiment.
Below: a selection of various Civil War lead bullets excavated in the Ball's Bluff vicinity. Courtesy Mike O'Donnell.

On this field the 15th Massachusetts and the 17th Mississippi regiments first clashed. The Yankees, positioned around the Jackson House (visible on the ridgeline to the right), fell under fierce fire from the Confederates who fought from the cover of large rock outcroppings in the middle of the field. Photo, Mike O'Donnell.

but few men, I thought it best to fall back about 300 yards, so as to command the main road from Big Spring to Leesburg thinking the enemy might throw a force in that direction and cut me off; but learning that some of our troops were on my right in the fortifications, I resumed my former position.

I captured 3 wounded prisoners and 14 or 15 stands of arms. I maintained my position in front and about 600 yards from the enemy under a scattering fire from their long-range guns. I had 1 man seriously wounded and 2 slightly wounded in the engagement.[44]

Three major factors hindered the Union and assisted the Confederate forces in this opening phase of the Battle of Ball's Bluff. First, the Union soldiers (especially the officers) were taken by surprise when attacked by the Mississippians coming from the north. Second, the Union soldiers and officers were completely green having never 'Seen the Elephant' whereas the Confederates were veterans of the Battle of Manassas. Third, the Union soldiers were armed with outdated smoothbore Austrian muskets which failed to hit most targets because they were so awkward to handle. The Confederate soldiers were armed with rifled muskets which enabled them to shoot straight at much longer distances than the smoothbore weapons of their foes.

Having been bloodied by the 17th Mississippi, Colonel Devens withdrew his battalion from the field in front of (i.e. west of) the Jackson House to the woodline in the rear (i.e. east of) the house. He regrouped his command for approximately half an hour before retreating back to the position of Colonel Lee and the 20th Massachusetts at the edge of Ball's Bluff. After meeting with Colonel Lee, Devens once again led his battalion of the 15th Massachusetts to the woodline at the east side of the Jackson House. He was joined there by Lieutenant Howe who informed him that the battalion was to stay where it was. Lieutenant Colonel Ward (Deputy Commander of the 15th Massachusetts) was about to reinforce Devens with the 2nd battalion of the regiment via Smart's Mill Ford. Lieutenant Howe further reported that ten Union cavalrymen were

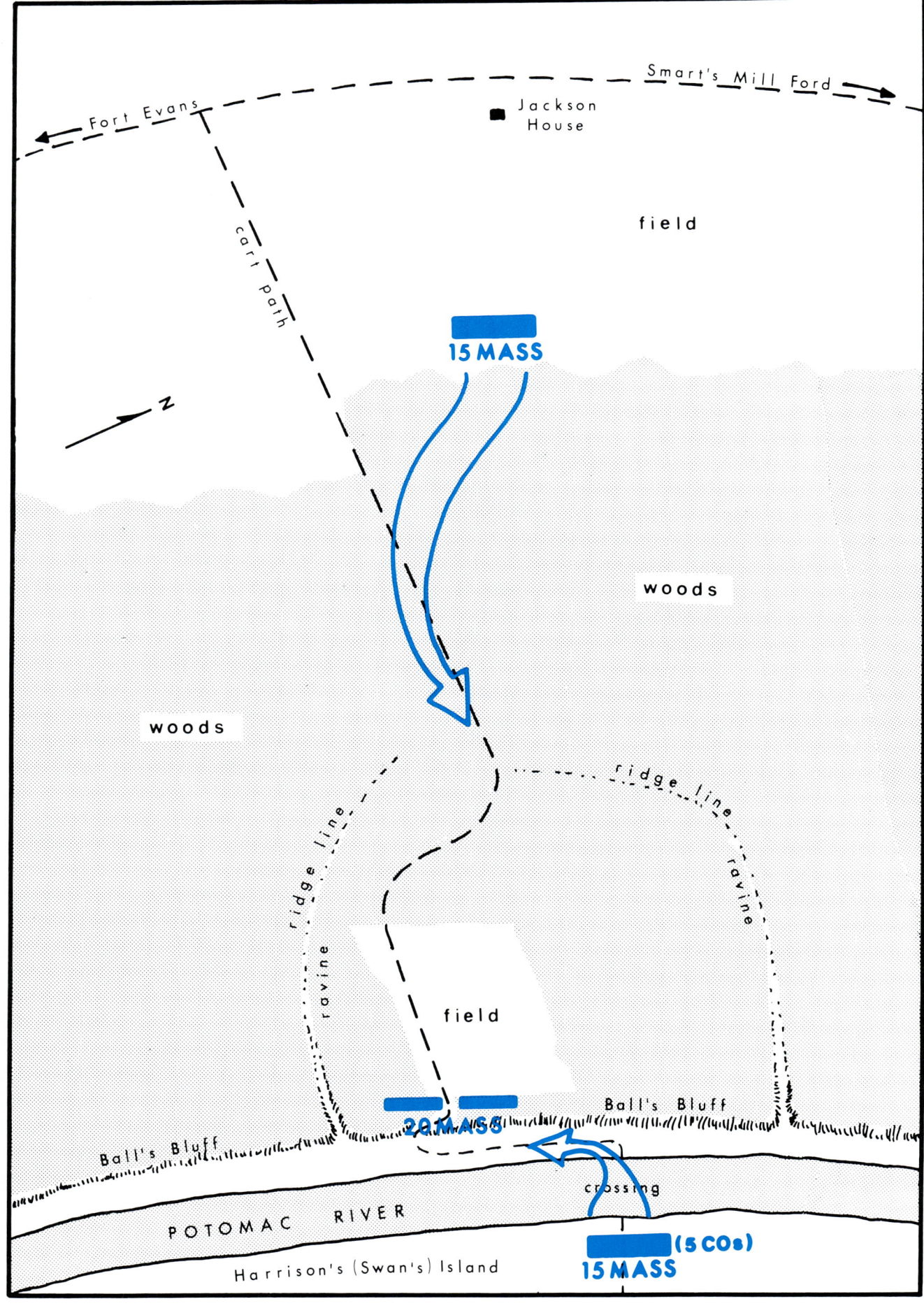

crossing at Smart's Mill Ford to assist Colonel Devens as flank guards, scouts and couriers.[45]

After receiving Lieutenant Howe's report Colonel Devens dispatched him back to General Stone at Edward's Ferry with a message concerning the morning skirmish. Upon reaching Harrison's Island Lieutenant Howe intercepted Lieutenant Colonel Ward with the 2nd battalion of the 15th Massachusetts Regiment preparing to cross at Smart's Mill Ford. An overly excited Howe conveyed to Ward a false report that Devens was being cut-up and therefore needed Ward's help immediately. Forego the crossing at Smart's Mill Ford and cross your battalion at Ball's Bluff in order to save Devens was the message that Howe gave Ward.[46]

Thus the entire axis of the battle was changed from the planned one at Smart's Mill Ford to Ball's Bluff. The Union infantry and artillery were about to be funneled into battle at the worst possible crossing site with inadequate boat transportation. The crossing at Smart's Mill Ford was easy. Soldiers could cross the Potomac River from Harrison's Island with little or no need of boat transportation. However, the crossing from Harrison's Island into Virginia via Ball's Bluff had to be made entirely via boats. This

MAP, opposite: at 8 a.m. the 15th Massachusetts retires from the woods east of the Jackson House to the Bluff. Meanwhile, Union reenforcements continue to cross over from Harrison's Island.

Federal issue accoutrement breast plate, above, unearthed near Fort Evans by Chuck Thompson.
Below: the road to Smart's Mill Ford has changed little since the battle. This particular section, southeast of the Jackson House, witnessed Philbrick's patrol on the 20th as well as Col. Devens' collision with the pickets of the 17th Mississippi the following morning.

Lieutenant Church Howe, adjutant of the 15th Massachusetts, whose false report to Col. Ward on Harrison's Island resulted in the difficult crossing at Ball's Bluff instead of the planned crossing at Smart's Mill Ford. Photo, Carlisle Barracks.

doomed the brave Union soldiers who were soon to fight there since boats were not available at Ball's Bluff in anywhere near the numbers required to transport the necessary reinforcements, ammunition, artillery, etc.

After delivering his fatal message on Harrison's Island, Lieutenant Howe reported to General Stone at Edward's Ferry. He described to Stone the situation at Ball's Bluff and Harrison's Island. Stone then sent a message to Colonel Edward Baker to proceed across the island to the bluff to take command with authority to reinforce or withdraw the Union forces atop Ball's Bluff as he saw fit.[47]

HEADQUARTERS CORPS OF OBSERVATION
Edwards Ferry, October 21, 1861.
Col. E. D. Baker, Commanding Brigade:

COLONEL: In case of heavy firing in front of Harrison's Island, you will advance the California regiment of your brigade or retire the regiments under Colonels Lee and Devens upon the Virginia side of the river, at your discretion, assuming command on arrival.

Very respectfully, colonel,
your most obedient servant,
CHAS. P. STONE
Brigadier-General, Commanding[48]

Unchanged since 1861 this view from beneath the Bluff looks downriver toward Harrison's Island. This placid looking surface of the Potomac belies the treacherous currents below. Photo, Mike O'Donnell.

Ball's Bluff today is still the same—a rock-strewn height so steep and dangerous as to be nearly impassable. General Stone had supposed it would be lightly guarded when he directed a party of the 15th Massachusetts to cross the Potomac and seize the cliffs. Photo, Mike O'Donnell.

Because of the major change in Union plans at Ball's Bluff, Smart's Mill Ford and Harrison's Island it is natural to ask why Stone did not proceed there to take charge of matters. First, Stone felt that Baker was a good subordinate who could size up the situation and make a proper decision as to the course of action. It should be remembered that Baker was one of the commanding figures of his day. A brilliant political orator, a radical Republican Senator, a personal friend of the President, a veteran of the Black Hawk War and a regimental/brigade commander in the Mexican War.[49] By turning the situation upriver over to Colonel Baker, General Stone was able to focus his attention on his primary feint movement at Edward's Ferry. By crossing there Stone felt that he could hold the main Confederate force at Fort Evans in place thereby enabling either General McCall to turn its right flank or Colonel Baker to turn its left flank, therefore enabling the Union forces to win a major victory at Leesburg.

Concerning his troop movements at Edward's Ferry, General Stone stated the following in his official report to General McClellan:

> In order to distract attention from Colonel Devens' movement and at the same time to effect a reconnaissance in the direction of Leesburg from Edwards Ferry, I directed General Gorman to throw across the river at that point two companies of the First Minnesota Volunteers under the cover of a fire from Ricketts' battery, and sent out a party of 31 Van Alen Cavalry, under Major Mix, accompanied by Capt. Charles Steward, Captain Murphy, Lieutenants Pierce and Gourand, with orders to advance along the Leesburg road until they should come to the vicinity of a battery which was known to be on that road and then turn to the left, and examine the heights between that and Goose Creek, see if any of the enemy were posted in the vicinity, ascertain as nearly as possible their number and disposition, the country with reference to the passage of troops to the Leesburg and Georgetown turnpike, and return rapidly to cover behind the skirmishers of the Minnesota First.
>
> The reconnaissance was most gallantly conducted by all in the party, which proceeded along

the Leesburg road nearly or quite 2 miles from the ferry, and when near the position of the hidden battery came suddenly upon a Mississippi regiment, about 35 yards distant, received its fire, and returned it with their pistols. The fire of the enemy killed 1 horse, but Lieutenant Gourand seized the dismounted man, and drawing him on his horse behind him, carried him unhurt from the field. One private of the Fourth Virginia Cavalry was brought off by the party a prisoner. This prisoner being well mounted and armed, his mount replaced the one lost by the fire of the enemy.[50]

A member of the First Minnesota remembered the morning's events somewhat differently:

The next morning, October 21, at the "unholy hour" of 1:30, raw and chilly and dark as pitch, the First Minnesota was routed out of their tents, took a hasty and ill-relished breakfast, and then, accompanied by the Eighty-second New York, with knapsacks and other equipment, marched down to Edward's Ferry again. The two regiments reached the Ferry at daybreak, and immediately began to cross the Potomac in flat-boats previously provided, two companies at a time. In a little while the regiment was in line. Two companies were sent out as skirmishers, covering the advance on the Leesburg road of Major Mix's detachment of thirty-five men of the Third New York Cavalry, that went up the road two miles but were finally driven summarily back by

Earthen ramparts of the "masked battery" still guard the old Edward's Ferry road. Rebel artillery posted here turned back the cavalry scouting party under Major Mix and discouraged General Gorman from advancing toward the fighting at Ball's Bluff. Photo M. O'Donnell.

Brass buttons bearing the state seals of New York and Massachusetts lost by troops of Gen. Stone's command while stationed near Poolesville, Maryland. Below: Colonel Edward Baker, U.S. senator from Oregon and confidante of President Lincoln, killed at Ball's Bluff. The image is a carte-de-visite. Author's collection.

detachments of the Thirteenth Mississippi and Jennifer's Cavalry. At 11 o'clock the Thirty-fourth New York came over from Seneca Mills. The Seventh Michigan, of Lander's Brigade, also came. The muskets of this regiment were worthless and it was made to dig rifle pits, and Gorman's command, 2,250 strong, remained here all day and the ensuing night.[51]

Meanwhile Colonel Evans, located at Fort Evans on the road from Edward's Ferry to Leesburg, was receiving his subordinate's reports. From Captain Duff he learned of the Union crossing at Ball's Bluff and subsequent skirmish.[52] Directly in front of him he could observe the Union crossing at Edward's Ferry.[53] He knew that McCall would not be advancing against him on the Leesburg-Alexandria Turnpike and that the Union forces were attempting to turn his left flank instead. Colonel Evans dispatched four companies of Mississippi infantry (two from the 18th Mississippi, one from the 13th Mississippi and one from the 17th Mississippi) plus three undersized troops (i.e. companies) of Virginia cavalry under the overall command of Lieutenant Colonel W. H. Jennifer to reinforce Captain Duff and contain the Union flanking column at Ball's Bluff.[54] At the same time Evans maintained his three Mississippi regiments at Fort Evans enabling him to contain the Union forces then crossing at Edward's

From a Harper's Weekly, Union artillery *is rushed into action along the Potomac.*
MAP, *opposite: the original Union plan of attack involved McCall's advance up the Leesburg Turnpike in conjunction with crossings by Stone at Smart's Mill Ford and Edward's Ferry.*

Ferry and reinforce either his left or right flank (the right flank at that time rested on the west side of the Burnt Bridge on the Leesburg-Alexandria Turnpike under the auspices of the 8th Virginia Infantry Regiment).⁵⁵ Colonel Jennifer's report of his engagement with the 15th Massachusetts Regiment that morning reads, in part, as follows:

> At 9 o'clock I received an order to report with my cavalry to you at Fort Evans. After obeying this order you gave me permission to take my cavalry near the enemy's position in order to make an attack should he again advance. I concealed the cavalry in a ravine near Mr. Trundle's house, ready to make a charge should an opportunity offer. The enemy at this time was under cover of the thick woods between the river and Leesburg, and reported by the prisoners just taken to be six full companies of 100 men each.
>
> At 11 o'clock I determined to attack the enemy, and, if possible, drive him from his strong position, and sent you a dispatch to that effect. Captain Campbell, of the Eighteenth Mississippi Regiment, with two companies of infantry, placed himself under my command. I then sent an order to Captain Duff to hold himself in readiness to attack the enemy's right flank. So soon as sufficient time had elapsed for Captain Duff to receive the order I advanced towards the enemy's position, and when within a few hundred yards of him two more companies of infantry joined me by your order. My whole command then consisted of three companies of cavalry, commanded respectively by Capt. W. B. Ball, Capt. W. W. Mead, and Lieutenant Moorehead (Captain Adams' company), and five companies of infantry, commanded respectively by Captains Campbell and Welborn, Eighteenth Mississippi Regiment; Captain Duff, Seventeenth Mississippi Regiment; Captain Fletcher, Thirteenth Mississippi Regiment and one other captain, numbering in all about 320 men.
>
> Captain Campbell was ordered to deploy one of his companies, Captain Wellborn's, as skirmishers, and to feel the enemy's position. The other companies were directed to advance in the following order: Captain Campbell on the right, Captain Duff on the extreme left, Captain Fletcher and the cavalry on the center. Capt. William B. Ball was placed in command of the cavalry.
>
> Upon a nearer approach to the enemy it was found to be impossible to charge with cavalry, owing

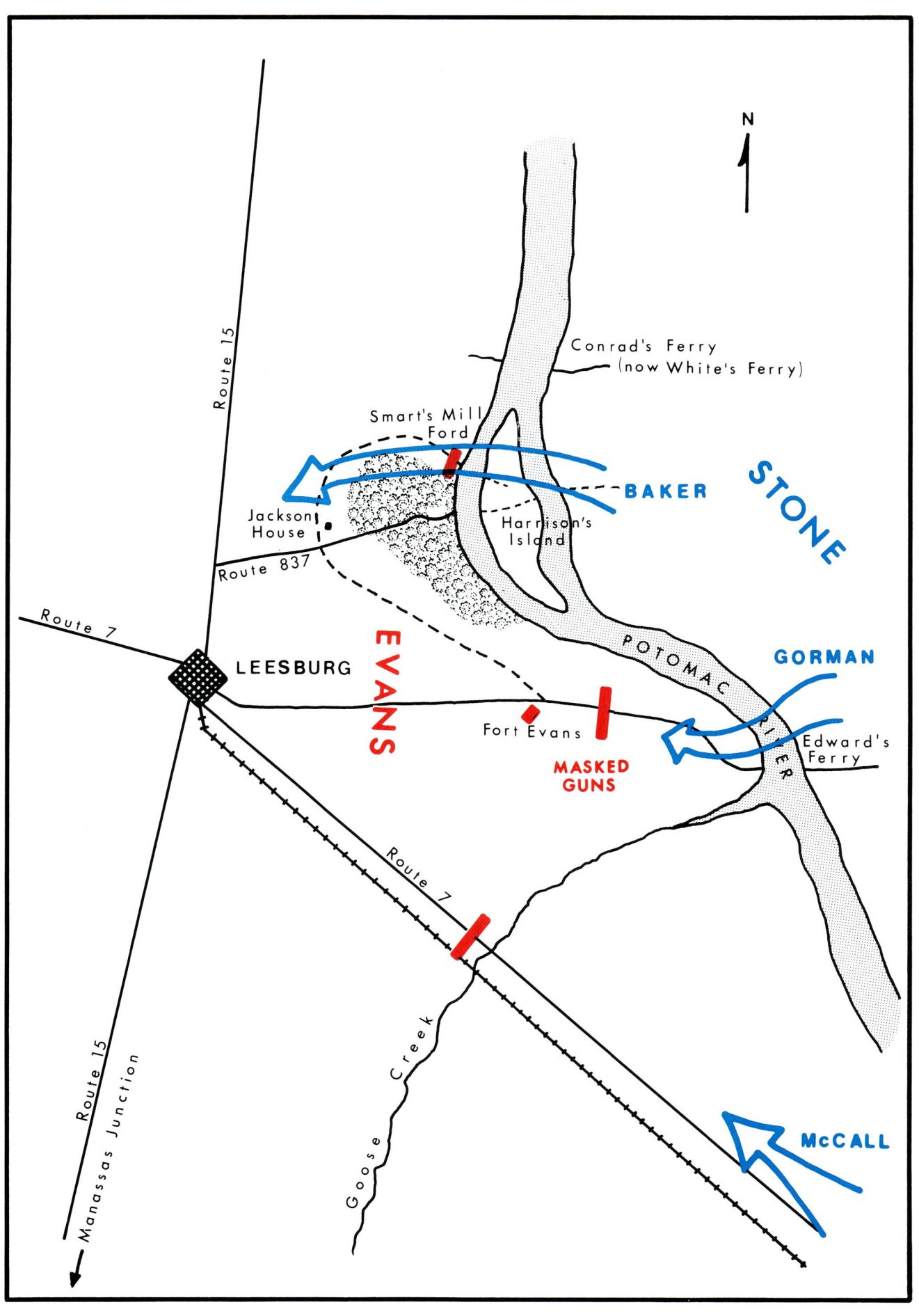

Two officers, above, of the 15th Massachusetts who survived Ball's Bluff. The young lieutenant, left, is Richard Derby. Captain Henry Bowman is to the right. Courtesy U.S. Army Center of Military History.
Below is an officer's sword belt and buckle with the state letters emblazoned on the face. This specimen was worn by a member of New York's Tammany regiment.

to a high and strong fence between the enemy and my command. I therefore ordered Captain Ball, at his request, to dismount his company and fight on foot. The attack was then made, and a brisk fire kept up through the fence. Finding the enemy was not disposed to fall back, I ordered a charge over the fence which order was promptly obeyed, and so soon as a portion of the fence could be torn down I leaped my horse over, followed by Captain Ball... The enemy was soon driven from his first position, but a heavy fire was kept up from the thick woods to which he had retreated. Fearing my small command would be led into an ambuscade, I ordered it to fall back and take position in rear of the fence it had just passed, and sent to you for re-enforcements.[56]

Receiving Colonel Jennifer's request for reinforcements at approximately 10 a.m., Colonel Evans pulled the 8th Virginia Regiment from its position at the Burnt Bridge and sent it double-timing toward Ball's Bluff. Company H of the 8th Virginia was left at the Burnt Bridge as a picket guard.[57]

Virginia state seal button, above, found at the hillside position of the 8th Virginia Regt. overlooking the Leesburg Turnpike at Burnt Bridge. Courtesy C. Thompson.

Modern view of the Burnt Bridge site which stood near the steel highway bridge at left. General Evans' Confederates were posted on the wooded eminence at right. Photo M. O'Donnell.

III

The Battle for the Bluff

Now began a race against time for the Confederates. Colonel Eppa Hunton double-timed his 8th Virginia Regiment from the Burnt Bridge, past Colonel Evans at the fort, northward to join Colonel Jennifer's command west of the Jackson House.[1] Upon his arrival at the Jackson House, Colonel Hunton posted his 8th Virginia Regiment (375 strong) south of the house and on the right of the Confederate battleline. The center of the Confederate line was occupied by four Mississippi infantry companies and the left of the line by three small troops of Virginia cavalry. Lieutenant Colonel Jennifer commanded the center and left elements of the Confederate battle force. At approximately 12:30 they attacked Colonels Devens and Ward and the men of the 15th Massachusetts Regiment east of the Jackson House.[2] A severe skirmish developed between 700 Confederates and 600 Union soldiers. With the danger of being outflanked becoming stronger every minute, Colonel Devens withdrew the 15th Massachusetts back to the cleared field at the edge of Ball's Bluff.[3] A survivor of the regiment remembered it this way:

Perhaps I should tell you that when deployed as skirmishers each man is about five paces from the next consequently our first platoon of only thirty-two or three men was extended over a line of as many rods. We had not been in this position long when we saw an officer ride in front of their infantry and wave his hand. Immediately the infantry advanced, and at the same time a rushing sound was heard in the woods on our left; someone said 'cavalry' and sure enough, the next minute a large body of them dashed upon us. It was impossible for so few of us, situated as we were, to withstand such a force. We fired upon them and did our best to get back to the reserve. As I turned to retreat I saw George Taylor a few rods from me, making his way off the field but as he did not get back to the reserve and has not since been heard from, I concluded that he was shot dead, being the only one that was killed in that skirmish, although two of our boys who were wounded and taken prisoners have since died from the effects of their wounds. I had not proceeded more than five rods on my retrograde march when I experienced a peculiar sensation in my right thigh. There was not much chance to doubt what hurt at that time; the balls were whistling on all sides, and I believed that I was carrying an ounce of lead besides the forty in my cartridge box. Such proved to be the case, for in a minute or two my shoe was full of blood and my pants saturated with same. Although wounded I still kept on, resolved to get back to friends or die. A body of the rebel infantry had got into the woods on the left and cut off our retreat through the open space; we therefore took to the woods on the right, which we knew led round to the reserve. Before I reached them, I saw Al Osborn and Albert Litchfield sitting behind a corn shock, both I believe were wounded and both were soon after taken prisoners. Stopping behind a little house, which was about three rods from the edge of the woods, for a minute, I found George Daniels, wounded in the wrist and shoulder. Lowell, another of our boys, was also there. I saw him go to the corner and fire. 'There,' says he, 'I've fixed him; I saw him fall.' Leaving the house, I reached the woods and was now comparatively safe.[4]

By 1:30 Colonel Devens had retired the bloodied elements of his regiment through the woods to the cleared field at the Bluff. There he found the relative security of friends in the 20th Massachusetts Regiment under Colonel William R. Lee. Five more companies of the 20th Massachusetts

Right: Col. Charles Devens, commander of the 15th Mass. Regt. at Ball's Bluff. He fought the initial action in the vicinity of the Jackson House. He served with distinction as a Brig. Gen. later in the war. Photo, courtesy National Archives.

Below: artist's rendition of the futile charge of the 15th Mass. against the Rebels at the Jackson House. Their rout ensured disaster. From The Illustrated London News, *November 23, 1861.*

The Jackson House as it appears today. On October 21, 1861 it was the scene of the opening conflict. The 15th Mass. held a position in this field east of the house until driven back to the bluffs. Photo, Mike O'Donnell.

Regiment arrived (under Major Paul Revere—grandson of the Revolutionary War Hero) and two 12-pound mountain howitzers of Battery B, 1st Rhode Island Light Artillery.[6] Their movement from Maryland into Virginia was described by a survivor:

> On October 21st Captain Vaughn was ordered to Conrad's Ferry, and with the left section proceeded to the river, where Colonel Baker's brigade was crossing to the Virginia side. As the landing was crowded with infantry waiting to be taken across, Captain Vaughn left the section in charge of Sergeant-Major Staples, and went down to Edward's Ferry to bring up the centre section. While the captain was gone the landing became partly clear of troops, and Sergeant Staples moved the left section down to the landing, where great confusion reigned. There seemed to be no one to command or dispatch the troops across as they arrived. At this time Colonel Cogswell, of the Tammany or Forty-second New York, arrived with his regiment, and, as the left section of Battery B occupied the landing, ordered it to cross. On learning that there was no commissioned officer of the battery with the section (Captain Vaughn not having returned from Edward's Ferry), he ordered Lieut. Walter M. Bramhall, of the Sixth New York Battery, to take command and cross as soon as possible so as to clear the way for his Regiment. The only means of crossing the river was by a large scow attached to a hawser, which had been stretched from the Maryland shore to Harrison's Island in the Potomac River. Sergt. Silas G. Tucker had his gun dismounted and placed on board of the scow. The scow was only large enough to take one gun detachment and horses, so Lieutenant Bramhall and Sergeant Tucker with the fifth piece and men crossed to the island. While they were crossing, Sergt.

MAP, opposite: battle situation at 8 a.m. is shown. The 15th Massachusetts withdraws to the Bluff after the initial skirmish, is reenforced, and resumes its position near the Jackson House. Again, the unit is attacked and driven back to the Bluff.

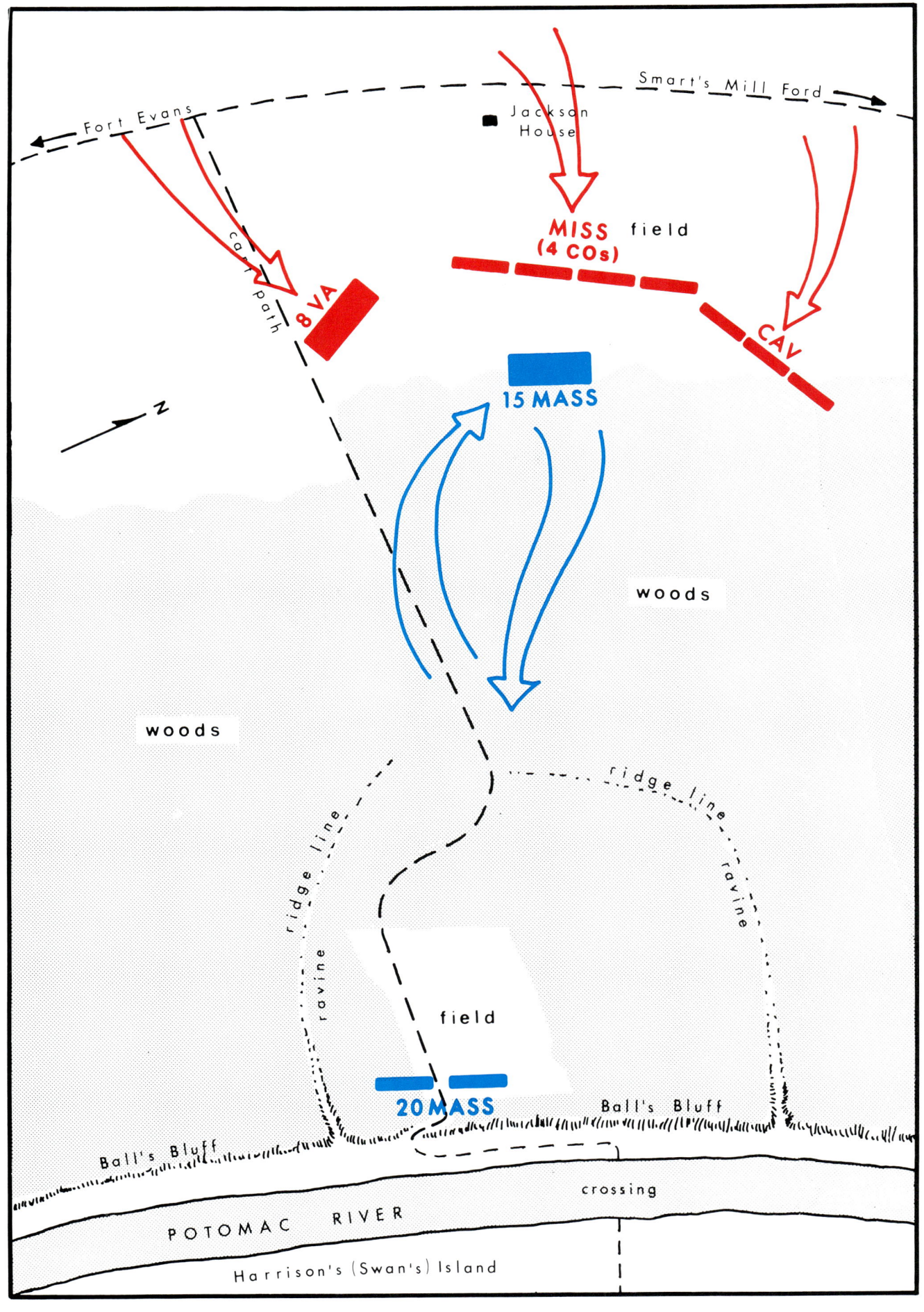

Charles H. Adams had his gun (the sixth) dismounted and made ready for embarkation, and, on the return of the scow, it was placed on board, and Sergeant Adams crossed to the island with his gun and detachment. As soon as the fifth piece was landed it was mounted and crossed the island. Here it was dismounted again, and the gun and carriage with the limber was placed in a small scow (or canal boat), and Lieutenant Bramhall and men crossed to the Virginia shore. Sergeant Tucker with the drivers and their horses followed in another scow. The river between the island and Virginia side was narrow, the water running very swift, and it was with great difficulty that the scows were propelled to the opposite shore. On landing the gun was mounted, when another difficulty was encountered. They were on a miry clay bank under a wooded bluff about seventy feet high, with rocks and fallen trees, making the passage for artillery very difficult. After

Col. William R. Lee, left, commander of the 20th Mass. Regt., crossed the Potomac in support of Devens and assumed a defensive position on the bluff. Photo, courtesy National Archives.
Below: the narrow and treacherous channel of the Potomac separating Harrison's Island (in the background) and the banks beneath Ball's Bluff. Photo, Mike O'Donnell.

Eyewitness sketch of the crossing of Federal reinforcements from Harrison's Island to the Virginia shore below the bluffs. Courtesy Battles and Leaders.

much severe labor and with the help of the infantry, Lieutenant Bramhall succeeded in reaching the summit of the bluff with one gun and limber, seven horses, and fourteen men. The gun was placed in position in line with, and to the left of, the seventy-first Pennsylvania, Colonel Baker's regiment (also called First California).

Following the crossing of the five companies of the 20th Massachusetts Regiment and two howitzers of the 1st Rhode Island Light Artillery came Colonel Edward Baker with four companies of his First California Regiment. During the late morning of 21 October, General Stone had ordered Baker to cross over from Maryland into Virginia to ascertain the condition of affairs opposite Harrison's Island. Baker's exact orders were:

HEADQUARTERS CORPS OF (OBSERVATION)
Edwards Ferry, October 21, 1861
Col. E. D. BAKER, Commanding Brigade:
   COLONEL: In case of heavy firing in front of Harrison's Island, you will advance the California regiment of your brigade or retire the regiments under Colonels Lee and Devens upon the Virginia side of the river, at your discretion, assuming command on arrival.
   Very respectfully, colonel,
   your most obedient servant,
   CHAS. P. STONE,
Brigadier-General, Commanding[9]

After receiving his orders to cross, Colonel Baker learned that the Smart's Mill Ford crossing site had been abandoned in favor of Ball's Bluff. Baker realized that this was a potential disaster for the Union effort. The crossing at Smart's Mill Ford necessitated few if any boats whereas the one at Ball's Bluff would require an extensive number of boats. Because he understood the desperate circumstances relative to the major crossing at Ball's Bluff, Colonel Baker spent the next few hours supervising the removal of a canal boat from the Chesapeake and Ohio Canal and into the Potomac River for use at Ball's Bluff.[10] Having shifted the canal boat into the

Portrait of Col. Edward Baker taken from a Matthew Brady photograph for publication in Frank Leslie's famous newspaper on November 9, 1861. The button shown is a Union officer's coat button of the type which adorned the tunics of Baker and many other Federal officers at Ball's Bluff. This specimen was excavated near the site of the battle by Charles Thompson. Photo, Mike O'Donnell.

river to assist in the transportation of men and material, Colonel Baker decided that it was time to cross over to Virginia. He proceeded to Ball's Bluff, arriving there at approximately 2:15.[11] In his official report Colonel Devens described the Union situation at the time of Colonel Baker's arrival:

> I returned to the bluff where Colonel Baker had already arrived. This was at 2:15 p.m. He directed me to form my regiment at the right of the position he proposed to occupy, which was done by eight companies, the center and left being composed of a detachment of Twentieth Massachusetts, numbering about 300 men, under command of Colonel Lee. A battalion of the California regiment, numbering about 600 men, Lieutenant-Colonel Wistar commanding; 2 howitzers, commanded by Lieutenant French, and a 6-pounder, commanded by Lieutenant Bramhall, were planted in front, supported by Company D, Captain Studley, and Company F, Captain Sloan, of the Fifteenth Massachusetts.[12]

The Union forces consolidated their position along the cleared field above Ball's Bluff. The Confederates moved toward them in a semicircle formation to prevent the Yankees from advancing a second time. On the extreme left of the Rebel line were three partially dismounted troops of Virginia cavalry. This was a perfect position for them because the left of the cavalry could keep a watch on the Union right and also keep an eye open for another Union flanking column from upriver. At the center of the Confederate line the four Mississippi infantry companies were positioned to strengthen the cavalry against a possible Union infantry assault and to provide the link between the cavalry on the left and the 8th Virginia Infantry Regiment on the right. By placing his regiment on the right of the line Colonel Hunton maintained the integrity of the attacking Confederate forces that struck the Union troops at the Jackson House at 12:30. He also used his regiment to block any further advance of Union forces westward along the cart path. Forward swept the Confederate battleline into the forest during the early afternoon of 21 October. Upon reaching the western edge of the cleared field the Confederates sent a "spitting fire"[13] into the ranks of the Union forces driving those in the cleared field back to the

MAP, opposite: between 1 p.m. and 2:15 p.m. the 15th Massachusetts has fallen back to the cliffs and formed with the 20th Massachusetts. Baker arrives at the head of his 1st California Regiment. Two howitzers are in the field and heavy firing is blazing along the entire front.

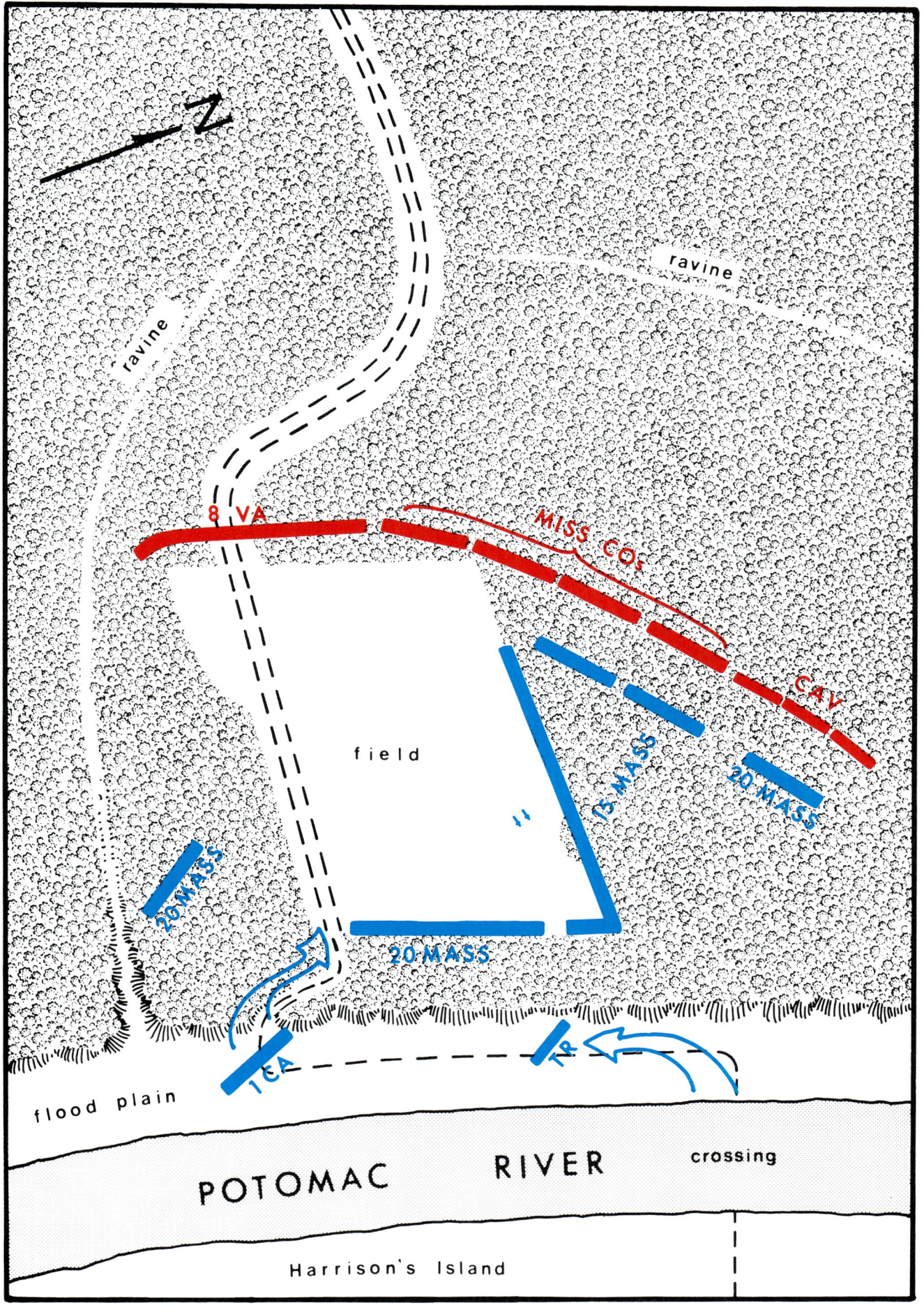

Sturdy log cabin of unknown vintage stands sentinel outside the grassy walls of Fort Evans near Leesburg, Virginia. Photo, Mike O'Donnell.

woods at the eastern edge.[14] Captain Duff, whose company fought the initial engagement with Colonel Devens, reported an incident he saw:

> I threw forward skirmishers ... in a dense thicket on the banks of a deep ravine. One of the skirmishers was halted within ten steps of my line by a man who proved to be an officer in the Tammany regiment of New York. He burst a cap at the skirmisher but Lieutenant Stephens saw him and shot him down before he could fire.[15]

As the Confederate forces under Colonels Hunton and Jennifer were preparing to begin the final engagement around the cleared field at 3 p.m., more Union reinforcements started to arrive. These were men of the famed Tammany Regiment (42nd New York Volunteer Infantry Regiment) under the command of Colonel Milton Cogswell. In his official report Colonel Cogswell made a number of insightful observations about the mismanagement of the boat transportation across the two branches of the Potomac River and the tactical mismanagement of the Union forces at Ball's Bluff by Colonel Baker.

> At about 2 o'clock p.m. on the 21st October I received orders to cross the Potomac at Harrison's Island taking with me the battery of artillery, which was posted at the same point with myself. Arrived at the landing opposite Harrison's Island, I found the greatest confusion existing. No one seemed in charge, nor any one superintending the passage of the troops, and no order was maintained in their crossing... I moved with one company of my regiment and two pieces of artillery, belonging to the Sixth New York Battery, to the island... I immediately crossed the island to make the passage of the second branch of the river, and there found still greater confusion existing than at the first landing. The California regiment had already gained the Virginia shore, and just as I arrived, Lieutenant-Colonel Wistar, its commander, was moving from the island landing in the lifeboat. I then crossed in a scow, taking with me Company C, Captain McPherson, of my regiment, and one piece of artillery, with its horses, under Lieutenant Bramhall, Sixth New York Battery.
>
> Ordering Lieutenant Bramhall to move his piece by a path to the left and report to Colonel Baker on the field, I ascended the bluff (about 70 feet high) and reported myself to the same com-

mander. I found Colonel Baker near the bluff, on the edge of an open field about eight or ten acres extent, trapezoidal in form, the acute angle being on the left front, the shortest parallel side near the edge of the bluff, and along this line was the First California Regiment, while the Fifteenth Massachusetts Regiment was formed in line in the open woods, forming the right hand boundary of the field, its line being nearly perpendicular to that of the California Regiment.

Colonel Baker welcomed me on the field, seemed in good spirits, and very confident of a successful day. He requested me to look at his line of battle, and with him I passed along the whole front. He asked my opinion of his disposition of troops, and I told him frankly that I deemed them very defective, as the wooded hills beyond the ravine commanded the whole so perfectly, that should they be occupied by the enemy he would be destroyed, and I advised an immediate advance of the whole force to occupy the hills, which were not then occupied by the enemy. I told him that the whole action must be on our left, and that we must occupy those hills. No attention was apparently paid to this advice, and Colonel Baker ordered me to take charge of the artillery, but without any definite instructions as to its service. About twenty minutes afterwards the hills on the left front to which I had called attention were occupied by the enemy's skirmishers, who immediately opened a sharp fire on our left. I

Above: Colonel Nathan "Shanks" Evans displayed cool courage and a military prowess which proved largely responsible for the Confederate victory at Ball's Bluff. Photo, National Archives.
Below: interior view of Fort Evans today looking across the parade ground toward the northeast bastion. Photo, Mike O'Donnell.

immediately directed the artillery to open fire on those skirmishers, but soon perceived that the fire was ineffectual, as the enemy was under cover of the trees, shooting down the artillerists at easy musket range. Soon Lieutenant Bramhall and nearly all the artillerymen had been shot down, and the pieces were worked for a time by Colonel Baker in person, his assistant adjutant general (Captain Harvery), Captain Stewart, assistant adjutant general of the division, a few other officers and myself.[16]

The battle at Ball's Bluff was now joined in earnest by both sides. Colonel Hunton sent a courier to Colonel Evans at Fort Evans to hasten forward reinforcements. Hunton reported that the 8th Virginia was running low on ammunition and that the Union forces were rapidly being reinforced not only with infantry but also with artillery.[17] Receiving this information at his command post on the Edwards Ferry Road, Colonel Nathan G. 'Shanks' Evans faced a critical decision demanding the utmost in command ability. Since the early morning of 21 October "Shanks" Evans had to be concerned about the unexpected threat at Ball's Bluff as well as the threat developing directly in front of him at Edward's Ferry. As General Stone stated in his official report:

> In order to distract attention from Colonel Devens' movement and at the same time to effect a reconnaissance in the direction of Leesburg from Edward's Ferry, I directed General Gorman to throw across the river at that point two companies of the First Minnesota Volunteers under the cover of a fire from Ricketts' battery, and sent out a party of 31 Van Allen Cavalry, under Major Mix, accompanied by Capt. Charles Stewart, assistant adjutant-general, Captain Murphy, Lieutenants Pierce and Gourand, with orders to advance along the Leesburg road until they should come to the vicinity of a battery which was known to be on that road and then turn to the left, and examine the heights between that and Goose Creek, see if any of the enemy were posted in the vicinity, ascertain as nearly as possible their number and disposition, examine the country with reference to the passage of troops to the Leesburg and Georgetown turnpike, and return rapidly to cover behind the skirmishers of the Minnesota First.

The reconnaissance was most gallantly conducted by all in the party, which proceeded along the Leesburg road nearly or quite 2 miles from the ferry, and when near the position of the hidden battery came suddenly upon a Mississippi regiment, about 35 yards distant, received its fire, and returned it with their pistols. The fire of the enemy killed 1 horse, but Lieutenant Gourand seized the

Below: 1st Rhode Island artillery shell a Rebel camp across the Potomac River. From Leslie's Illustrated Newspaper, October 5, 1861.
MAP, opposite: reveals the final troop dispositions as the final phase of the battle develops at the bluff at about 3 p.m. Both sides are rushing forward with reenforcements.

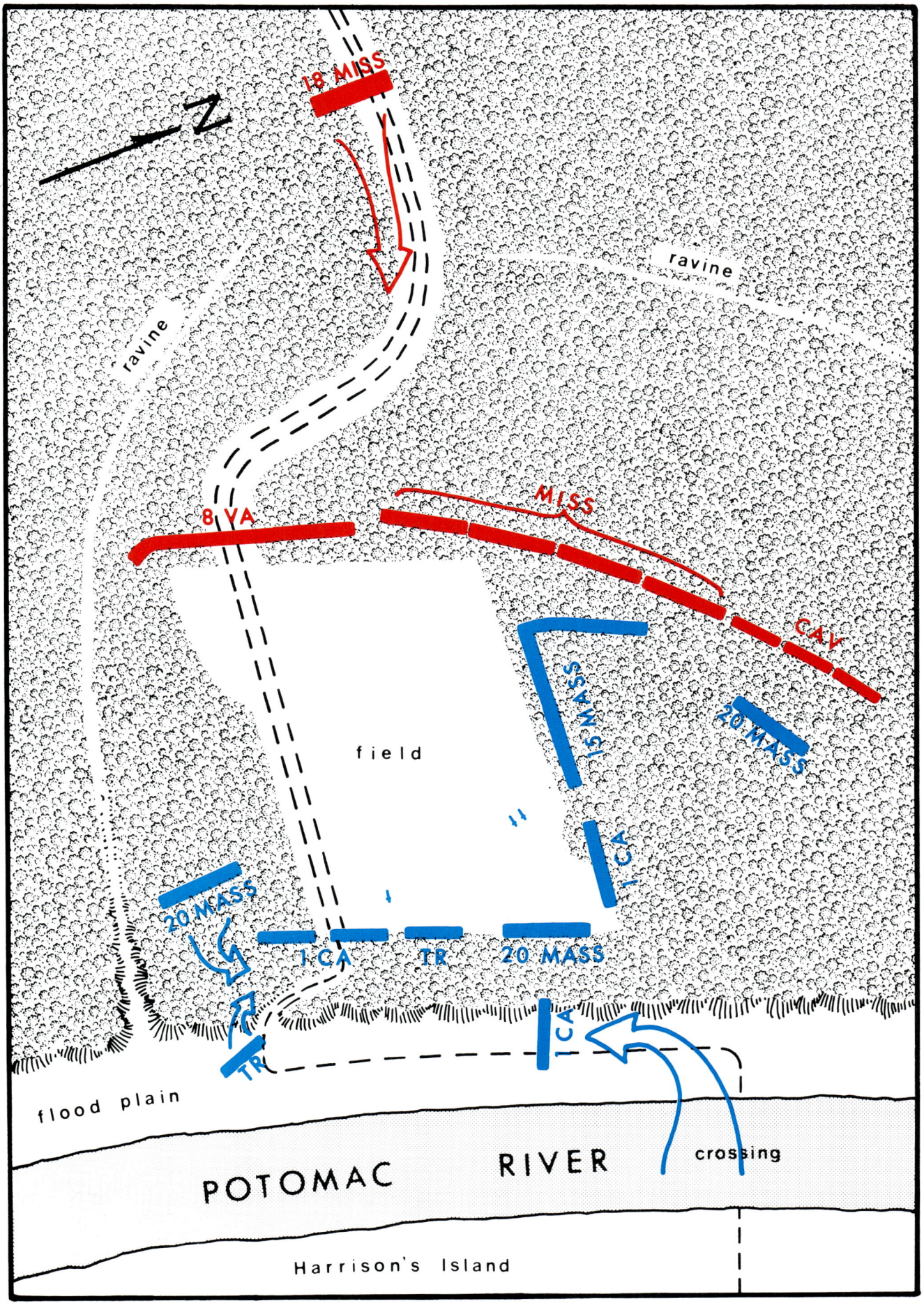

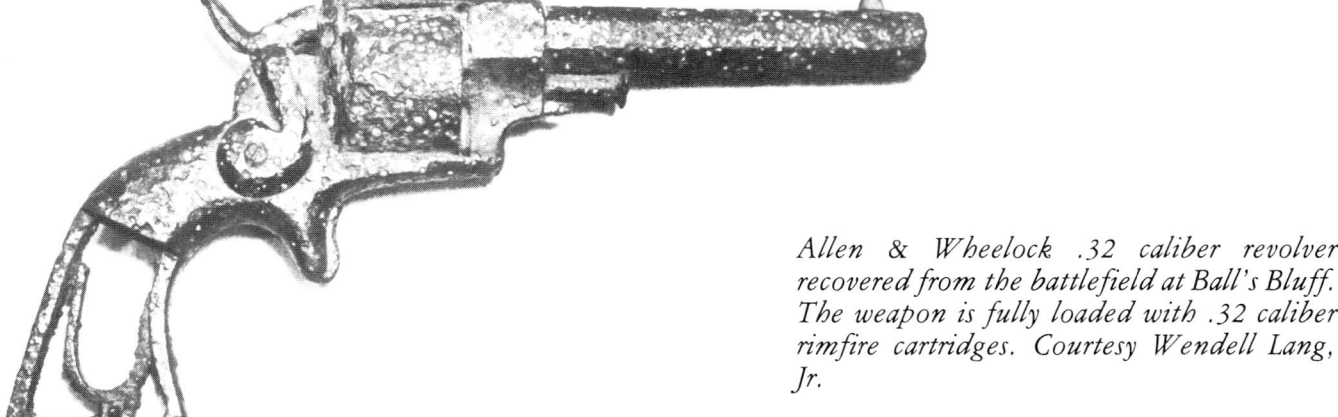

Allen & Wheelock .32 caliber revolver recovered from the battlefield at Ball's Bluff. The weapon is fully loaded with .32 caliber rimfire cartridges. Courtesy Wendell Lang, Jr.

dismounted man and, drawing him on his horse behind him, carried him unhurt from the field. One private of the Fourth Virginia Cavalry was brought off by the party a prisoner. This prisoner being well mounted and armed, his mount replaced the one lost by the fire of the enemy.[18]

To counteract this Union threat at Edward's Ferry, Colonel Evans ordered the 13th Mississippi Infantry Regiment forward at 1:30. Its commander, Colonel Barksdale (later killed at Gettysburg), wrote the following report about holding the Union forces in check at Edward's Ferry on 21 October:

> About 1:30 o'clock I was ordered by you to advance in the direction of Edward's Ferry, and to ascertain the position and number of the enemy. I marched at once in that direction and halted in a skirt of woods near the Daily house, at the same time directing Captain McIntosh to skirmish in the woods and near the river on the left, and Captain Ecksford, with a platoon of his company, to skirmish on the right of that house, and report without delay the result of their observation. Both reported that the enemy was in force in large numbers on this side of the river and just beyond the Daily house. I immediately ordered the regiment to advance, and when near the house a number of shots were fired by the advance guard on both sides, killing 1 man of my regiment. The loss of the enemy not ascertained.
>
> Perceiving that the object of the enemy was to outflank me on the right, and learning that Colonels Burt and Featherston, with their respective commands, had been ordered in another direction, I formed my regiment on the right of the Edward's Ferry road, intending to commence the attack from the woods stretching along the Daily plantation and to the right of the house, at the same time directing Captain Bradley to skirmish on the left and Captain

Selection of revolver and carbine bullets excavated from cavalry picket posts along the Potomac River. In 1861 the Potomac was heavily patrolled by Union and Confederate forces on opposite sides of the river. Photo, Mike O'Donnell.

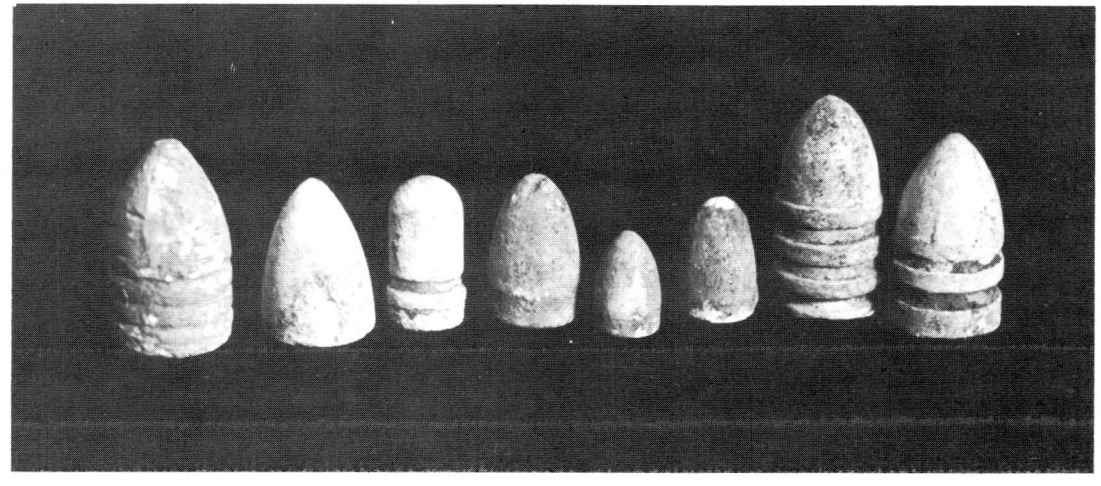

Worthington on the right.

I am satisfied that the presence of my command in position at Edward's Ferry prevented the advance of a large column of the enemy, which was intended to reinforce General Baker's command near Conrad's Ferry, then engaged in battle with our forces.[19]

It had been three months to the day that "Shanks" Evans had seen a similar feint at a stone bridge along Bull Run Creek near Manassas Junction. Realizing that the Union forces were again feinting directly at him while swinging a column around his extreme left, Colonel Evans held over 2,000 of them at bay with one regiment (the 13th Mississippi) and one battery of artillery (the Richmond Howitzers). He proceeded to hasten reinforcements to his left. First to start the double-time march toward Ball's Bluff from Fort Evans was the 18th Mississippi Infantry Regiment under the command of Colonel Erasmus R. Burt.[20]

Since the 18th Mississippi Regiment started its two mile double-time march to Ball's Bluff the combat on the bluff had intensified. Captain William F. Bartlett of the 20th Massachusetts Regiment described this phase of the battle in a letter to his Mother dated 25 October.

> Well the first volley came and the balls flew like hail. You can see from our position on the plan (i.e. map) that we were exposed to their full fire. The whizzing of balls was a new sensation. I had read so much that I was curious to experience it. I had a fair chance. An old German soldier told me that he had been in a good many battles, but that he never saw such a concentrated fire before. They fired beautifully, too, their balls all coming low, within from one to four feet of the ground. The men now began to drop around me; most of them were lying down in the first of it, being ordered to keep in reserve. Those that were lying down, if they lifted their foot or head it was struck. One poor fellow near me was struck in the hip while lying flat, and rose to go to the rear, when another struck him on the head, and knocked him over. I felt that if I was going to be hit, I should be, whether I stood up or lay down, so I stood up and walked around among the men, stepping over them and talking to them in a joking way, to take away their thoughts from the bullets, and keep them more self-possessed. I was surprised at first at my own coolness. I never felt better, although I expected of course that I should feel the lead every second, and I was wondering where it would take me. I kept speaking to Little, surprised that he was not hit amongst this rain of bullets. I said two or three times, "Why Lit., aren't you hit yet?" I remember Macy was lying where the grass was turned up, and I "roughed" him for getting his coat so awfully dirty. Lit. was as cool and brave as I

Col. Van Alen, above, commanded the cavalry attached to Gen. Stone's Corps of Observation. A scouting party of 31 of his men under Major Mix was sent out from Edward's Ferry on October 21, 1861. Before they could fully reconnoiter they were turned back by the Confederates' "hidden battery."

> knew he would be. The different companies began to wilt away under this terrible fire. Still there was no terror among the men; they placed *implicit confidence* in their officers (I refer to our regiment particularly), and you could see that now was the time they respected and looked up to them.[21]

At the same time Confederate reinforcements were moving toward Ball's Bluff, additional Union infantry and artillery were crossing over from Maryland into Virginia and joining the battle atop Ball's Bluff. Among the reinforcements arriving in mid-afternoon for the Union were the rest of the companies of the 1st California Regiment under Lieutenant Colonel Isaac J. Wistar and a twelve-pounder James Rifle under the command of Lieutenant Bramhall (the two mountain howitzers that Lieutenant Bramhall had earlier brought over were under the command of a Lieutenant French of the 1st U.S. Artillery).[22] Colonel Wistar left this account of his crossing and impression of the battlefield:

> I had two scows, of the capacity of forty men each, on the Maryland side of Harrison's Island, and one on the Virginia side, of the capacity of fifty men. I had got four companies on the Island and one on the Virginia side (having been delayed at the second crossing by other troops) when General Baker arrived on the Island and crossed at once to the Virginia side.
>
> After crossing six companies to the Virginia side, I left the Island and passed over myself, leaving Captain Ritman to hurry on the transportation.
>
> The Virginia side of the river was a bluff, eighty feet high, nearly perpendicular, and covered with rocks and a dense thicket.
>
> When I reached the top of the bluff, General Baker immediately explained his plan of battle stating his whole force to be twelve hundred men, at the same time reading to me your dispatch, announcing the approach of four thousand of the enemy from Leesburg, and expressing his own serious doubts of the result. The detachment of the Fifteenth Massachusetts was drawn up in the edge of the woods on the right, facing up the river. The rest of our forces were arranged across the edge of the open field, at right angles with the former, their backs towards the river; my battalion having the left, three companies being in reserve and one deployed as skirmishers to cover the left flank.
>
> From the left of our position at the edge of the woods, the ground fell rapidly to the left, about thirty yards, to a gully, on the other side of which it rose to a hill higher than the ground on which we stood, at short distance.
>
> The enemy's first fire was scattering, some of it from tree-tops around the field, where they had placed their marksmen—our men lying down for shelter, by command.[23]

At approximately the same time that Colonel Wistar was arriving atop Ball's Bluff, Colonel Eppa Hunton prepared for the arrival of the 18th Mississippi Regiment from Fort Evans. In so doing he moved the majority of his regiment to the north side of the cart path in order to allow the Mississippians an unmolested passageway to the battlefield and a

The old road to Edward's Ferry follows its wartime route towards the abandoned river crossing. Traces of the feared "masked battery" remain in the woods at the crest of the hill in the foreground. Photo M. O'Donnell.

MAP, opposite: decisive action occurred between 3 and 4 p.m. First, the 1st California assaults the 8th Va. and is repulsed. Then the 18th Miss. arrives, immediately charges the two howitzers, and is repulsed. Finally, the 18th Miss. occupies the dominant ridge on the Union left flank which rendered the Federal position untenable.

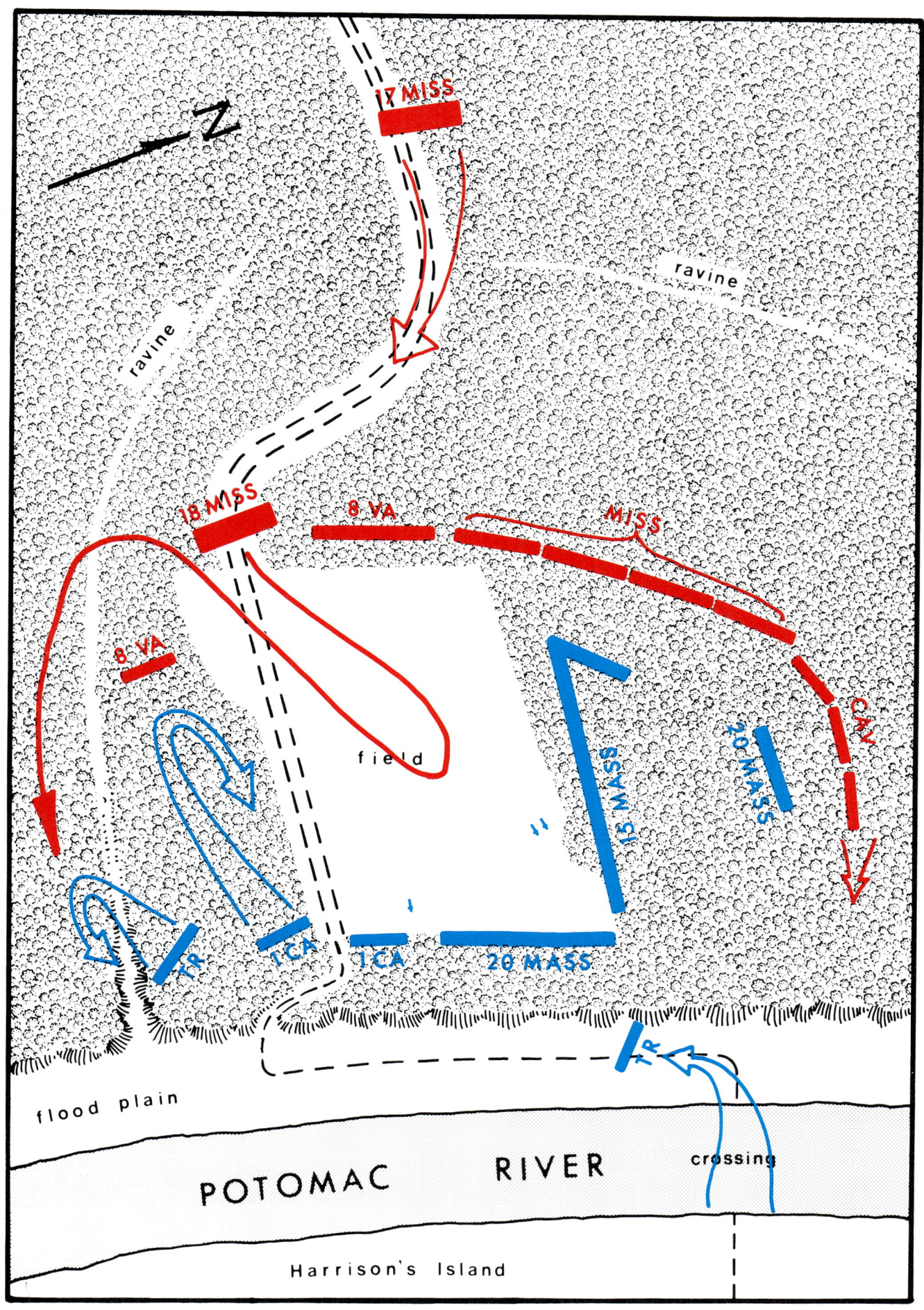

position on the Confederate right flank. Hunton retained one company of Virginians on the south side of the cart path to act as a blocking force to prevent the Union forces from securing the ridgeline behind the ravine on the southern side of the cleared field. In addition, the Virginians would temporarily act as a flank guard until the arrival of the Mississippians. Noticing this isolated company of Confederates on the southern side of the cart path, an attack was made upon them by two companies of the 1st California Regiment. An intense fire-fight broke out between these two relatively isolated elements of the Blue and Gray resulting in one Confederate officer and 14 enlisted men being taken prisoner.[24] Colonel Wistar described the fire-fight as follows:

> After comprehending the general condition, I requested permission to make a change in the disposition of our skirmishers on the left, and make any disposition I saw fit. In pursuance of this order I returned, and after a brief consultation with Colonel Cogswell and myself, he directed me to throw out two companies as skirmishers to feel the woods in front for the precise location of the enemy's right, getting as much cover for the movement as possible from the woods on the left, with directions if attacked in force, to contest the ground and fall back, fighting.
>
> In the execution of this order, Captain John Markoe, with his company (A), immediately moved out, Company D following in support under Lieutenant Wade—the latter company being short of officers—and the bulk of my command needing no immediate attention I accompanied the movement myself.
>
> The two companies moved rapidly up under cover of the woods on the left, until reaching the triangular open space before mentioned, when they were met by a galling fire from the enemy's riflemen on their front and left. Company A, led by Markoe and closely followed by D, rushing quickly over the open ground entered the woods, when a whole regiment of the enemy (8th Virginia) rose up from the ground at thirty paces distance and charged with the bayonet. A severe contest ensued, but our skirmishers somewhat checked the enemy's charge by taking trees and throwing an effective fire into their crowded ranks, at close distance. The right wing of our skirmishers was soon destroyed, but the left continued to hold ground for some time until Markoe was wounded and taken prisoner, when the survivors slowly fell back, bringing with them several prisoners, including an officer of the 'Eighth Virginia' whom I had the honor of sending to you the following morning.
>
> These two companies suffered severely in this gallant effort, company A having lost three of its officers, and all its sergeants, except two, one of whom is wounded.[25]

Mississippi button found on the Ball's Bluff battlefield along the Rebel lines. Traces of red enamel indicate that it may have belonged to a member of the red-trimmed 17th Mississippi Regt. Courtesy Dalton Rector.
Sketch illustrates the movement of C.S. reenforcements into battle. Courtesy Battles and Leaders.

This prominent ridge, overlooking the killing field below it, was held by the Mississippians. The Federals made a weak and ineffectual attack upon the position and were beaten back. The three-ring minie ball, right, was fired in the action and remained lodged in wood from the tree that it struck. Photo, Steve Sylvia.

As the fire-fight between the 1st California and 8th Virginia died off a calm returned to the battleground around the cleared field only broken by the sound of the 18th Mississippi Regiment doubletiming eastward on the cart path toward the cleared field. Although Colonel Burt was their leader, the Mississippians were guided on the battlefield by Elijah V. White, a local resident, who because of his knowledge of the terrain at Ball's Bluff, had been acting as guide and courier for Colonel Hunton all during the battle.[26] Elijah White was the personification of a local boy who made good. Because of his bravery and resourcefulness at Ball's Bluff he was commissioned Captain in the Confederate Cavalry eventually becoming Colonel of the 35th Virginia Cavalry, "The Commanches." At the end of the war he commanded the famed Laurel Brigade.[27]

Arriving at the cleared field, the 18th Mississippi went from columns of fours into a line of battle with Colonel Burt on horseback leading the charge. It was as gallant as it was doomed. Now the position of the two howitzers under Lieutenant French and the 15th Massachusetts Regiment along the northern side of the cleared field became evident. The howitzers were placed the moment they arrived atop Ball's Bluff to fire into any attacking Confederates coming into the cleared field via the

"Cannonading on the outposts of the Army of the Potomac" illustrates the activities of General Stone's Division guarding the Potomac River north of Washington, D. C. From Harper's Weekly, *October 19, 1861.*

cart path. The same was true for the 15th Massachusetts who added their volleys of musketry with that of the howitzers to stop the Mississippians,[28] mortally wounding Colonel Burt. As the 18th Mississippi retreated into the woods at the southwestern corner of the cleared field, one of them remembered an incident:

> An amusing incident occurred at this time. Our first lieutenant, Bostick, was a big, fat ole man, nearsighted and hard of hearing. Not hearing the order to halt, he rushed on... by himself, pistol in one hand and sword in the other. We screamed to him to come back, but he did not hear us, and continued... When near the (battery) he was wounded and fell.[29]

After the 18th Mississippi retreated to the cover of the woods, a majority of the regiment marched onto the high ridge overlooking the ravine which bordered the south side of the cleared field. They continued eastward along this ridgeline until close to the river where they were attacked by two companies of the Tammany Regiment and one company of the 1st California Regiment causing the 18th to stop their eastward advance.[30] A member of the 18th Mississippi who stayed in the ravine to fire at the Union troops remembered:

> We dropped into a small ravine that ran parallel to the river. Our regiment was on the slope of a hill behind us and many feet above us. In our front was a thicket, very dense, of mountain laurel, and I could see nothing. To me it was like looking for a bear in a Mississippi canebrake, where the dogs are braying around you, and the animal not in sight. The little drain that I was in was about three feet deep, and a sapling about eight inches in diameter was just in front of me, not more than a foot from my head. I at once saw the great advantage and protection I had, if we could only hold our position. Soon the rattle of the musketry began, and the

bullets flew high out of the laurel thicket, and the roar was deafening. We shot volley after volley into this obstruction that hid our view, and soon the thicket seemed to melt, and disappear. Here and there a glimpse of a Yankee could be caught, and our fire from the skirmish line began to increase. Before an hour had elapsed the laurel thicket had been mowed down, and our field was clear. I then began to single out my Yank, and with a steady, deadly aim I hunted a belt buckle as my target.[31]

Once the 18th Mississippi ended its bloody initial encounter at Ball's Bluff, it was joined by the 17th Mississippi Regiment. The commanding officer

Above: artillery friction primers found near the position of the two Yankee howitzers at Ball's Bluff by field researcher, Chuck Thompson.
Below: artillery projectile and chunks of iron shrapnel recovered from the hillsides along the Potomac near Ball's Bluff.

Dramatic depiction of the mortal wounding of Colonel Baker at the head of his troops. Though a man of unquestionable bravery, Baker's tactical decisions reveal his lack of military expertise. From Frank Leslie's Illustated Newspaper, *Nov. 9, 1861.*

of the 17th, Colonel Winfield Scott Featherston, wrote in his official report of the battle:

> About 3 o'clock p.m. I was ordered to advance rapidly to the support of these regiments, which were then engaged with a greatly superior force of the enemy, and accordingly we moved at a double-quick a distance of more than 2 miles to the field, when, perceiving that there was an interval of about 200 yards between the two other regiments, I immediately occupied it with my regiment. Learning that Colonel Burt had been dangerously wounded and borne from the field, I conferred with Lieutenant. Col. T. M. Griffin, commanding the Eighteenth Mississippi Regiment, and formed my regiment on the center of our line, in the edge of the woods and immediately in front of the enemy, who were drawn up in the woods upon the opposite side of a small field.[32]

The situation of the Union forces was becoming more desperate. It was now after 4 p.m. and they had been on the move since the early morning hours of 21 October. They had been without food for an extended period of time and were greatly fatigued from having been in combat since 7 a.m. Added to this were other problems with reinforcements and evacuating the many wounded caused by the inadequate boat transportation. The situation was desperate among the Union infantry and even more so with its artillery support. Lieutenant Bramhall in his official report stated:

> Upon order of General Baker I moved my piece

Amid the panic and chaos of defeat survivors of Col. Baker's shattered command carry his bullet-riddled corpse down the cliff, above.
Right: the same location today shows little change since the Union debacle of 1861. Photo, Mike O'Donnell.

forward into position in the center... I had hardly got into position when the enemy, who occupied the woods in front at the other extremity of the opening and a portion of the distance down the right and left, opened upon us a severe fire, wounding two of my cannoneers. I immediately responded, and continued a rapid fire until all but two of my cannoneers were wounded and left me. Among these, most unfortunately, was No. 4, who took with him the tube pouch and lanyard. Finding no other lanyard nor any primers in the limber chest, I obtained the assistance of some infantry soldiers and hauled the piece down to the rear. After a few moments the missing tube pouch was found and brought to me, the blood which covered it showing plainly the cause of its disappearance. At this time there was but one cannoneer (Carmichael) by the piece. The piece was brought into position by the aid of General Baker, Colonel Cogswell, Colonel Lee (I think that is his name), and Captain Stewart of General Stone's staff. Assisted by these gentlemen the firing was resumed and maintained until they were obliged to leave and go to their several commands. I then called for volunteers, whom I soon obtained from the infantry. I would be glad to have been able to distinguish who they were that came to my aid, for they worked with great zeal and coolness, but the similarity of uniforms prevented. I would beg, however, to call attention to one young fellow whose name I obtained. He is a private (Booth) of Company L, California regiment, who rendered me great assistance, at times being the only one with me at the piece. I do not know how long a time the piece was engaged, but I judge it to have been about half an hour... The last round which I fired was when the enemy had flanked us on the left and were pouring in a deadly fire from that quarter as well as from the front at about the moment when General Baker fell at the head of his men.[33]

While the Union forces battled against a steadily deteriorating situation, the dismounted Virginia Cavalry under Lieut. Col. Jennifer continued to work their way eastward toward the bank of Ball's Bluff. This enabled the Confederates to cut off the Union escape route to the north via Smart's Mill Ford.[34]

As this was transpiring Colonel Baker continued to walk up and down the front ranks of his soldiers posted at the eastern edge of the cleared field. His bravery was exemplary but his leadership in directing his forces was non-existent. Baker had given up the battle as lost.[35] His final hour of combat is best described by his aide and brigade quartermaster, Captain Francis Young, in his official report.

Colonel Baker was at all times in the open field, walking in front of the men lying on the ground,

Below: small stone tablet marks the location of Baker's death on the now tranquil heights of Ball's Bluff. Photo, Mike O'Donnell.
MAP, opposite: the battle situation betwen 4 and 5 p.m. shows a company of the 18th Mississippi maneuvering against the Federal left flank and being repulsed by the 1st California. Baker is killed and replaced by Col. Cogswell who orders the 15th Massachusetts to shift left preparatory to the breakout attempt.

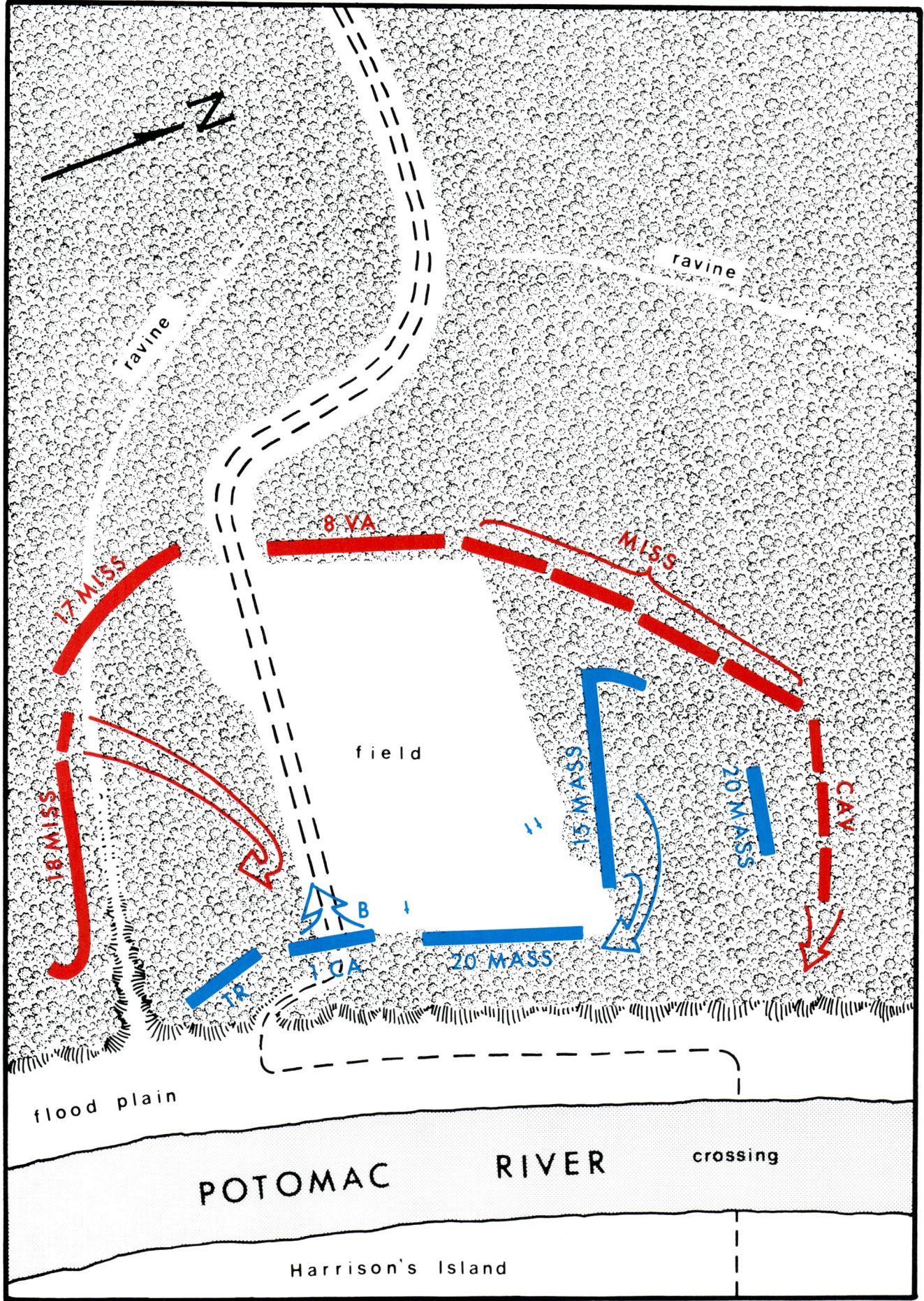

exhibiting the greatest coolness and courage. The fire of the enemy was constant, and the bullets fell like hailstones... Colonel Baker fell about 5 o'clock. He was standing near the left of the woods, and it is believed he was shot with a cavalry revolver by a private of the enemy, who, after Colonel Baker, crawled on his hands and knees to the body and was attempting to take his sword when Captain Bieral with 10 of his men rushed up and shot him through the head and rescued the body. At the time Colonel Baker was shot he was looking at a mounted officer, who rode down a few rods into the field from the woods and appeared to be falling from his horse. Colonel Baker, turning about, said, "See, he falls." and immediately fell, receiving four balls, each of which would be fatal.[36]

With the death of Colonel Baker a crisis of command descended upon the Union leadership. Colonel Lee of the 20th Massachusetts and Colonel Devens of the 15th Massachusetts wanted to order an immediate retreat across the river. Just then Colonel Cogswell, commanding the Tammany Regiment, arrived and took command forbidding any attempt to retreat across the river at that time. As senior officer on the field, Colonel Cogswell ordered an attempt at a breakout toward the Union forces downriver at Edward's Ferry. Colonel Devens was ordered to shift his 15th Massachusetts Regiment from the Union right flank to behind the 20th Massachusetts, and then move in a column of assault against the Mississippians to enable the Union forces to punch their way through to Edward's Ferry. Colonel Devens was to be joined by companies from the Tammany Regiment and the 1st California Regiment then on the Union left flank.[37] The best account of this attempted breakout is in the regimental history of the 15th Massachusetts.

As a preliminary step to the movement towards Edward's Ferry Colonel Cogswell ordered the Fifteenth to move from the right to the left of the line. Colonel Devens says of this movement: "The cool manner in which the regiment marched from the right to the left of the line, to protect the left, would have won for it an historic name if it had been done on one of the battlefields of Europe."

There was again confusion in transmitting or receiving orders. Colonel Cogswell says that he commanded all the troops to advance to the left in a solid body on the enemy's line, that he advanced with the two Tammany companies and a portion of the California Regiment, but that the Fifteenth and Twentieth did not follow. Colonel Devens says: "Confusion was created by the appearance of an officer of the enemy's in front of the companies of the Tammany Regiment who called on them to charge on the enemy. The detachment of the Tammany Regiment, probably mistaking this for an order from their own officers, rushed forward to the charge and a part of the Fifteenth Massachusetts, supposing that an order had been given for the advance of the whole line, rushed forward with eagerness, but was promptly recalled by their officers, who had received no such order." One of the men of the Fifteenth says: "The battle again commenced by one of the rebel leaders, who was mounted on a bay horse, riding out of the woods and shouting, 'Come on, boys, we have them now!' ... The rebels drove back the Tammany companies, which retreated in such a way as to produce considerable confusion.

At last Colonel Cogswell gave the order to retreat to the river bank. Colonel Devens said to him, "Sir, I do not wish to retreat. Do you issue it as an order?" "Yes sir," Cogswell replied. "I would like to have you repeat it in the presence of my major, then," said Devens. "I order you to retreat," Cogswell commanded again.[38]

The spirit of defeat now made itself felt throughout the Union officer corps. Captain Bartlett of the 20th Massachusetts in a letter to his Mother wrote:

For I knew then, that we should either be killed or taken prisoners. The field now began to look like my preconceived idea of a battlefield. The ground was smoking and covered with blood, while the noise was perfectly deafening. Men were lying underfoot, and here and there a horse struggling in death. Coats and guns strewn over the ground in all directions. I went to the Colonel and he was sitting behind a tree, perfectly composed. He told me there was nothing to be done but "surrender and save the men from being murdered." Most of the men had now got down the bank.[39]

This spirit of defeat was noticed in the Confederate ranks. As Private Randolph Shotwell of the 8th Virginia remembered:

Then ensued an awful spectacle! A kind of shiver ran through the huddled mass upon the brow of the cliff; it gave way; rushed a few steps; then, in one wild, panic-stricken herd, rolled, leaped, tumbled over the precipice! The descent is nearly perpendicular, with ragged, jutting crags, and a water laved base. Screams of pain and terror filled the air. Men seemed suddenly bereft of reason; they leaped over the bluff with muskets still in their clutch, threw themselves into the river without divesting themselves of their heavy accoutrements—

MAP, opposite: following the death of Baker command devolved upon Col. Cogswell, who ordered a series of moves designed to effect a breakout. The map illustrates the failed attempt.

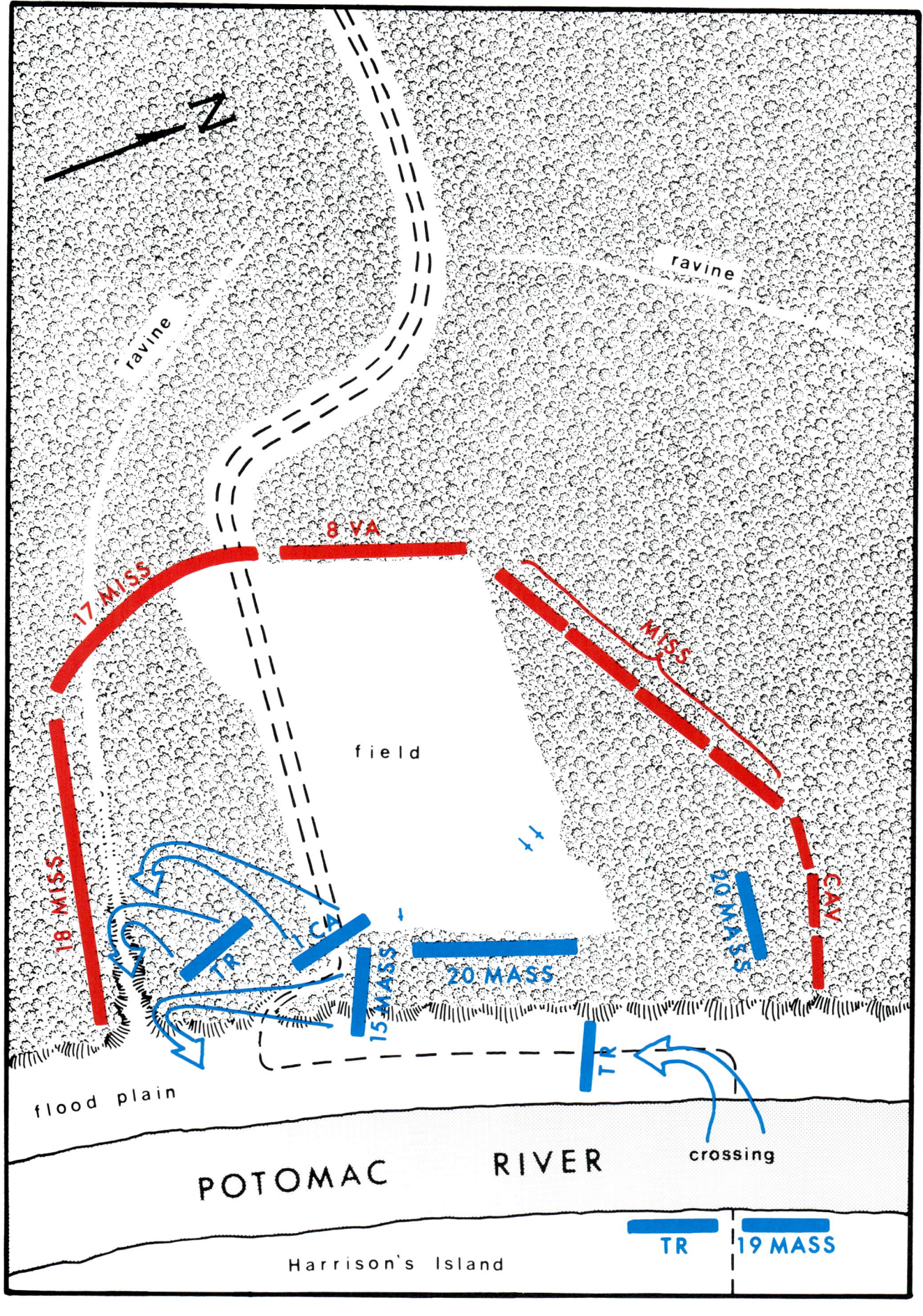

hence went to the bottom like lead. Others sprang down upon the heads and bayonets of those below. A gray-haired private of the First California was found with his head mashed between two rocks by the heavy boots of a ponderous "Tammany" man,

The state seal of Virginia adorns the face of this brass cuff button lost on the battlefield at Ball's Bluff by a member of the 8th Virginia Regiment. Courtesy Chuck Thompson.

The view below looks west across the dirt access road built by the U.S. Army in 1908. Traces of the old cart path run parallel in the woods to the left. A section of the original clearing can be seen to the right. The stone marker in the background indicates the spot where Clinton Hatcher fell. Hatcher was color bearer of the 8th Virginia killed in the final charge. Photo, Mike O'Donnell.

who had broken his own neck by the fall! The side of the bluff was worn smooth by the number sliding down.[40]

However, all was not lost on the Union side. On both the Union right and left flanks small counterattacks took place as brave soldiers sold their lives as dearly as possible in order to buy time for their comrades to escape to Harrison's Island. On the Union right this counterattack was led by Captain William Bartlett of the 20th Massachusetts who described it as follows (Special note: The Confederate flag bearer referred to here was the brave Clinton Hatcher of the 8th Virginia Regiment. He gave his life in this final Confederate charge. His marker stone stands just west of the National Cemetery where he fell. The local Sons of Confederate Veterans Camp is named in his honor.):

> I called for Company I for one last rally. Every man that was left sprang forward, and also about six men (all who were left) of Captain Dreher's company, and ten men of Company H under Lieutenant Hallowell, all of whom followed me up the rise. As we reached the top, I found Little by my side. We came upon two fresh companies of the enemy which had just come out of the woods; they had their flag with them. Both sides were so surprised at seeing each other—they at seeing us coming up with this handful of men, we at seeing these two new companies drawn up in perfect order—that each side forgot to fire. And we stood looking at each other (not a gun being fired) for some twenty seconds, and then they let fly their volley at the same time we did. If bullets had rained before, they came in sheets now. It is surprising that anyone could escape being hit. We were driven back again. I had to order sharply one or two of my brave fellows before they would go back. Everything was lost now.[41]

On the extreme Union left a counterattack was led by two fresh companies of the gallant Tammany Regiment after they landed on the Virginia shoreline. They attacked up the cart path striking the 18th Mississippi on its exposed right flank thereby enabling more of the retreating Union forces to reach temporary safety along the beach below the bluff.[42]

The charge of the 17th and 18th Mississippi Regiments was reported by Lieutenant Colonel John McGuirk, deputy commander of the 18th Mississippi:

> Col. W. S. Featherston ... ordered the right and left wings up, thus forming a crescent line, which enabled us with raking fire to cut down the advancing enemy. The men manifested confidence

"So near and yet so far" must have struck home in the hearts of the fleeing Federals who stood on this spot and gazed across the river to Harrison's Island. Photo, Moss Publications.

under the coolness of their officers. They seemed fighting a sham battle when above the roar of musketry was heard the command of Colonel Featherston, "CHARGE, MISSISSIPPIANS, CHARGE! DRIVE THEM INTO THE POTOMAC OR INTO ETERNITY!" The sound of his voice seemed to echo from the vales of Maryland. The line arose as one man from a kneeling posture, discharged a deadly volley, advanced the crescent line, and thus encircled the invaders, who in terror called for quarter and surrendered.[43]

A private with the 17th Mississippi Regiment wrote in his diary the following remarks concerning the charge:

> We formed about five o'clock when the firing was very heavy. When we were formed we advanced firing as we advanced & when we had gotten within about 60 yards of a 12-lb. cannon, orders were given by Col. Featherston to charge & drive the enemy into the river or drive them into eternity. His clarion voice rung up and down the lines was heard by the enemy on this side & rung among the hills of Md. & struck terror to the enemy. The cannon was taken & the enemy driven back under the bluff of the river.[44]

All of the Confederate forces swept forward to the edge of Ball's Bluff. The bloody struggle atop the bluff was now ending. Lieutenant Colonel Thomas McGriffen of the 17th Mississippi summed up the action in his official report:

> The Federal force fought well. A number were killed with the bayonet by my men.[45]

At this point Ball's Bluff is practically a vertical rise of some 70 feet. Scores of panic-stricken Federals plunged from the heights to the rocks and water below.
MAP, opposite: from 6 p.m. to 9 p.m. the Union withdrawal becomes a rout. Several Yankee companies executed desperate counter attacks—then the Rebels push an all-out attack which sweeps the field.

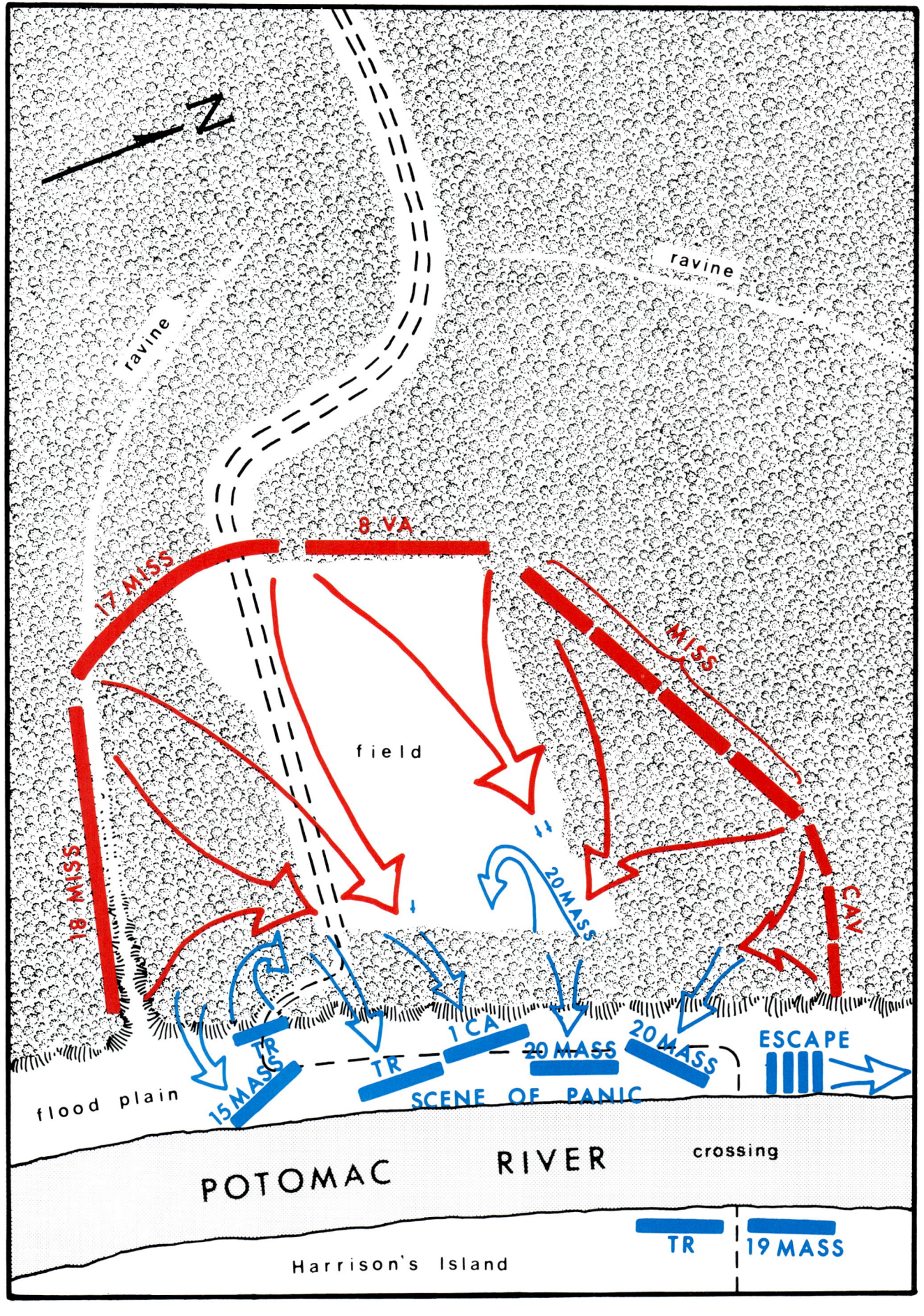

IV

Panic on the Heights

As the struggle atop Ball's Bluff was coming to an end the struggle on the beach/bench, an area of flood plane between the base of Ball's Bluff and the Potomac River, was increasing. All day long this area had been the focal point for fresh Union soldiers arriving in Virginia and for the wounded and dying evacuating from Virginia. With the pall of defeat upon them hundreds of Union soldiers sought safety there in the dying twilight. The 15th Massachusetts recorded the following incident in their endeavor to recross to Harrison's Island:

Lieutenant Charles H. Eager of Company B thus described his experience and the rescue of Colonel Devens:

After the order had been given to retreat, we rallied in a kind of bridle-path under the bluff, and near the river, when Colonel Devens ordered us to throw our arms into the river and take care of ourselves as best we could. There were a good many of the company who said they could not swim, or did not dare undertake it. I told them I could not swim, but we could keep together as much as possible, make our way up the river, and perhaps find a boat in which we could cross. George L. Boss, upon hearing me say I could not swim, said two or three of them could take me across, and soon appeared with Corporal Fred H. Sibley and Alvan A. Simmonds, who insisted upon my going with them. I told them I might be the means of drowning them all, and they had better go without me, but they insisted, and seemed so confident of success, I told them that if I could find anything that would float I would make the attempt. Upon going to the river edge, we found a limb some six inches through at the butt and perhaps ten feet long, and in pulling that out, pulled up a common floor joist about the same length. Upon seeing that, I told them I could 'make the trip' with it on my own hook, and not endanger their lives, but they would not hear a word to that and said I must go with them. At this point Walter A. Eames offered his services in assisting us across, and which proved to be very valuable. I certainly think without his help we should have had hard work to have reached the opposite shore. Just as we were about to embark, Colonel Devens came to the water's edge and stripped of his equipment and clothing. When Eames asked him if he could swim, he replied that he could not. Eames said to him, 'Hop on to our craft and we will take you across, too.' After satisfying himself that they were all swimmers but me, he waded in.

In spite of all our efforts we drifted quite a distance downstream, the current being strong, and finally landed on a small island separated from Harrison's Island by a stream some twenty-five feet wide, which proved to be fordable, only about waist deep.[1]

Just upriver from the 15th Massachusetts was their brother regiment, the 20th Massachusetts. For the latter the situation grew more desperate as described in their regimental history:

It was now dusk. The rebels could not come down the bluff without entirely breaking up their own organization, and moreover could not see very well what was doing, owing to the bushes and trees and darkness. The line of skirmishers and the firing of scattered groups of men warned them of the danger of approaching the 'last ditch,' and kept them at bay for several hours. They therefore remained on the bluff and kept up a continual firing on the men among the trees, in the boats, and swimming.

The scow was immediately filled with wounded and started back for the island. It made one trip in safety, and the little boats also carried over their loads, but some of the wounded and many uninjured men were shot in the boats.

The scow, having now returned was again filled with wounded for her second trip, but as she was pushed off, a rush of uninjured men was made who loaded her so that her gunwales were almost level

Panic-stricken Federal soldiers flee the triumphant Confederate forces on the crest. Their only avenue of escape was the Potomac—an even more treacherous and merciless foe.

Left, Sgt. Eames of the 15th Massachusetts who was credited with assisting the wounded Gen. Devens to safety. Courtesy, U.S.A. Military History Institute.
Below: modern view of Harrison's Island from the base of Ball's Bluff. Photo, Moss Publications.

Captain William Bartlett of the 20th Massachusetts Regiment. Bartlett was one of the Yankee heroes of the engagement. Rather than surrender on the beach, Bartlett led 100 men to a safe crossing upriver at Smart's Mill Ford. This courageous soldier served with distinction for the remainder of the war losing an arm and a leg in the process.

with the water. But even in this condition she had reached the middle of the stream in safety, when some of the men poling her were shot and fell on the gunwale. This of course disturbed the trim of the boat, and the frantic endeavors of the occupants to steady her again served only to make matters worse. She rolled completely over, and everybody was thrown out. As they came up to the surface again after their first plunge, they looked like a huge ball of men, entangled together and holding on to each other, rolling over and over in their desperate attempts to break apart and swim ashore. It was a fearful and heart-rending sight! Only one man is known to have escaped out of this entire boat-load. The scow floated down the stream and was lost. The metallic lifeboat was soon riddled by bullets and sank. The two little skiffs also disappeared. Within half an hour not a single boat of any description was within reach. There was no hope of escape now for those who could not swim unless they could find relief above or below.[2]

As hundreds tried to escape across the river and hundreds more shivered along the banks of the Potomac there were some enterprising Union soldiers who decided to escape upriver. These were the remnants of four companies—one each from the 20th Massachusetts, 15th Massachusetts, 1st California and the Tammany Regiment—each one clustered around their surviving officers or non-commissioned officers. Under the overall command of Captain Bartlett of the 20th Massachusetts they made their way upriver to the crossing area near Smart's Mill Ford. Captain Bartlett had this to say regarding his escape:

> I started up the river, followed by about twenty men of the Twentieth Regiment, twenty of the Fifteenth, and forty of the Tammany and California regiments. Captain Tremlett, Company A, Twentieth, Lieutenant Whittier, ditto, and Little Abbott went with me. An officer of the Fifteenth also was with the party. We followed up the edge of the river, and came to an old mill which we knew was up in this direction. It was owned and run by a man named Smart, who lived in Leesburg, so the negro told me, whom I questioned as to who was there. We expected to stumble on a party of the rebels every step. I asked him where his boat was. He wondered how I knew that they had one, and said it was up in the mill-way.
>
> I went up there and found a skiff under water, twenty rods away from the edge of the river. It was capable of holding five persons. Those with me declared it useless and impracticable, and proposed going into the mill, get a good night's rest, and give ourselves up in the morning. I thought, though, that if I only got one load of five over, it would be worth trying; so we got it down to the river and began the transportation, expecting every minute to be discovered and fired at by the rebels. When the boat was put into the water, the whole crowd made a rush for it. I had to use a little persuasion by stepping in front of it, drew my pistol (for the first time this afternoon), and swore to God that I would shoot the first man who moved without my order. It was the only thing that saved them. They were obedient and submissive, and avoided being shot by me or taken prisoners by the enemy. I selected five men of my own company and sent them across first, with a man to bring back the boat. So, by degrees, I got those of the Twentieth, next those of the Fifteenth

(whose officer, by the way, sneaked off, got across on a raft, and left his men on my hands), and lastly those of the Tammany and California regiments. I sent Lieutenant Whittier over in the second load, to look out for the men as they came over. It was a tedious job. At last I went over with Tremlett and Little, and was once more back on the island. We thus saved eighty men and officers from being taken prisoners... We went down to the hospital opposite our battlefield, where we found the wounded being cared for. They had heard, and believed, that I was shot, and the welcome that the men gave me brought tears to my eyes.[3]

Meanwhile the Confederate forces, exhausted by their long struggle atop the bluff and not desiring to enter into further combat on the beach at night, retired to Fort Evans to nourish themselves with food and rest. For the 8th Virginia Regiment and others it was also necessary to restock their empty cartridge boxes with ammunition.[4] Colonel E. V. White left this remembrance of his return to Ball's Bluff that night and subsequent capture of the remainder of the Union forces there:

> We reported promptly to Colonel Hutton, who ordered me to remain with Lieut. Charles Berkeley, who, with a detail of seventeen men, had been instructed to picket the ground during the night.
> Except Lieutenant Berkeley's little party all of our forces had retired to the vicinity of the Fort for rest and rations, and we took up our solemn vigil over the 'dark and bloody ground.' It was presently suggested that we go to the river, for although our battle had rolled to the very edge of the Bluff, none of our people had been quite there.
> Reaching the bank we sat down to listen, and heard a man struggling out in the river, crying

General Devens and staff pose for the camera. Devens survived his wound received at Ball's Bluff and became a noted infantry commander. Courtesy National Archives.

Elija White, raised in the Leesburg/Ball's Bluff vicinity, served as a guide during the battle and led a sortie onto the beach beneath the bluff to capture some 350 Federal soldiers later that night. Courtesy, Irwin Rider.

"Help, help, or I shall drown." The agonized voice of the despairing wretch, as it wrung out over the broad water, amid the stillness and darkness of inevitable death, conveyed to the mind an image of the horror which must weigh upon the heart of one doomed knowingly to eternal death. We could hear his strangling effort as he spouted the gurgling water from his mouth, and then another cry for help, answered this time by a voice calling from the gloom beyond, "Hold up a little longer, we are going." The first impulse, dictated by the desperate and savage experiences of the day, was to open fire and drive off his rescuers, but a more humane feeling prevailed, and we quietly listened, soon dimly discerning the boat rapidly approaching the Virginia shore, and landing two or three hundred yards above us, where the Federals had been crossing all day.

The space of beach or shore from the foot of the bluff to the water's edge is about sixty yards wide, and after crossing from the island, the Federals had to go down the river the two hundred or more yards to reach the road leading up on the bluff.

This space was still strewn with dead and wounded men waiting removal or burial, so that when we moved up towards the landing place we found it difficult, in the deep darkness prevailing under the bluff, to avoid stepping on bodies, those with life still in them always giving us notice of it.

Approaching the landing I suggested to Lieutenant Berkeley that he hold his men while I went forward alone to reconnoiter, which he did, and I walked up to the mass of people gathered about the landing. It was so dark they could not distinguish me from their own men, and making the best investigation I could, I reported to Berkeley that there were 1,500 of them.

On hearing my report the Lieutenant said, "Don't you think we can capture them?" Here was no taking counsel of fear—fifteen against fifteen hundred... It was then agreed that I should mount the captured horse, ride to the Eighth Virginia and ask them to come over and help us. Reaching their bivouac I found Lieutenant-Colonel Tebbs in command, and upon stating the situation to him and asking for the regiment, he said the men were so worn out with the exertions of the day that he would not order them for the expedition but that if any chose to volunteer for it they might go... In all fifty-two came forward promptly.

Moving rapidly back to Berkeley, we found we had come up on the Bluff and as not a man among us, except myself, knew a foot of the ground, they unanimously made me leader, and I placed Lt. Berkeley, with his original squad of a dozen, on the Bluff, to wait until the balance opened fire under it, when he was to open rapidly, making all the noise possible and shouting every order he could think of.

The remainder of the party descended the bluff to the beach or shore, and when near the landing we heard the boat returning from the island. How many trips it had made in my absence I do not know, but the number of men on shore had very perceptibly diminished. Here I halted my little army, and having witnessed the confusion among the Federals at a previous landing, I instructed my men to wait until the boat reached the shore. As it came to land we moved forward, and when nearly up with them I called for a surrender, but receiving no reply I ordered "Fire!" and our guns blazed into them. There was a general stampede of those who were able, a large number of them jumping into the river.

All their officers who could do so had left these poor fellows to their fate sometime before, except one, a gallant Irish Captain of the California regiment, who had swam over to the island to try for some way to get his men over, but failing that had swam the river back again to share the fate of his company. I think his name was O'Meara, and he

Surgeon Joseph Bates, 15th Mass. Regt., attended the masses of injured soldiers from the fight.
Below: a Civil War surgeon's kit, pocket type, which belonged to Dr. John Beckenbaugh of Sharpsburg, Maryland who cared for the wounded from several battles during the war. Courtesy, Doug Bast.

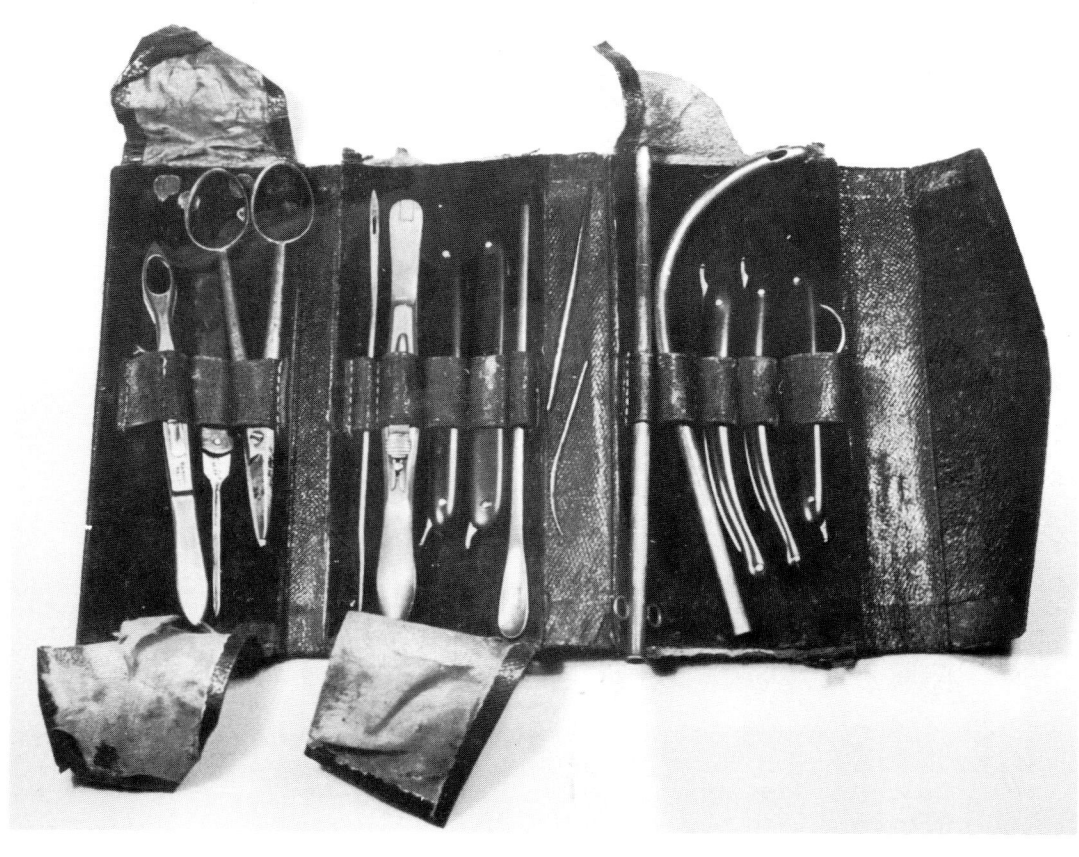

deserves the Medal of Honor. This brave gentleman called out, as a last resort in the wreck and confusion, "We surrender, who is in command? Capt. W. N. Berkeley replied, "General White," and Captain O'Meara asked, "General White, what terms will you give us?"

My unofficial promotions this day had been much too rapid for my scant military knowledge, and for want of a more professional answer I replied, "The terms of war, sir," which seemed to suit the Captain, for his clear voice called, "Men, General White gives us the terms of war; come out of the river and surrender," which they did, and then the brave fellow went up the river and brought back a number who had been in hiding there, when gathering them all together, he marched them up the bluff to the plateau where he formed them in line, and handed over to our charge three hundred and twenty-five prisoners, with many arms, ammunition.[5]

While this was going on along the Virginia shoreline the 19th Massachusetts Regiment was extremely busy on Harrison's Island receiving the survivors and preparing to defend the island. The night of 21/22 October was a hectic one for the men and officers of the 19th Massachusetts. In their regimental history they wrote:

Instinctively there was a hush along the entire line, and hats were raised as the body of Gen. Baker, covered with an American flag, was tenderly lifted out of the scow and slowly borne along the front. This incident had almost a demoralizing effect, but the command to 'Pile in lively, boys' occupied the attention at once and the men of the Nineteenth jumped into the scow and hauled it back over to the island, just at dusk.

The regiment marched in line across the island at sunset, just in time to see the worsted Union

General Gorman's troops march toward the Potomac River at Edward's Ferry, Maryland. From Harper's Weekly, *Nov. 9, 1861.*

forces, hotly pursued, flying in disorder down the opposite bank, and at once took a stand where they could aid in repelling the advance of the enemy.

In consequence of the shooting of wounded men by the enemy on the bluff, Col. Hinks, who retained command of the troops on the island, determined to do something to stop it. Lieut. Reynolds was detailed, with 16 men, to proceed under the cover of the darkness to the front of the island, dig a number of holes—like post holes—throw up the dirt as an embankment in front and drop a man into each, to fire across the river and thus protect, as far as possible, the retreat of the wounded.

It was the season of moonlight nights, but on this occasion clouds providentially obscured the moon. The detail worked away, digging their holes until a break in the clouds occurred, the moon shone brightly for a few minutes giving us 'dead away' and we were 'peppered' from the Virginia shore. No rabbits ever hunted their holes quicker. We dropped into them, behind the dirt already thrown up, crouching in a heap like lumps of putty, until the clouds again shut out the moon and the work was resumed and completed.

Although he could ill be spared, one man from Company F was sent over three times with the boat and he rescued fifteen men. Out of this number not one could be found who would return for his comrades.

During the night Lieut. Dodge asked for more men as pickets and a detail from Company H, under the command of Lieut. Hale, was sent out, completing the line along the shore. It was a terrible night for those on picket. The wounded on the Virginia side of the river, cut off from all help, could plainly be heard crying for water and begging that a boat be sent over to them. Now and then one could be heard as he waded out into the water, and, with strong and steady strokes, breasted the current. Little by little his strokes became weaker, then less steady, then mere splashes, in the frantic endeavor to hold out. Then a gurgling sound, a cry for help, and all was still again. All this passed under the senses of willing comrades, powerless to give aid. Now and then, one who was more successful would creep, cold, benumbed and almost dead up the bank.[6]

Meanwhile General Stone, now fully alerted to the disaster that had occurred at Ball's Bluff, telegraphed both President Lincoln and General McClellan as to the death of Baker and the need for

General Gorman, brigade commander in Gen. Stone's Corps of Observation, posed with his wife for this image. During the campaign Gorman had crossed at Edward's Ferry and was halted by a lone regiment of Barksdale's Mississippians. Courtesy National Archives. Below: an illustration of a Federal battery firing support for Gorman's invasion force on Oct. 22, 1861. From Frank Leslie's Illustrated Newspaper, *Nov. 16, 1861.*

Camp of the 19th New York—a part of General Bank's division which marched to the relief of General Stone's shattered command. From Leslie's Illustrated Newspaper, *Sept. 14, 1861.*

assistance. To President Lincoln he sent the following telegram:

October 21, 1861
Edwards Ferry, 10:35 P.M.

His Excellency the President

It is impossible to give full particulars of what is yet inexplicable to me. Our troops under Col. Baker were reported in good condition and position within 15 minutes of the death of Col. Baker. We have still possession of Harrison's Island and some fifteen hundred men on the Virginia side opposite Edward's Ferry. Six hundred more going over. We have lost several field officers killed and wounded and Colonels Lee and Cogswell are said to be prisoners. Colonel Ward wounded. The enemy has not thus far attempted any attack of our positions. We have lost 2 mountain howitzers and one Rifled James Gun. The enemy was undoubtedly reinforced in the evening but how much it is impossible to say. The report of killed by me half an hour before the disaster was 30. Our killed and wounded may reach 200, numbers of prisoners unknown.

C. P. Stone
Brig Genl[7]

Just as General Stone was alerting the President he also alerted Generals Banks and McClellan about the disaster at Ball's Bluff and the position of the Union forces still in Virginia at Edward's Ferry. General Banks and General McClellan immediately sent reinforcements in the form of General Banks' division with Banks himself arriving at 3 a.m. on the morning of 22 October.[8]

A member of the 9th New York State Militia Regiment recorded his impressions of that forced night march to rescue his comrades in arms:

As we pursued our march passing through Poolesville, we saw a guard stationed before a house, on inquiry we learned that it contained the body of Colonel Baker of the First California Volunteers, who was killed that day, in the Battle of Ball's Bluff, which was fought by Brigadier General Stone's Division, the command devolving upon Colonel Baker: now we understood why our march was hurried, it was to reinforce Stone's Division in case of an attack the next day; we willingly quickened our speed, all along the road, men in a state of almost nudity, some with nothing more than a blanket thrown over their shoulders, still others barefooted, suffering from the cold, having swam the Potomac near Conrad's Ferry, to prevent their being taken prisoners by the rebels, and they were going as fast as possible to Poolesville, some of them being badly wounded; we also met government wagons filled with wounded men, going to Poolesville. Halted along the road to rest awhile, after which we crossed the Chesapeake and Ohio Canal, on a boat laid across the canal, a plank reaching from the boat to the towpath, and halting long enough to load our muskets, we pursued our march quietly, the rain coming down in torrents, and about 4 a.m. halted on the banks of the Potomac, half a mile below Conrad's Ferry, and laid down in our blankets to sleep, being fatigued, after a quick march of 16 miles.[9]

The Chaplain of the 2nd Massachusetts Regiment wrote of his regiment's march to the relief of Stone's command:

It was at Poolesville that the first news met us of the defeat. There was the camp of the Fifteenth Massachusetts, and there some of its sentries informed us of the result. All along the road from that point we met fugitives straggling back to their camp. By the road were many men utterly worn down with fatigue, sleeping on the ground; and now and then were groups around a fire hastily built on the roadside, dejected, but still burning with a desire for a new struggle. Many were but half clothed; some without even trousers or shoes; some wrapped only in blankets.[10]

With the situation at Ball's Bluff quieting down and, at the same time, being stablized by the influx of fresh Union forces, General Stone turned his attention to his forces in Virginia at Edward's Ferry. He had approximately 4,500 men under the command of General Gorman facing an undetermined number of Confederates.[11] These Union forces were attacked on the afternoon of 22 October by Colonel William Barksdale and his 13th Mississippi Regiment. In his official report Colonel Barksdale stated:

On Tuesday morning I was ordered by you to reconnoiter the enemy at Edward's Ferry, and attack him if in my judgment his numbers and position would warrant me in doing so. Reaching the ground I occupied the day before, I ordered Captain Randell

Bivouac along the Potomac rendered a somewhat romantic view of the war to the civilian readers of Harper's Weekly *in the October 5, 1861 edition.*

These two illustrations from Leslie's *September 14, 1861 edition protray the troops of General Banks' command trudging through the mud and rain of western Maryland.*

General Nathaniel Banks whose division reenforced General Stone's command near Poolesville. Courtesy National Archives.

Below is a view of Harrison's Island and the Maryland shore from the crest of Ball's Bluff. Union sharpshooters, concealed along the river bank in the foreground provided covering fire for their routed comrades huddled on the beach beneath the bluff. Photo, Mike O'Donnell.

to skirmish on my left and Captain Eckford on my right. They reported that the enemy in very large numbers were stationed, as on the preceding day, near the banks of the river. From their movements, which could be easily seen from my position, I supposed they were planting a battery at the point of woods jutting out into the field to the right of the Daily house. I determined to make the attack at that point, and accordingly, ordered Captain Eckford to commence the engagement, and to charge and take the battery, if one should be found there.

Taking the road leading to Kephart's Mill, I halted the regiment in the woods to the right of the Daily plantation, and in a few minutes Captain Eckford commenced the attack upon several companies of pickets which were stationed along the field, charging upon and driving them in great disorder and confusion before his fire. I ordered the regiment at once to advance, and the engagement in a moment became general. Under a heavy fire from the enemy's batteries on both sides of the river and an incessant fire from his lines on this side the regiment continued to advance some 400 yards, firing as it advanced, driving the enemy before it back to the river, and killing, so far as I have been able to learn, 35 or 40 of their number. The enemy having been driven back behind his field works, and greatly outnumbering my command, having also artillery on both sides of the river, I did not deem it proper further to continue the assault, and hence withdrew the regiment to its position near Fort Evans, which I reached some time after dark.[12]

The night of 22 October saw the Union forces pulled out of Virginia at Edward's Ferry and returned to the safety of the Maryland shore. A member of the 1st Minnesota Regiment remembered it this way:

As soon as it was dark General Gorman

While Gen. Gorman withdrew his men from their toe-hold in Virginia at Edward's Ferry on the night of October 22, citizens of Leesburg searched the grisly battlefield by candlelight for friends and relatives. This brass candlestick holder (ca. 1830) was excavated in 1973 at Ball's Bluff. Courtesy Dalton Rector.

Frank Leslie ran this graphic, if somewhat erroneous, depiction of the nighttime withdrawal of Gen. Gorman's 2,500 men from their trenches on the Virginia shore at Edward's Ferry. The 13th Mississippi had prevented them from assisting Stone at the bluff nearly two miles away.

General Frederick Lander, U.S. Army, as he appeared during the war. Wounded in action at Edward's Ferry, he wrote a poem dedicated to the courage and nobility of his men. Courtesy, National Archives.

launched several canal boats into the river and manned them with lumbermen (mainly from the Stillwater, Minneapolis and St. Anthony companies) who with poles handled the boats expertly. General Stone attended personally to the withdrawal of the troops and I was detailed to act as his messenger or orderly and carried verbal messages from him and made reports to him personally during the entire night, and can vouch for his constant, watchful personal supervision of every movement, and his solicitude and care that no munitions, provisions, or materials of any kind should be destroyed or abandoned; and the writer can also testify to the great skill exhibited in conducting the withdrawal as rapidly as the boats could carry the men, but without chance of disorder or panic.

The First Minnesota, reduced by the detail handling the boats, was selected and placed in position to become the rear guard. All the other troops were new and such withdrawal in the night (after knowledge of Baker's disaster) might easily have been so mismanaged as to cause trepidation and disorder. But the movement was effected in perfect quiet and order. The troops nearest the river were first crossed, then others apprised of the retreat only as they received orders to move to the boats at once and in silence. There was no crowding and no delays. When nearly all had crossed, the picket was withdrawn, the writer traversing its length in the darkness and timber and communicating the order to each reserve. As the picket fell back, the First Minnesota alone was left and it was also called in the east, General Stone being the last man to embark.[13]

Thus ended the physical fighting of 21 and 22 October at Ball's Bluff and Edward's Ferry. Though casualties on both sides at Edward's Ferry had been exceptionally light—their official reports to the contrary—the cost of Ball's Bluff proved to be just the opposite. Of the 1720 Union soldiers engaged in combat at Ball's Bluff a total of 49 were killed, 158 were wounded, 553 taken prisoner and 161 were missing and presumed drowned in the Potomac River. On the Confederate side a total of 1709 infantry participated with 36 killed in action, 117 wounded in action and two (from the 8th Virginia) captured. Over half the Confederate casualties were in the 18th Mississippi Regiment—a result of their charge and sustaining two attacks by the Tammany Regiment.[14]

When Union General Frederick Lander (wounded at Edward's Ferry) heard that the Confederates had stated that "fewer of the Massachusetts officers would have been killed, had they not been too proud to surrender"[15] he wrote the following poem. (It is best read when standing at the National Cemetery at Ball's Bluff.)

Aye, deem us proud, for we are more
Than proud of all our mighty dead;
Proud of the bleak and rock-bound shore,
A crowned oppressor cannot tread.

Proud of each rock, and wood, and glen,
Of every river, lake and plain;
Proud of the calm and earnest men
Who claim the right and will to reign.

Proud of the men who gave us birth,
Who battled with the stormy wave,
To sweep the red man from the earth,
And build their homes upon his grave.

Proud of the holy summer morn
They traced in blood upon its sod;
The rights of freemen yet unborn:
Proud of their language and their God.

Proud that beneath our proudest dome
And round the cottage-cradled hearth,
There is a welcome and a home
For every stricken race on earth.

Proud that yon slowly sinking sun
Saw drowning lips grow white in prayer,
O'er such brief acts of duty done,
As honor gathers from despair.

Pride, 'tis our watchword; "clear the boats,"
"Holmes, Putnam, Bartlett, Peirson- Here"
And while this crazy wherry floats
"Let's save our wounded," cries Revere.

Old State—some souls are rudely sped—
This record for thy Twentieth Corps,—
Imprisoned, wounded, dying, dead,
It only asks, "Has Sparta more?"[15]

Modern view of sunset over Ball's Bluff. It was this time of day that Baker was killed and the Federal rout began in earnest. Photo, Mike O'Donnell.

V

Congressional Investigation

The combined Union defeats at Bull Run and Ball's Bluff, along with the death of Colonel (also United States Senator) Edward Baker, gave birth to the Joint Congressional Committee on the Conduct of the War on 10 December 1861.[1] This committee consisted of three Senators and four Congressmen.[2] Originally, it sought the reasons for the Union defeats at Bull Run and Ball's Bluff and the causes behind the inactivity of the Army of the Potomac.[3] Later, it investigated other Union defeats, ferreted out corruption in the Union war effort, and sought to direct and control the overall Union war effort.[4]

(Prior to the establishment of this particular Joint Committee on the Conduct of the War, Congress had twice attempted to establish such investigative bodies. The first attempt was in the 1790's following the failure of the U.S. Army expedition against the Indians of the Northwest Territory. The second attempt was in 1813 concerning the various defeats of the U.S. Army in 1812 and 1813 against the British.)[5]

This Joint Committee was composed mainly of Radical Republicans from both the Senate and the House of Representatives. Five of the original seven members of the committee were Radical Republicans.[6] Just who were these Radical Republicans? Basically, they were those members of the Republican party who were strong believers in, and workers for, the immediate emancipation of the slave in the South. Once the Civil War started in April of 1861, these men were for a strong prosecution of the Union war effort to crush the rebellion and bring about a speedy restoration of the Union. Their third main war aim continued to be the immediate emancipation of the southern slave.[7] The committee members, at the time of the Ball's Bluff hearing in early 1862, were as follows: Senator Benjamin Wade of Ohio, Senator Zachariah Chandler of Michigan, Senator Andrew Johnson of Tennessee, Congressman George Washington Julian of Indiana, Congressman Daniel Gooch of Massachusetts, Congressman John Covode of Pennsylvania, and Congressman Moses Odell of New York.[8]

Foremost of the Radical Republicans in the Senate and the chairman of the committee was Senator Benjamin Franklin Wade of Ohio.[9] Originally a lawyer, Wade entered Ohio politics in the 1830s identifying himself as an anti-slavery politician even at that early date. Because of his solid work in the Ohio legislature, they elected him to the United States Senate in 1851. This was at a time when the slavery issue was beginning to become the major national issue between the North and the South. Wade came out against the Fugitive Slave Law and the Kansas-Nebraska Bill. When war broke out in 1861, Wade came to the forefront in demanding a hard and fast victory for the Union accompanied by the destruction of slavery.[10] His appointment as chairman of the committee came about due to the influence of his fellow Radical Republican Senator, Zachariah Chandler of Michigan. Chandler was the author of the resolution creating the Joint Committee on the Conduct of the War and, as such, was entitled to claim its chairmanship. Chandler declined on the grounds that he was not a lawyer and suggested that his lawyer colleague Senator Wade was best suited to chair such a committee. Thus, Benjamin F. Wade, a hard core anti-slavery and strong war effort proponent, became chairman of the Joint Committee on the Conduct of the War. Wade was not content with being just the

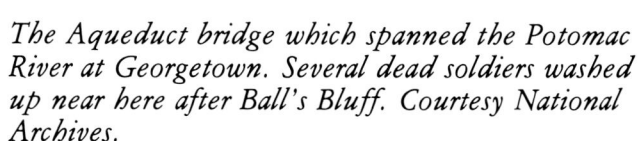

The Aqueduct bridge which spanned the Potomac River at Georgetown. Several dead soldiers washed up near here after Ball's Bluff. Courtesy National Archives.
A drowned soldier is removed from the icy waters near Great Falls.

chairman of the committee but with his dominating personality and strong viewpoints he also became its dominant member. It was soon realized by all of the Washington political scene that the committee and Wade were as one.[11]

The second most powerful member of the committee was its creator, Senator Zachariah Chandler of Michigan. Chandler preceded his political career with an extremely successful financial one in commerce and banking. In 1854, he helped to found the Republican Party in Michigan. In addition, he was a strong advocate of aiding the Free Soilers then moving westward to populate the Kansas Territory. Elected to the United States Senate in 1857, Chandler joined the Radical Republican faction and later became one of the strongest opponents of secession.[12] Chandler maintained his political power not only through his personality, but also his chairmanship of the Committee on Commerce which controlled jurisdiction over funds for river and harbor improvements.[13]

The only Democratic Senator to sit on the initial membership of the committee was a War Democrat, Andrew Johnson of Tennessee. Johnson came from the non-slave holding class of white southerners. He entered local politics in 1828 and continued in Tennessee state politics through 1843 when he was elected to the U.S. House of Representatives. He continued in the Congress until 1853, then returned to Tennessee as governor from 1853 to 1857. In 1857, he was elected to the United States Senate.[14] At the outbreak of the Civil War in 1861, Johnson, alone of all the southern senators, remained loyal to the United States. For this he was welcomed in the North and hated in the South. He was an active member of the committee until appointed War Governor of Tennessee by President Lincoln in March of 1862.[15]

Of the four members of the House of Representatives who were members of the committee, the one considered to be the "most able"[16] and the "most active"[17] was Daniel W. Gooch of Massachusetts. Gooch entered state politics in 1852 after having been a practicing attorney since 1846. In the late 1850s, he entered the U.S. House of Representatives. Once there he supported antislavery publications such as *The Impending Crisis in the South: How to Meet It* by Hinton Helper.[18] As a skilled lawyer, he conducted many of the committee's cross-examinations and became in addition the committee's legal advisor.[19]

If Daniel Gooch was considered the "most able" of the congressmen on the committee during its investigation of Ball's Bluff, then Congressman George Washington Julian was considered by many to be the most radical. Julian was born in Indiana in 1817 and entered the Bar there in 1840. He began his political career in state politics in 1845. In 1848, the Free Soil Party elected him to the U.S. House of Representatives and he became their Vice Presidential candidate in the election of 1852.[20] He was one of the organizers of the Republican Party at its Pittsburgh Convention of 1856. In 1860, he sought and won election once again to the U.S. House of Representatives.[21] Although initially a supporter of Lincoln, as time went on, he attacked Lincoln from his position on the committee. He was considered to be a most thorough and probing questioner on the committee.[22]

Another Radical Republican from the House of Representatives, who was appointed to the committee, was John Covode of Pennsylvania. Covode first gained political experience by serving in the Pennsylvania House of Representatives. Though elected to the U.S. House of Representatives in 1854 as an anti-Mason Whig, he switched to the Republican Party in 1856. He first became prominent in Congress by his chairmanship of the Covode Investigating Committee. This committee investigated charges of bribery against President Buchanan. In the 1860 election, Covode became a member of the influential Republican Executive Congressional Committee.[23]

The only War Democrat to be initially appointed to the committee was Moses Fowler Odell of New York. He was born in 1818 and entered New York City politics in 1845. In 1860, he was elected to the U.S. House of Representatives.[24] Odell was considered an extremely hard-working member of the committee. He himself considered McClellan to be "treasonable incompetent."[25]

Next to the members on the committee, the most important political personage who dealt with the Battle of Ball's Bluff was Edwin M. Stanton. Before the Civil War Stanton had held many important positions both in and out of the Federal Government. Admitted to the Bar in 1836, he made his mark as a lawyer of hard work, honesty, and overall ability. From 1849-56 he was counsel for the state of Pennsylvania during which time he gained a national reputation in his field. His practice in civil law brought him into association in the late 1850s with Abraham Lincoln. In 1858, he journeyed to California to represent the United States against fraudulent land claims. He won the important cases for the United States, thus saving over $1,500,000,000 for the government. As the country stumbled toward Civil War in late 1860, Stanton was appointed Attorney General, by President Buchanan, on 20 December 1860. After the outbreak of the war, Stanton became legal advisor to the Secretary of War, Simon Cameron.[26]

Senator Zachariah Chandler of Michigan, author of the resolution creating the Joint Committee. Chandler worked closely with Senator Wade and the other Radical Republicans to control the committee. Courtesy National Archives.

Senator Benjamin Franklin Wade of Ohio, chairman of the powerful Joint Congressional Committee on the War. Courtesy National Archives.

Representative Daniel W. Gooch of Massachusetts, a skilled lawyer considered the "most able" committee member. Courtesy National Archives.

Senator Andrew Johnson of Tennessee, a Democratic member of the committee. Courtesy National Archives.

Representative George Washington Julian of Indiana, a founder of the Republican Party in 1856. Julian was considered the "most radical" committee member. Courtesy National Archives.

When McClellan made his appearance on the Washington scene, Stanton soon became both his friend and his advisor. Because of his outstanding ante-bellum legal career, and his acquaintanceship with Lincoln, Stanton was made the Secretary of War on 15 January 1862. He reorganized the War Department along more efficient systems, and sought a hard war effort to restore the Union. In light of the Battle of Ball's Bluff and its subsequent investigation by the committee, it is worth noting that Stanton had had the control of emergency arrests transferred from the State Department to the War Department. In addition, upon becoming Secretary of War, he maintained a close relationship with the Radical Republicans on the committee.[27] His 1861 friendship with McClellan therefore waned until he became a bitter foe of the general. It was Stanton who issued the orders for General Stone's arrest in February of 1862.[28]

As mentioned in the opening paragraph of this chapter, the death of Colonel Edward Dickinson Baker was one of the major causes of the development of the Joint Committee on the Conduct of the War. Baker had been born in England and was brought to America in 1815 when he was four years old. Showing high intelligence early in life, he was admitted to the Bar in 1830 in Illinois. After that he was a junior officer in the Black Hawk War, a law and political associate of Abraham Lincoln, a brilliant orator, and a member of the Illinois State Legislature.[20] When war broke out with Mexico in 1846, he raised and became the Colonel of the 4th Illinois Volunteer Infantry Regiment.[30] He served with great distinction at the Battle of Cerro Gordo where he assumed command of General Shield's Brigade after the general was wounded. In 1852, he left Illinois for California where he became famous for his legal and oratorical skills.[31] Twice in 1855 and 1859 Baker was unsuccessful in running for the United States Senate from California which went solidly Democratic and strongly pro-slavery. He then left California for Oregon where he won election as United States Senator in the election of 1860. Besides his own election victory, Baker, through his oratorical ability and personal magnetism, helped Lincoln to narrowly carry both Oregon and California with his rallying slogan of: "Free Men, Free Speech and Freedom."[32] Arriving in Washington, D. C. for the inauguration of his old friend and associate, Abraham Lincoln, he became Lincoln's principal advisor on political conditions on the West Coast. Lincoln selected him to ride in his carriage to the inauguration and to have Baker introduce him before his inauguration speech.[33] During the early months of the Civil War, Baker served both as a United States Senator and as Colonel of the 1st California Regiment.[34] His magnificent speeches against those leaving Washington for the South and in support of the Union at various rallies in the North won him overwhelming fame as the orator of the Union.[35] He declined appointments as both a Brigadier General and as a Major General in order to maintain his seat in the U.S. Senate.[36] At the time of the Battle of Ball's Bluff, he commanded a brigade consisting of the 1st, 2nd, 3rd & 4th California Regts in Stone's Division (i.e., the Corps of Observation).[37] Though not an instigator of the Union reconnaissance into Virginia he was given discretion to either retire the troops at Ball's Bluff or reinforce them. Baker decided upon the latter and then failed to make the proper tactical dispositions to command the high ground on his left and front. Baker died a brave colonel at the head of his brave men.[38]

With the death of their distinguished colleague at Ball's Bluff, the Radical Republicans searched for the individual responsible for Baker's death and the Union defeat along the Potomac. Their suspicions fell upon Baker's commanding officer, General Charles Pomeroy Stone.[39]

Initially General Stone, though greatly upset by the losses and defeat suffered at Ball's Bluff, felt no apprehension over his person or his career because of what had happened. This was so because on 22 October General McClellan appeared, and after an inspection/inquiry into what had occurred informed Stone that he did not find him responsible for the defeat at Ball's Bluff. This professional exoneration was reassuring to Stone, yet Stone was concerned about what the President thought of him and the events of Ball's Bluff. McClellan informed Stone that he had told the President that Stone was not at fault for the defeat at Ball's Bluff.[40] A short time afterwards, in November, General Stone appeared before Lincoln to clear himself of charges of misconduct concerning the Battle of Ball's Bluff. This he was able to do to the Presidents satisfaction.[41]

However, for General Stone, vindication from his military superior (McClellan) and his civilian superior (Lincoln) would not be enough to save him or his career. Due to earlier troubles he had had with the Radical Republicans, Stone soon became the victim of malicious gossip against him in Washington.[42] It seems that during the Autumn of 1861, Stone had returned fugitive slaves to their owners in Maryland. Now this was in accordance with Lincoln's policy in the border states and also with the laws of the United States. Unfortunately for Stone, some of his Massachusetts officers, who were involved in these matters, were strong anti-slavery men, who complained to their governor, John Andrew, about being forced to return runaway slaves. Governor Andrew was furious and wrote a letter of reprimand

Governor John Andrew of Massachusetts whose anger over Gen. Stone's apparent mishandling of the state troops at Ball's Bluff boiled over the issue of returning fugitive slaves. Courtesy National Archives.

to the colonel of the 20th Massachusetts.[43] General Stone reacted strongly against what he considered to be civilian interference in his military chain of command. He wrote General McClellan the following:

> The fact that most of the soldiers in the regiment referred to were enlisted into the service of the United States in the State of which the governor referred to as the respected chief magistrate does not I conceive give his excellency a right to assume control of the interior discipline of the regiment, nor does it give him authority to command the punishment of a meritorious officer for any offence, either real or imaginery.[44]
>
> The usurpations of those ambitious state authorities commenced in much smaller matters than this of assuming authority in a national regiment serving in the field against the public enemy far removed from the State of which his excellency is governor. And it matters little to me whether the usurpation comes from South or North, Georgia or Massachusetts, I feel it my duty to bring the matter at once to an issue and if possible to arrest the evil before its natural fruits—open rebellion—shall be produced.[45]

Upon receipt of this letter, McClellan forwarded it to Governor Andrew. Governor Andrew was so upset at Stone's letter—and McClellan's apparent endorsement of—that he replied as follows:

> The Regiment was raised in the State under my authority in response to a certain requisition, not for soldiers, but for "ten Regiments," from the Department of War. I appointed and commissioned its officers, and the regiment was recruited here, on our own soil, at Camp Massasoit in the town of Dedham and the county of Norfolk, and marched from here to Washington with every kind of equipment and furniture recognized by the Army Regulations of the United States—and all of it provided and paid for by this Commonwealth—from its army wagons, ambulances, and horses, and its Enfield rifles (imported by Massachusetts from England under contracts made by an agent sent there by the State, the next week after the fall of Sumter) down to shoe-strings and tent-pins. Nor did we omit to supply anything for which the gallant Colonel William Raymond Lee (now a prisoner in a felon's cell at Richmond)—himself a regularly-educated officer and distinguished graduate of West Point, suggested to me even a wish.[46]

I would to Heaven that he were back now, at the head of his regiment—or that the Army of the Potomac were hammering at his prison door with both hands—and neither cause of all this war.[47]

The entire situation had now gone too far for Governor Andrew who instructed Senator Charles Sumner of Massachusetts (a Radical Republican) to attack General Stone on the floor of the U.S. Senate. This Senator Sumner did as follows:

Sir, my special object now is, to exhibit wrong here at home rather than in distant Missouri. Brigadier General Stone, the well-known commander at Ball's Bluff, is adding to his disaster there by engaging in the surrender of fugitive slaves. He does this most successfully. If a fugitive slave is to be handed over to a Rebel, the General is easily victorious.

Sir, beside my constant interest in this question, beside my interest in the honor of the national army, I have a special interest at the present moment, because Brigadier General Stone sees fit to impose this vile and unconstitutional duty upon Massachusetts troops. The Governor of my honored State has charged me with a communication to the Secretary of War, treating it as an indignity to the men, and an act unworthy of the flag. I agree with the Governor, and when I ask your attention to this outrage, I make myself his representative, as well as my own.

Others besides the Governor of Massachusetts complain. There are two German companies in one of the Massachusetts regiments, who entered into the public service with the positive understanding that they should not be put to any such discreditable and unconstitutional service. They complain, and with them all their own compatriot fellow citizens, the enlightened, freedom loving German population throughout the country.

The complaint extends to other quarters. Here is a letter from Philadelphia, interesting and to the point. I read a short extract only.

"I have but one son, and he fought on Ball's Bluff in the California regiment, where his bravery brought him into notice. He escaped, wounded, after dark. He protests against being made to return fugitive slaves, and if ordered to that duty, will refuse obedience and take the consequences. I ask, Sir, shall our sons, who are offering their lives for the preservation of our institutions, be degraded to slave catchers for any persons, loyal or disloyal? If such is the policy of the Government, I shall urge my son to shed no more blood for its preservation."

With such communications, some official and

Radical Republican Senator Charles Sumner of Massachusetts vehemently denounced Gen. Stone on the Senate floor. Sumner later declined Stone's request for a duel. Courtesy National Archives.

others private, I feel that I should not do my duty, if I failed to implore the attention of the Senate to this intolerable grievance. It must be arrested. I am glad to know that my friend and colleague, the Chairman of the Committee on Military Affairs (Mr. Wilson), promises us a bill to stop this outrage. It should be introduced promptly and passed at once. Our troops must be saved from such shame.[48]

Senator Sumner's denouncement was so strong that Stone promptly sent him a challenge to a duel of honor. Being a politician, Sumner took the letters to Lincoln who upon reading the various speeches and letters remarked to Sumner concerning Stone's letter and challenge:

I don't know that I would have written such a letter; but if I had wanted to, I think, under the circumstances—under the circumstances, mind you—I would have had a right to do so.[49]

Not only was General Stone wading into a deep political quagmire with the Radical Republicans—concerning not only the issue of slavery but also the relationship of the military to civilian government in time of civil war—but his superior, General McClellan was also on the edge of this quagmire.[50]

McClellan had come to the military forefront in Washington following his victories in western Virginia and the defeat of the Union Army at the Battle of Bull Run on 21 July 1861.[51] The basic problem that McClellan had was that he was a conservative Democrat general who believed the war was being fought to preserve the Union and not for the abolition of slavery. This brought him into direct and strong confrontation with the Radical Republicans. They viewed the war not only in terms of restoring the Union but also in the immediate emancipation of the southern slave. The Radicals viewed McClellan, and other generals who were Democrats and/or not abolitionists like themselves, as being soft in their desire to win the war and crush the southern states. Furthermore, the Radicals viewed McClellan's lack of activity in advancing against the rebels at Manassas Junction as an open indication that he really did not want to defeat his southern friends. All of this combined with the two facts that McClellan was Stone's military superior and had supported Stone after Ball's Bluff put McClellan into extremely bad favor with the Radical Republicans both in Congress and the country.[52]

In the rebuttal of these ill-founded suspicions concerning McClellan, the historian T. Harry Williams has written:

The suspicion had no basis in fact. The super caution of the generals was the result not of any sympathy for the enemy but of their military education. They had been educated in eighteenth-century ways of warfare. They thought of war as bloodless strategy. They believed that wars were won by maneuvering, as on a gigantic chessboard, and that hardly ever did armies come to combat. They viewed war as a kind of game. It was played by professionals and it had no relation to the society that supported the war. Generals fought battles when the conditions were exactly right. They did not fight because the civil authorities wanted a battle to sustain popular morale. In short, many of the generals were unfit to command in a modern political war like the Civil War.[53]

Basically, McClellan did not think that overall conditions favored an advance against the Confederate fortifications at the Manassas Junction/Centreville area in the autumn of 1861 for basic military reasons. With the advent of rain the Virginia roads would become quicksand of bottomless mud; there was no railroad to support the Army beyond Alexandria, and the Confederate defenses were exceedingly strong.[54] The Union soldiers, though better than the army that had run at Bull Run five months before, were still in desperate need of training as shown by their performance at Senator Baker's funeral:

In drill and training, the soldiers were far from precise. Infantrymen, standing at salute while Baker's coffin was carried to the hearse, were looking over their shoulders, talking aloud, lounging on one leg, wriggling and scratching. Their guns were pointed in all directions, and some held them like fish poles. In the grand military procession which escorted the bier, some companies were all in a muddle, and at times ran to keep up with the men ahead. "No Coasack or Bashi Bazouk," wrote the *Tribune* man, "was ever half so rude, raw, undisciplined and uncivilized in appearance as this cavalry selected for a purpose of ceremony."[55]

What had happened at Ball's Bluff underscored all of the above events in McClellan's thinking that the Army of the Potomac was still too green to advance into a major campaign, especially one against the massive Confederate fortifications at Centreville/Manassas Junction, with the onset of winter weather just around the corner.[56] Ball's Bluff had been fought between 1700 men on either side in a small area. Union advances had been made without clearcut purposes, orders had been misinterpreted and wrongly given, staff officers did not comprehend their duties; the Army was still too green. Better to wait until spring, McClellan reasoned, than to risk another Bull Run/Ball's Bluff debacle.[57]

Where was all of this leading Generals Stone

and McClellan, especially in their relationships with the Radical Republicans in Congress and their Joint Committee on the Conduct of the War? It can best be summarized in the words of the noted Civil War historian Bruce Catton:

> General Stone had run into very bad luck and had suffered atrocious injustice. Yet what had really wrecked him was not so much the vengeful suspicion of ruthless politicians as the sunken reef of the slavery issue. He had been taught, suddenly and with great brutality, what other soldiers were being permitted to surmise for themselves—that the issue was not going to stay submerged, that it was going to become central, that sooner or later the war was going to adjust itself to it.
>
> Like the lamented Colonel Baker, the principal men in the Republican party believed in bold and determined war, and it did not seem to them that they had been getting it lately. It had been hard enough for them to keep quiet while McClellan leisurely perfected his army's organization and training; they found it altogether unendurable when the first aggressive move made by any piece of that army proved to be the halfhearted thrust at Ball's Bluff, productive of shameful disaster. When the man responsible for that fiasco turned out to be one who had steadfastly refused to let his part of the army take an anti-slavery stand, the inference seemed irresistible.
>
> For the Republican leaders in Congress—men like Ohio's Senator Ben Wade, Michigan's Senator Zachariah Chandler, Pennsylvania's Congressman Thaddeus Stevens—believed not only in hard war but also in the abolition of slavery. Hard war meant smiting the Confederacy quickly and with vigor; also, as they saw it, it meant destroying what the Confederacy stood on, the institution of slavery. The two must go together, and a general who had no interest in striking down slavery probably had no real interest in striking down the Confederacy either. That the President of the United States had flatly refused to let abolition be made official policy made no difference. Notice had been served that softness on the slavery issue would ultimately be equated with softness in regard to victory itself.[58]

Following the defeat at Ball's Bluff, any plans for an advance of the Army of the Potomac against the Confederates at Centreville/Manassas came to a halt.[59] Instead, as the noted Civil War historian Dr. B. Franklin Cooling has written:

> The spring campaign of 1862 began as early as November of the preceding year—at least in terms of planning and resulting controversies which engrossed key military and civilian officials of the Lincoln administration.[60]

As the days progressed beyond the debacle at Ball's Bluff events moved on in the war for the Union. Skirmishes continued from Missouri to Virginia wherever the army's outposts were stationed. On 1 November, McClellan replaced General Winfield Scott as Commander-in-Chief of the Union Armies. Now, in addition to the Army of the Potomac, McClellan found himself responsible for the land military forces of the Republic. The Federal Navy successfully captured a number of Confederate coastal positions, but made a diplomatic mistake inviting war with Great Britain by seizing the Confederate diplomats Mason and Slidell. By 1 December, President Lincoln was inquiring of McClellan as to when the Army of the Potomac would advance. The next day the second session of the 37th Congress convened amidst the depression over Ball's Bluff, concern over the *Trent* affair, frustration over lack of movement by the Army of the Potomac, and the rising question of slavery as more and more of an issue. Just one week later the U.S. Senate approved, by a vote of 33 to 3, the organizing of a Joint Committee on the Conduct of the War. On 10 December, the U.S. House of Representatives approved the Senate's resolution for a Joint Committee on the Conduct of the War. It was in this atmosphere of late November and early December that the committee first met on 27 December 1861.[61]

The very first witness that the committee called in front of it was Brigadier General Frederick W. Lander of Massachusetts. General Lander had been a private railroad engineer prior to the Civil War. At the outbreak of the war he was sent on a secret mission to Texas. Thereafter he served on McClellan's staff in the western Virginia campaign at Philippi in June and later at Rich Mountain in August.[62] Upon the organization of "The Corps of Observation" at Poolesville in October, he took command of a brigade under Stone.[63] Two of the regiments from his brigade, the 15th and 20th Massachusetts, were engaged in the Battle of Ball's Bluff. His other two units, the 7th Michigan Infantry Regiment and a company of Massachusetts sharpshooters, were engaged at Edwards Ferry on 21 and 22 October.[64] Though not at the battles on 21 October, he did arrive on 22 October in time to receive a severe leg wound in the skirmishing at Edwards Ferry.[65] In response to questions from the committee he stated that he had not observed any rebel fortifications that would have prevented Union troops from advancing from Edwards Ferry to reinforce their comrades at Ball's Bluff. However, he felt that General Stone had based his plans on erroneous information due to Captain Philbrick's inaccurate reconnaissance report about the Confederate camp that actually was not there. In a startling item of disclosure, he stated that he had

Lieutenant William L. Putnam was laid to rest in the Lowell family plot at Mt. Auburn Cemetery in Cambridge, Massachusetts. Courtesy B. Pohanka.

discussed bridging the Potomac for a massive Union offensive just twelve days before the Battle of Ball's Bluff.[66] This last statement would indicate Union plans to cross the Potomac prior to the Battle of Ball's Bluff.

Following General Lander into the witness chair was Brigadier General George A. McCall, commander of the Pennsylvania Reserve Division in the Army of the Potomac. An 1822 graduate of the military academy at West Point, he later fought the Seminole Indians in Florida and was twice brevetted for gallantry in the Mexican War. Afterwards he became a colonel and one of two Inspector Generals of the Army before resigning in 1853.[67] When war broke out in 1861 he was commissioned first a Major General of Pennsylvania forces and later a Brigadier General of U.S. Volunteers.[68] When McClellan reorganized the Army of the Potomac in October, McCall commanded a division of three brigades made up entirely of Pennsylvania volunteers.[69]

Though not engaged in Ball's Bluff directly, it was his reconnaissance to Dranesville on 19-20 October that had precipitated Stone's demonstration at Edwards Ferry on October 20 and crossing at Ball's Bluff on 21 October.[70] (Late in December in a second reconnaissance at Dranesville, General McCall had defeated a Confederate foraging party there under the command of General Jeb Stuart.)[71]

In response to questions by the committee, General McCall described his advance to and operations around Dranesville in detail. In particular, he reported that though he had been ordered by McClellan to return to Langley (where his division was encamped) on the evening of 19 October, he had not done so until 10:00 A.M. on the morning of 21 October due to mapping projects carried out by his engineers. The committee wanted to know if McCall could have advanced further toward Leesburg and Ball's Bluff. General McCall replied in the negative, stating that such a move would have opened his left flank to an attack by the Confederates based at Centreville. However, the members of the committee did not think that this was a correct position since they felt that McCall could have been supported by the Division of General William F. Smith. McCall corrected the members of the committee by informing them that General Smith would have had a march of twenty-eight miles, along the Leesburg Turnpike, to have reached Leesburg; whereas, the Confederates would only have to march fifteen miles from Centreville to reinforce Colonel Evans at Leesburg. Had the United States forces taken Leesburg would there have been any value in doing so, the committee asked. Once again, General McCall had to reply in the negative since he felt that Leesburg was too far in advance of the main Union lines to have been permanently held and that General McClellan did not desire to bring on a major battle there, so far from his logistical base at Washington.[72]

In answering the committee's questions concerning General Stone, McCall stated that he felt that Stone had made a serious mistake when he informed McClellan that there were enough boats to successfully cross the Potomac. This had misled McClellan into thinking that Stone could successfully cross and recross his men across the Potomac River without endangering them in being stranded in Virginia due to a lack of boat transportation.[73]

McCall answered the committee's final two questions concerning the lack of a Union advance on Centreville and his policy toward fugitive slaves in the following manner. In his opinion General McClellan had not advanced against the Confederate fortifications at Centreville because they were too strong and the Virginia roads—in case of rain/sleet/snow—were not capable of logistically supporting the Army. As far as fugitive slaves were concerned, General McCall was taking in all that came into his lines and forwarding them to Washington.[74]

After questioning Generals Lander and McCall, the committee called General William F. Smith to testify in front of them. General Smith was an 1845 graduate of West Point and a veteran of many survey and exploration travels. At the outbreak of the Civil War he became Colonel of the 3rd Vermont Regiment and participated in the Battle of Bull Run.[75] In August he was commissioned a Brigadier General of U.S. volunteers and given command of a brigade in the Army of the Potomac. On 3 October he was given command of a division.[76] It was Smith's division that the committee thought was in supporting distance of McCall when McCall had marched to Dranesville. The committee asked General Smith if he was in supporting distance of McCall at Dranesville if McCall should have been attacked by Confederates from Centreville. General Smith replied yes.[77]

The committee's line of questioning of Generals Lander, McCall, and Smith indicates that it was interested in three major areas of concern. These were: (1) support for Stone at Ball's Bluff by McCall and Smith, (2) reasons why the Army of the Potomac did not attack Leesburg for a decisive battle, and (3) the status of contraband slaves in the Union camps. The first concern is a natural one considering what had happened to Stone at Ball's Bluff. The second concern shows the committee's interest in strategic military movements. The third concern is a political one since the committee consisted of Radical Republicans, one of whose goals was the immediate emancipation of slaves in the Confederacy.[78]

The questioning of Generals Lander, McCall, and Smith in late December was preliminary to the final and major witness to appear before the committee in their first hearing; that witness being Brigadier General Charles P. Stone. In early January, General Stone received a summons to appear before the committee in regards to Ball's Bluff. This summons reached Stone in Washington, D.C., where he was at the bedside of his ill wife.[79] He requested a delay due to his wife's condition but the committee would have none of that and ordered Stone to report in front of them on 5 January.

Stone went before the committee believing that they were gathering facts concerning the reasons for, and lessons to be learned from, the Battle of Ball's Bluff. Initially, the committee asked basic questions concerning Stone's rank and position in the Army, the number of men in his command and their state of health, the location of his regiments around Poolesville plus their health and armament, and the condition of roads in his area in relationship to troop movements.[80]

The committee next moved to one of its favorite themes, the lack of an aggressive forward movement by the Army of the Potomac against the Confederate army at Centreville/Manassas Junction. Stone would not comment directly upon this since he felt that it was in the command responsibility area of General McClellan. However, when pressed about the feasibility of a winter campaign, Stone cited as examples the Quebec Campaign of 1775, the Moscow Campaign of 1812, and Hannibal's crossing of the Alps.[81] (It is interesting to note that the first two campaigns cited by General Stone were total failures due to winter weather and the logistical problems that it causes. Hannibal's crossing of the Alps was a spectacular accomplishment which did lead to some tactical victories but never to a strategic victory.)[82]

After finishing their questioning on the

General George A. McCall, commander of the Pennsylvania Reserve Brigade, was the second witness called before the committee. McCall's advance to Dranesville precipitated Stone's actions at Edward's Ferry and Ball's Bluff. Courtesy National Archives.

strategic rationale for the Army of the Potomac to move forward, the committee got to the heart of their questioning of General Stone, which was the Battle of Ball's Bluff. The committee asked General Stone questions concerning how long he had been in Poolesville and how far his headquarters was from that of General Banks. Specific questions came next concerning why the crossing of the Potomac was made at Ball's Bluff and what troops were at Edwards Ferry when that crossing was made. Stone replied that the initial crossing at Ball's Bluff was a reconnaissance under Captain Philbrick and that the crossing at Edwards Ferry was a demonstration to occupy the Confederates' attention.[83] Using a large map that he had brought along, General Stone proceeded to show the committee members the specific locations of places and the troop movements involved at Ball's Bluff and Edwards Ferry.[84] He further explained to the committee that he had no intention for his main troop movement to cross at Ball's Bluff (which was to be used only as a reconnaissance crossing site), but rather at Smarts Mill Ford.[85]

General Stone proceeded to go into detail for the reasons of Baker's defeat at Ball's Bluff. These were: the inaccurate report of Captain Philbrick concerning the Confederate camp which did not exist; the lack of a cavalry scouting party that had advanced to Smarts Mill and then turned back; the incorrect crossing of the second battalion of the 15th Massachusetts Infantry at Ball's Bluff instead of at Smarts Mill Ford due to Lieutenant Howe's wild report; the mishandling of the boat transportation at the two crossing sites by Captain Young; the mistake of Colonel Baker in spending an hour and a half in getting a canal boat into the river when the job should have been handled by a junior officer; discretionary orders had been given to Colonel Baker to retire the troops in Virginia or advance reinforcements to their aid—he chose wrongly to reinforce without first crossing to check the situation in Virginia; and finally the poor tactical disposition of troops made by Colonel Baker once he arrived at Ball's Bluff.[86]

Had General Stone given Colonel Baker orders to cross as was rumored, the committee requestioned. Stone replied that he had not and had the actual orders to prove his statement.[87] This order read as follows:

H.Q. Corps of Observation
Edwards Ferry, October 21, 1861
Col. E. D. Baker, Com. of Brigade:
COLONEL: In case of heavy firing in front of Harrison's Island, you will advance the California regiments of your brigade, or retire the regiments under Cols. Lee and Devens, now on the Virginia side of the river, at your discretion—assuming command on arrival.
Very respectfully, Col. your most obt. servt.,
Chas P. Stone
Brigadier-General Commanding[88]

General Stone proceeded to answer questions concerning who had ordered the reconnaissance across the Potomac—he had done so, and was it to the Union's advantage to take Leesburg—only on a temporary basis due to it being untenable. Had General Stone been aware of McCall's movement to Dranesville—only in regards to his demonstration he held at Edwards Ferry on 20 October. Once again Stone put forth the statement that the reconnaissance on 21 October was his own idea. The committee queried Stone as to the reasons why Colonel Baker had not been reinforced by the Union forces in Virginia at Edwards Ferry. For basically two reasons, replied Stone. First, there was a Confederate masked battery located between Edwards Ferry and Ball's Bluff that would have torn the Union troops to pieces. Second, the terrain was both wooded and hilly, a perfect place for the rebels to have ambushed Union troops advancing toward Ball's Bluff from Edwards Ferry.[89]

The final two major questions that the committee had were in regards to the Confederates building fortifications along the river and General Stone's policy toward fugitive slaves. Because of the briefing that he had received at McClellan's headquarters before meeting with the committee,[90] General Stone refused on grounds of military security to discuss this matter with the committee.[91] This was a significant factor later on in February when the committee forwarded charges against Stone to the Secretary of War.[92] The truth of the matter was that what newspaper reporters saw and wrote about as Confederate fortifications having been built near the Potomac River were, in actuality, Union fortifications built during their demonstrations at Edwards Ferry on 21 and 22 October.[93]

The end of the committee's interrogation of General Stone on 5 January focused on Stone's policy toward fugitive slaves. This was a matter dear to the philosophy of the Radical Republicans as they were strongly for the immediate emancipation of the southern slave.[94] The committee informed Stone that they had read in the newspapers that Stone was returning fugitive slaves to their rebel masters. Outraged, Stone replied that this was "slander," the likes of which had even been stated on the floor of the U.S. Senate. Stone further informed the committee that upon a number of occasions, Negroes—either free or slave—would situate themselves around

Confederate earthworks guarding the approaches to Leesburg, Va. General Stone was accused of allowing the Rebels to construct fortifications along the river. In actuality, the earthworks in question were those belonging to the Union forces that crossed the river at Edward's Ferry on October 21, 1861. Harper's Weekly, *October 12, 1861.*

the edges of his camps selling whiskey to his soldiers. This was extremely bad for the discipline of the soldiers and as such Stone could not tolerate it. Therefore, the Negroes were sent away from the camps into other parts of Maryland. As far as turning fugitive slaves over to their former masters, Stone informed the committee that he had never done so in regards to slaves escaping from Virginia but was required, under Maryland state law and the policy of the Lincoln Administration, to do so in regards to Maryland slaves. The committee reminded Stone that the U.S. Congress had passed a law in the summer of 1861 informing the U.S. Army that fugitive slave policy was a political not a military policy area. Stone informed the committee that the only time a fugitive slave from Virginia had been requested by his Virginia owners to be returned,

Stone had refused to do so. Furthermore, Stone informed the committee, all fugitive slaves coming into his camps from Virginia were first, personally given an intelligence debriefing by himself, and were then put to work around the camps doing useful work. If the fugitive slave could not or would not do useful work, they were turned loose in the Maryland countryside to make their own way.[95]

At the end of this first session, General Stone asked for a copy of the transcript and was assured he would receive one. He never did. Furthermore, the committee members rose and thanked Stone for his testimony[96] thereby giving Stone the false impression that he had successfully answered the Committee's concerns regarding himself and the battle of Ball's Bluff.

VI

Imprisonment and Release

The month of January 1862 was a most difficult and trying one for the Lincoln Administration. Though able to solve the *Trent* Affair and thereby avoid war with Great Britain, the domestic situation seemed as gloomy as the winter weather.[1] The General-in-Chief of the Armies of the United States, George B. McClellan, had been stricken with typhoid fever since mid-December, thus grinding to a halt the hope of operations by the Army of the Potomac.[2] Serious accusations against the honesty and integrity of the Secretary of War, Simon Cameron, had forced his resignation early in the month. Within a week he was replaced by Edwin Stanton, former Attorney General of the Buchanan Administration.[3] The overall mood of Lincoln himself is shown in his meeting with his Quartermaster General, Montgomery C. Meigs:

> Montgomery Meigs, the Quartermaster General, was getting settled in his new office in Winder's Building, when the President visited him in great distress. He had been unable to gain admittance to McClellan's sickroom. Sitting down in a chair before the open fire, Mr. Lincoln said, "General, what shall I do? The people are impatient; Chase has no money and he tells me he can raise no more; the General of the Army has typhoid fever. The bottom is out of the tub. What shall I do?"[4]

It was in such an atmosphere of depression, suspicion and scapegoating that the second session of the Joint Committee hearings on Ball's Bluff got underway on 9 January 1862.[5]

Following the conclusion of General Stone's first session before the Joint Committee, a letter had been received by Congressman Roscoe Conkling. This letter was dated 8 January 1862, and was from Major J. Dimmick of the 2nd New York State Militia Regiment, part of Gorman's Brigade of Stone's Division.[6] It read as follows:

> Confidential
> 2nd Regt NYS Militia
> near Poolesville,
> Jan 8, 1862
>
> Hon. Roscoe Conkling, M.C.
> Washington, D. C.
> Sir:
> I notice by yesterday's Washington paper that in the House of Representatives on Monday, the resolution i.e. investigation of the affair at Ball's Bluff etc. was called up on your motion. Presuming you would like to obtain any and all information in regards to the subject I have taken the liberty of addressing you & state these facts.
>
> *Previous* to the crossing by Col. Baker, Gen. Stone sent for *Lieut Bloodgood* of Battery B, Rhode Island Artillery (stationed at Poolesville) and gave him *verbal* orders to this effect—that he was to take a section of his battery to the bluff on the Maryland side of the Potomac opposite the center of Harrison's Island and *protect the crossing* of Col. Baker's troops. This order he obeyed & remained at the post designated until after the crossing was accomplished, and was then ordered over to take the place of Lieut Broomhall who was wounded on the other side. It is understood here that it is *denied* that Gen. Stone gave orders for the crossing, but the facts stated by Lieut Bloodgood he is willing to substantiate in a court of inquiry or any proper place. The Feeling is general here that *somebody* is responsible for the *military murder* of that day.
>
> As I am situated here it would be very unpleasant to have my name used in connection with this matter, but I would respectfully refer you in

regard to myself to either of the Senators or Representatives from Connecticut, all of whom are well acquainted with me.

Very Respectfully
Your obdt servt
J. J. Dimmick
Major, 2d Regt N.Y.S. Mil[7]

Prior to General Stone's testimony in this second session, the committee heard from twenty-three witnesses. A detailed look at these so-called witnesses to Ball's Bluff shows that nineteen of them were not veterans of the battle. Of the five witnesses who were, one was only on Harrison's Island and two others—Lieutenant Howe and Captain Young—were the main officers responsible for the disaster at Ball's Bluff. (Lieutenant Howe had misdirected the second battalion of the 15th Massachusetts Regiment away from their planned crossing at Smarts Mill Ford to

Congressman Roscoe Conkling presented as evidence to the Joint Committee a letter from an officer in General Stone's command which suggested Stone's culpability in the debacle at Ball's Bluff. Courtesy National Archives. Artillerymen with the 34th New York Regiment shell a Rebel camp along the Potomac River. From Frank Leslie's Illustrated Newspaper, *November 2, 1861.*

that of Ball's Bluff, thus changing the entire Union axis of the battle. Captain Young had been the Quartermaster of Baker's Brigade at the time of the battle and in such a position had been the officer responsible for the boat crossings from Maryland to Harrison's Island and then from the island to Virginia. The total failure of the boat system in both instances was constantly remarked upon by most officers and many of the enlisted men who were engaged at Ball's Bluff.)[8]

Besides being a major cause of the disaster at Ball's Bluff, Captain Young had been politically active—with President Lincoln—trying to save his reputation and his army commission. His first letter to the President was on 7 December 1861, part of which follows:

To the President
Sir

In the letter you gave me yesterday to Genl McClellan it appears that you have misunderstood my case & my wants and you will pardon me for saying that you have unintentionally done me an injustice.

You have deemed me to be an obscure and friendless person seeking your favor through your affection for Col Baker.

If services rendered to you and the Republican cause in New York are claim upon your consideration, I could have preferred my claims before I had met Col Baker. But I pass all that—I submit my letters, such as I could put in one day away from home. I had been misled by the counsel of friends, who believed you would not require testimonials of me who had been commissioned by my commander.

I did not know that you thought me untruthful and unworthy of your friendship.

If you could know, as you probably will in time, all the facts of the Battle of Ball's Bluff you would have no trouble in recalling all my statements to you.

I am not asking any favor or clemency of Genl McClellan. He cannot keep me. I wish an appointment as Brigade Quarter Master and Genl Gorman (?) will at once transfer me to a new service—I could not deliver to Gen McClellan—But Gen Gorman (?) in reading it agrees with me that the only help is as stated. I had been regularly by Col Baker and he promised to see to my commission. Two days before he was killed he told me and several officers that he intended to write a private letter to

View from the crest of Ball's Bluff overlooking Harrison's Island and the Potomac River. Harrison's Island was the Union staging area during the battle of Ball's Bluff and a scene of disarray in its aftermath. Photo, M. O'Donnell.

Secretary of War and have me appointed.

This is my case. I wish to remain in the service to the end of the war and if there was any other course for doing so I would not address you—all of my intimate associates in the Cal Regt have left it and I cannot return to it.[9]

On 7 January 1862, Captain Young wrote a second letter to President Lincoln which read as follows:

To the President
Sir

By order of General McClellan I am cashiered and dismissed from the service of the United States.

My overzeal for my Regiment and in defending the memory of Col Baker are the real cause of my trouble.

My court martial has found me guilty of the charge of leaving camp without the permission of Genl Burns.

I sincerely believe that I was authorized by the order of the Commandant of the California Regt and by my pass as Quartermaster signed by Genl McClellan to go to Washington on Regimental duty without the leave of Genl Burns. The Court Martial has found otherwise.

Mr. President, it is my first offence in a service of seven months.

Col Wistar now stopping at Willards can inform you as to my standing in the Regiment and perhaps may be able to explain away the seeming discrepancies in my report to you of the Battle of Ball's Bluff.

Mr. President as God knows all things, I am not deserving of this terrible punishment upon me and all those who bear my name.

I am Sir Your obedient
Servent
Francis G. Young[10]

Willards Hotel
Jan 7 1862

Eight of these first twenty-three witnesses were from the 2nd New York State Militia Regiment. This unit was an ante-bellum militia unit and very much a social club. Its membership greatly resented the regular army discipline as enforced by General Stone. Their attitude is best summed up by the historian, T. Harry Williams:

Now followed a long parade of witnesses consisting of volunteer officers in Stone's command and civilian residents from his district. The great majority of these men nourished bitter grievances against Stone because of the iron, West Point discipline which he enforced and his supposed prejudice against civilian soldiers. They regaled the Committee with fantastic tales of his alleged treason. Culled from campfire gossip, their evidence asserted that Stone had been guilty of criminal negligence at Ball's Bluff; his troops distrusted his loyalty; secessionists applauded him "above all other men"; he had permitted the enemy to erect fortifications near his lines; he carried on a mysterious and probably treasonable intercourse with the Confederates across the river; and once he had actually engaged in a conference with rebel officers under a flag of truce.

Wade and Chandler ran the entire investigation with flagrant unfairness. They asked leading questions designed to produce criticisms of Stone, and they bullied witnesses into giving the right answers. Nearly every officer was asked a question of this nature: "So far as you know, is not there such a general suspicion of General Stone among officers

Lieutenant Church Howe testified prior to Stone's second session before the Joint Committee. Lt. Howe had misdirected the Union reinforcements from their planned crossing at Smart's Mill Ford to Ball's Bluff. Courtesy, U.S.A. Military History Institute.

and men that they would be unwilling to go into battle with him?"

On one occasion the stern chairman asked an officer why Stone had not destroyed a certain flour mill near his lines. The officer professed ignorance. With the air of one revealing a great secret, Wade said, "He did not tell you why he had not battered it down, as it was supplying the rebel army with flour?" When another witness condemned Stone's laxity in permitting Confederate sympathizers to pass through his lines, Wade observed approvingly, "Then it is no mystery to you that the secessionists should have accounts of everything going on on this side?"[11]

A Captain James Brady of the 2nd NYSM testified against General Stone. He stated that Stone had not sent reinforcements from Edwards Ferry to help those caught at Ball's Bluff and that Stone had allowed mysterious letters and packages to be sent across the Potomac. He concluded his testimony by stating that General Stone had refused him permission to go home to New York City in regards to a business matter thereby costing him the $3,000 business deal. The only way he finally got there was to resign his commission thereby costing him his captaincy and four years service in the regiment.[12] (Is it any wonder that such men hated Charles P. Stone and were willing to spread gossip to discredit him?) Major Dimmick, who had written to Congressman Conkling on 8 January, also testified against Stone. He claimed that Stone allowed mysterious packages and letters to cross the Potomac; that the secessionists thought of Stone in the highest possible regard; that many of his men thought General Stone a traitor and disloyal; and finally, General Stone had permitted the rebels to build fortifications along the Potomac within range of the Union artillery.[13]

Countering such biased hearsay testimony against General Stone was that given by two officers who had actually fought at Ball's Bluff: Lieutenant

Infamous Libby Prison in Richmond, Va., home of several hundred prisoners captured at Ball's Bluff. General Stone was accused of corresponding with the enemy when in actuality he was forwarding mail to his men in captivity.

Colonel Wistar of the 1st California Regiment and Colonel Charles Devens of the 15th Massachusetts Regiment. Both men and their regiments still had full confidence in General Stone. Wistar stated, in answer to a question from the committee, that it would have been impossible for Stone to have reinforced Ball's Bluff from Edwards Ferry. As to the mysterious packages and letters being sent across the Potomac, Colonel Devens informed the committee that he was sending these items to the men of his regiment who, as a result of Ball's Bluff, were prisoners of war in Richmond.[14]

On 31 January, the committee recalled General Stone to appear in front of them. Stone had been informed on the day before, by the new Secretary of War Edwin Stanton, that certain witnesses had appeared in front of the committee who had impugned Stone's loyalty. Upon appearing in front of the committee, the Chairman, Senator Ben Wade, informed Stone that his conduct in regards to the Battle of Ball's Bluff had been called into question. Five major points had been brought against General Stone concerning not only the battle, but also other events surrounding his tenure as commander of the Corps of Observation. These were as follows:

1. Inadequate boat transportation had been supplied Colonel Baker at Ball's Bluff

2. Reinforcements had not been sent from Edwards Ferry to Ball's Bluff

3. There was excessive written communications with the enemy across the Potomac River in Virginia

4. Stone had allowed the rebels to build fortifications along the Potomac well within the range of U.S. artillery

5. Stone had not destroyed a rebel flour mill along the Potomac

Stone answered each of these false charges against himself in minute detail. Regarding boat transportation for Colonel Baker, since Baker had been given discretionary orders in regards to crossing into Virginia or retreating from Virginia, it was his responsibility as the officer in charge to see to his boat transportation. In point of fact, his boat transportation had been totally mismanaged by Lieutenant Howe of the 15th Massachusetts Regiment and Captain Young of the California (Baker's) Brigade. As far as lack of reinforcements from Edwards Ferry to Ball's Bluff was concerned, General Stone told the committee that he would be willing to lead them to the battle area to judge for themselves how impassable the terrain was for troop movements under battle conditions. Stone was told by committee members that they would not go since they could not judge terrain due to their lack of military education and experience. Stone could only point out to them their total hypocrisy in judging him, a military man. The committee glossed over Stone's statement of fact. As far as excessive communication with the enemy was concerned, that charge was completely without foundation. In great detail Stone informed the committee how each letter and package coming and going into his area of responsibility was examined in order to gain any intelligence information concerning the rebels and to make certain that no intelligence information concerning Union forces reached the rebels. In actuality, many letters and packages being sent south were going from Union soldiers whose comrades had been captured at Ball's Bluff and were prisoners of war in Richmond. Regarding the erection, by the rebels, of fortifications near the Potomac, the fact of the matter was that it had never occurred. Fortifications seen on the Virginia shore near Edwards Ferry were actually built by Union soldiers on 21 and 22 October. The only Confederate fort since constructed was Fort Johnston well west of Leesburg and out of range of Stone's artillery. As to the rebel flour mill, Stone told the committee that he had not destroyed it because he did not believe in making war on civilians.[15]

As historian Margaret Leech has written concerning Stone's second testimony in front of the committee:

> Ben Wade and his colleagues passed judgment on Stone in January. Unfriendly officers had come down from the upper Potomac to blacken Stone's name with the charge of disloyalty. Republicans lent a willing ear to the slander of a general who had been lenient in his treatment of Maryland slaveholders. In his absence, Stone was tried, condemned and sentenced in the star-chamber court, and Mr. Stanton issued an order for his arrest. At McClellan's request that Stone might be heard in his own defense, he was called before the Joint Committee. None of his detractors confronted him. The vague accusations of communicating with the enemy were repeated; and Stone sat staring at the Committee, a reserved and fastidious man. . . . In his outrage, his words tumbled over each other. "That is one humiliation I had hoped I never should be subjected to," he cried to Ben Wade. "I thought there was one calumny that could not be brought against me. I raised all the volunteer troops that were here during the seven dark days of last winter. I could have surrendered Washington." He had hardly been out of his clothes for the last year, he went on. Guarding the outposts of the capital, he got into his blankets every night without undressing. The most he had ever done was to pull off his boots.
> "If you want more faithful soldiers you must find them elsewhere. I have been as faithful as I can be. . . ." General Stone might have saved his breath. He was arrested and sent to Fort Lafayette.[16]

After General Stone had given his testimony on 31 January, the committee heard from eleven witnesses from 7 February through 27 February. Of these eleven witnesses, only three had been involved in the Battle of Ball's Bluff, a fourth had been on Harrison's Island, and two had been at Edwards Ferry. Colonels Lee and Revere who had fought at Ball's Bluff commented only about the lack of boat transportation. Chaplain Kellen of the 1st California claimed that Stone had given Baker a written order to cross the river.[17] However, a report published in Volume 3 of *The Rebellion Record* refutes that charge. It reads as follows:

> GEN. STONE'S ORDERS TO COL. BAKER - The following are exact copies of the orders from Gen. Stone to Col. Baker, which were found beneath the lining of the latter's hat by Capt. Young, his aide, after the body had been taken from the field. Both were deeply stained with Col. Baker's blood, and one of the bullets, which went through his head, carried away a corner of the first:
> H.Q. CORPS OF OBSERVATION
> EDWARDS FERRY, OCTOBER 21, 1861
> COLONEL: In case of heavy firing in front of Harrison's Island, you will advance the California regiment of your brigade, or retire the regiments under Cols. Lee and Devens, now on the Virginia side of the river, at your discretion—assuming command on arrival.
> Very respectfully, Col., your most obt. servt.,
> CHAS. P. STONE,
> Brigadier-General, Commanding

The second order which follows, was delivered on the battlefield by Col. Cogswell, who said to Col. Baker, in reply to a question what it meant. "All right, go ahead." Thereupon Col. Baker put it in his hat without reading. An hour after he fell:

> E. D. BAKER, COMMANDING BRIGADE:
> COLONEL: I am informed that the force of the enemy is about four thousand, all told. If you can push them, you may do so as far as to have a strong position near Leesburg, if you can keep them before you, avoiding their batteries. If they pass Leesburg and take the Gum Springs road, you will not follow far, but seize the first good position to cover that road.
> Their design is to draw us on, if they are obliged to retreat, as far as Goose Creek, where they can be reinforced from Manassas, and have a strong position.
> Report frequently, so that when they are pushed, Gorman can come up on their flank.
> Yours respectfully and truly,
> CHARLES P. STONE
> Brigadier-General Commanding[18]

Colonel Hinks of the 19th Massachusetts stated that there was great confusion on Harrison's Island—a factor to be found, it should be noted, in any battle situation. Mismanagement was the concern of Colonel Patrick of the 30th Pennsylvania Regiment. Colonel Dana of the 1st Minnesota Regiment had been at Edwards Ferry. He reported the same old stories about letters and packages being allowed to cross the Potomac and that his men thought General Stone disloyal. Colonel Van Alen, who testified next, had been in Washington the day of the battle. However, Colonel Tompkins of the 1st Rhode Island Artillery supported General Stone in regards to the shelling of Confederate fortifications. He told the committee that Fort Johnston was out of range of his artillery. In addition, when the Confederates did build fortifications close to the river, it was done at night. When discovered the next morning they were always shelled by his artillery.[19]

In regards to this second session of the Joint Committee hearings on the Battle of Ball's Bluff, General Stone was found guilty according to camp gossip, by statements made by individuals not even at the battle, half-truths, innuendos, and the like. Stone was, at this time, never given a copy of the transcript for review nor was he allowed to know who had said what to impugn his loyalty. It was as if he had been blindfolded and left in the fog and then found guilty of not knowing where he was and where he was going. And that is pretty much what happened. Stone was never allowed to have an attorney present, nor was he ever allowed to cross-examine those who had testified against him. In final notation on these two hearings it should be pointed out that of the thirty-nine witnesses called in front of the committee only eight were from those units that had fought at Ball's Bluff.

A review of the first half of testimony of the second session held by the Joint Committee on the Conduct of the War will show how damaging against General Stone it must have appeared. Conferences held with rebel officers in midstream, mysterious letters and packages allowed across the Potomac at will, failure to destroy rebel fortifications along the river, and a general consensus of disloyalty of him held by many of the officers and men under his command.[20]

Though writing of the time period of the Second Bull Run Campagin, the mood in Washington in early 1862 is best described by Bruce Catton as follows:

> The colonel of the 55th New York Infantry, landing at the Alexandria wharves next morning, noted an air of great depression as soon as he stepped ashore. Nobody knew just what had happened, but

all sorts of rumors were afloat; he found the word "treason" being used freely.

Treason: betrayal, treachery, a will to lose when the means to win are at hand; a dark, frightening word, coming up out of the shadows, carrying fear and distrust and panic unreason with it, so that the visible enemies in gray and butternut . . . seemed less to be feared than those who might be standing, all unsuspected, at one's elbow. The word was used everywhere: in the President's Cabinet, in the War Department, in the tests of the generals, and—most disastrously of all—in the ranks of the . . . army. All of the disillusionment . . . all of the sudden war-weariness which had come so soon to a land that had been long at peace, all of the bewilderment felt by men who saw themselves striking ineffectually at targets that mysteriously shifted and dissolved as one struck—all of this, welling up in the hearts of men who had done their best to no avail, began to find expression in that word. There had been betrayal: of high hopes and noble purposes, of all the army meant to itself and to the country. The country had suffered more than a defeat. What was happening now was the beginning of disintegration.[21]

On 28 January, the new Secretary of War, Edwin Stanton, issued the necessary orders that General Stone be arrested for suspicion of disloyalty. Upon hearing of Mr. Stanton's order, General McClellan requested that General Stone be allowed to testify in his own behalf.[22] Stone proceeded to do so on 31 January, but was undermined by two factors. The first being that upon arriving in Washington he had stopped at General McClellan's headquarters. There he was told to say nothing to the Joint Committee concerning the past, present or future military plans of General McClellan to the committee. To military men this would seem reasonable for security reasons, but to the Joint Committee it would appear that Stone was trying to hide information because that information would prove disloyalty.[23] The other major problem that Stone would face would be in front of the Joint Committee. There he would face—without benefit of a lawyer—a court-like situation in which he could neither know nor face his accusers and whose accusations would be stated to him only in general terms thereby making his generalized testimony appear that he was trying to hide damaging evidence against himself.[24]

General Stone's testimony delayed his arrest for eight more days. During that time the Joint Committee proceeded to take the testimony of witnesses concerning the Battle of Ball's Bluff.[25]

At the same time, General McClellan had started to feel the fury of the Joint Committee against himself. This was caused by his not advancing against the rebels in Virginia which some of the Radical Republicans on the committee took as a sign of treason.[26] McClellan's personal situation and his relationship vis-a-vis Stone are insightfully related in the following report that Colonel Van Alen (whose cavalry regiment was in The Corps of Observation) had with McClellan on 1 February:

Feb. 3. Note. Col. Van Alen told me Saturday night that it was reported that the Joint Committee of Congress had deemed of the Secretary of War to remove Genl. Stone from command (which would let Gorman in). That he had a talk about it with McClellan, who said "They want a victim" to which the Colonel answered—"Yes, and when they have once tasted blood, got one victim, no one can tell who will be the next victim!" Thereupon the Genl. colored up, and the conversation ceased.[27]

On 6 February, Allan J. Pinkerton, civilian head of McClellan's spy service, wrote a report to McClellan concerning Stone. Pinkerton had just finished interviewing a Mr. James Shorbs, civilian refugee from Loudoun County, Virginia. (Mr. Shorbs had been born and raised in Leesburg until age ten when his family moved to Ohio. He had returned to Loudoun just prior to the war, to settle family business, and had been caught there at the outbreak of the war. Confederate authorities in Richmond had refused him passage north until early 1862.)

At the top of his report detailing his interrogation of Shorbs, Allan Pinkerton had written: Brig. Gen. Charles P. Stone, U.S.A. suspected of disloyalty.[28] Mr. Shorbs made the following statements about General Stone. General Stone is very popular with the rebels and is the only Union officer they call a gentleman. There are frequent flags of truce to allow people to cross the Potomac River both coming from and going to Maryland. In particular, a Mrs. White, whose husband is a rebel cavalry officer, is a frequent river crosser. The rebels had told him that if just one Union regiment had advanced from Edwards Ferry to Ball's Bluff, the Union troops at the bluff would have been saved. Stone must have known what was going on at Ball's Bluff, yet continued to send troops across the river to their death. There were many mysterious flags of truce seen along the Potomac and along with these flags of truce many mysterious letters were passed across the river. Stone had returned escaped slaves and horses to a Mr. Ball on Mason's Island. He personally heard a Mississippi officer state that if the authorities in Washington, D.C. kept fooling around with General Stone that Stone would go South to join the Confederacy. On a number of occasions he heard rebel officers state that they often crossed the Potomac and visited with General Stone.

Allan J. Pinkerton, civilian head of McClellan's spy service, presented dubious evidence which cast doubt on Gen. Stone's loyalty. Courtesy National Archives.

General Evans, the rebel commander in Leesburg, stated that Stone was both a good officer and a gentleman. Furthermore, the majority of citizens in Leesburg thought highly of General Stone. Last, but not least, Stone had allowed a rebel fort to be built along the Potomac within the range of his artillery.[29] At the end of his report Mr. Pinkerton wrote:

> The statements of this man, James Shorbs, were given very freely and with apparent candor and sincerity, yet his general appearance did not impress me very favorably. He had been committed to the Old Capitol Prison to await your decision as to his further disposal.[30]

On the very back envelope of this report is written:

> Mr. President: These are the papers left with General McClellan in General Stone's case.[31]

After the report by Pinkerton on the Shorbs testimony, General McClellan was unable to delay Stone's arrest any further. General McClellan sent Pinkerton's report to Secretary of War Stanton.[32] He, in turn, sent the report to President Lincoln[33] and possibly to the Joint Committee.[34] The effect of all of this was that at 2:00 A.M. on the early morning of 9 February 1862, General Stone was arrested by Brigadier General Sykes, deputy commander of the Provost Guard of the City of Washington.[35] In a lengthy letter, dated 5 November 1866, General Stone described his arrest scenario to historian Benjamin J. Lossing as follows:

> Having, as I supposed, relieved the patriotic anxiety of the Committee, I was anxious to return to my command, and use the twelve thousand good troops belonging to it in capturing Hill with his 4,500 lying opposite to me and thirty miles from his support. But it was not so written. On the 8th of February I was engaged with some gentlemen at Willard's hotel looking on a map of the southern states just compiled, on which great care had been taken to lay down every railroad then working in those states. I remained with them until nearly midnight, and on reaching my residence I found a man walking up and down before the door. In my surprise and pleasure I saw it was General Sykes, an old comrade, and major of the same regular regiment to which I belonged. We had not met for some time and I greeted him cordially, congratulating him on his fine command. He replied very cordially but said that while he had fine troops to command his duties (as Commander of the City Guard) were very disagreeable, "and" said he "Stone, I have now the most disagreeable duty to perform that I ever had—it is to arrest you"— "Arrest me! and for what?" He replied that he did not know—could not conceive—but that he was ordered to arrest me and place me in close custody. I was astounded as you may well believe. Sykes then told me that I had better put on citizens clothes, for said he "I maybe will tell you that you are to be sent to Fort Lafayette." I then said, "Why Fort Lafayette is where they send secessionists!" "Yes" "Well, said I, this is astonishing, they are now sending there me who has been as true a soldier to the Government as any in Service." "That" said Sykes, "is just what three officers of your own rank said a few minutes ago when the order for your arrest was received."
>
> I went into my house, changed my dress, said a few words to my wife to quiet her, and left with General Sykes, who I found was attended by a Lieutenant and squad of soldiers who had been kept back a little bit. I was conducted to the quarters of

Brigadier General George Sykes, deputy commander of the Provost Guard of the City of Washington, arrested General Stone at 2 a.m., February 9, 1862. Courtesy National Archives.

the lieutenants of the City Guard, one of whom kindly gave up his room and bed to me, and although for the first time of my life in arrest of any kind, slept soundly until daylight. My first request was for writing materials, which were used in writing a letter to the Adjutant General, notifying him of my arrest and requesting information of charges with privilege of immediately meeting them. I suppose there was some strange misunderstanding with all connected with the Government and they would be happy to have cleared up, and such little uneasiness beyond the disagreeableness of the occurrence. I expected to be back with my command within a week.

Learning that a guard was to accompany me to Fort Lafayette I told Genl. Sykes that there was no necessity for that, or if Genl. McClellan would order me to report in arrest at Fort Lafayette, his order would be as effectual as any guard. But this would not do. General Sykes would gladly have assented, but *somebody* who I cannot say willed that I should be escorted as a dangerous person. A kind and gentlemanly lieutenant and two detectives were sent with me, and my parole of honor was taken that I would not attempt to escape! We left Washington on Sunday afternoon 9th.[36]

The version of General Stone's arrest as it appeared in a newspaper of 9 February—and therefore the version that the public was acquainted with—is as follows:

> Charles P. Stone was arrested in Washington this morning, at two o'clock by a posse of the Provost Marshal's force, and sent to Fort Lafayette, New York harbor. The charges against Genl. Stone are: First, for misbehavior at the battle of Ball's Bluff; second, for holding correspondence with the enemy before and since the battle of Ball's Bluff, and receiving visits from rebel officers in his camp; third, for treacherously suffering the enemy to build a fort or strong work, since the battle of Ball's Bluff, under his guns, without molestation; fourth, for a treacherous design to expose his force to capture and destruction by the enemy, under pretense of orders for a movement from the commanding general, which had not been given.[37]

What role did the Joint Committee play in the arrest of General Stone? The original arrest order issued by Secretary of War Stanton on 28 January was done so, as Stanton reported to McClellan, "at the solicitation of the Committee."[38] In the final analysis, regarding the second arrest order for General Stone issued on 8/9 February there can be

113

little doubt that the Joint Committee did not have any input since that arrest order was generated by Shorbs' testimony to Pinkerton.[39]

What were the reactions, private and public, military and civilian to Stone's arrest? The *New York Tribune* wrote that: "The knell of traitors within already tolls."[40] George Templeton Strong wrote in his diary:

> February 12. Monday afternoon, everybody was astounded by the news that General Charles P. Stone had been arrested. He is now at Fort Lafayette, charged, it is said, with treasonable correspondence. Very marvellous. That there has been treason somewhere in high quarters is certain, and if Stone be guilty, I hope he may be speedily hanged. He has had certain strong Southern affinities, vehement anti-Abolition tendencies, undoubtedly. Having been under a cloud ever since the Ball's Bluff disaster, for which he was generally held responsible, rightly or wrongly, and sharply censured and abused by the press and perhaps by his military superiors, it may be—it is at least conceivable—that he has become disgusted with the cause of the country and has listened to overtures from old friends in the rebel army. He was certainly not reputed a rebel when I saw him last June. People then gave him credit for having saved Washington from an eruption of wild Virginians, when the city was at their mercy and the railroad torn up, by his presence of mind and forethought in taking military possession of certain steamboats running on the Potomac.[41]

The Provost Marshal General of the Army of the Potomac, Brigadier General Marsena R. Patrick, wrote:

> Tuesday night, 11 February, 1862. Gen. Stone has been taken to Fort Lafayette, as a prisoner. Why is not stated. I do not believe he is disloyal, but no man can say that.[42]

Private Frederick Wight of the 9th New York State Militia Infantry Regiment (Stiles Brigade of General N. P. Banks Division)[43] wrote the following on 12 February:

> You have doubtless heard of the arrest of Gen. Stone. You can't imagine how astonished our regiment was when they heard of his arrest. Gen. Stone was the *Idol* of the 9th Regt and we were a favorite regiment with him. He has paid us many and many a beautiful compliment, on our behavior and thrice when we passed him in Poolesville each company gave him a good hearty cheer, now if he is guilty, we want to see him strung up without mercy.[44]

In the middle of February, Secretary of War Stanton received the following letter from Mr. Henry Toland of New York:

> Edwin M. Stanton, Esquire   New York
> Secretary of War   Feb 11/62
> Sir:
>
> I have not the pleasure to be personally acquainted with you, but if our friend General Robeson of Pittsburgh should visit Washington, he will tell you all about me. We were all astounded last evening, by the arrest of Genl Stone for treason. This induced me to refer to a letter from my son Washington of Nov 1, 1861, and I have transcribed a short extract from it, showing to you, what was at the time, the opinion of a young gentleman of very good sense, and which opinion was concurred in by every one here.
>
> We all believed in the ineptitude of Genl Stone, but no one, until now, ever believed him to be a traitor.
>
> My son has been in that division of the Army, confided to the command of this *miscreant,* since May last, who it cannot now be doubted has ever since been seeking means for his destruction, and for that of many men under his orders.
>
> Mercy or pity are not to be thought of in "this" case. He has been guilty of the deliberate murder of hundreds, and he wants to have destroyed every man in the Army, if he had the power to do so. He merits the death of a felon, not that of a soldier. It should appear to me to be exceedingly proper that his aide de camp should be carefully looked after. It cannot be expected that men of this Division (Stone's), will suffer the presence of officers so closely connected with him as Aide de camp.
>
> If they be not removed, and their participation in the treason investigated, I will advise my son to quit the Service, which he never intended to do, until the rebellion was at an end.
>
> I am very respectfully
> Henry Toland
> No 20 Exchange Place[45]

These viewpoints, expressing either certainty of guilt or at least possibility of guilt, are balanced by a letter written on 7 February by Brigadier General Willis A. Gorman of Stone's Division:

> Maj Genl G. B. McClellan   Feb 7th 1862
> Commander in Chief, etc.
> General
>
> The officers of this division of the Army of the Potomac are daily in receipt of newspapers containing, direct and indirect attacks upon Brig. Genl C. P. Stone, sometimes charging or intimating that he is not loyal—that he has forcibly returned fugitive slaves to disloyal Masters, that he was to blame for the repulse of our troops at Ball's Bluff, on the 21st of Oct last.
>
> I have been here, and along the Potomac ever

since Genl Stone took command of this Division, and was here before he arrived. As a gentleman, in all the social walks of life I have seldom met his superior, and quite rarely his equal. As an officer and soldier I hold him in equally high estimation, and he has my *entire* confidence as a true, loyal patriot. Every act, word and deed of his coming under my observation has only tended to confirm this judgment. As to the repulse at Ball's Bluff, he has even expressed to me the most earnest wish to have it investigated. I was not cognizant of his plans, except so far as to receive and obey his orders. I shall be more than happy to attack, or defend, under his Military skill and judgement. I have never known of his returning fugitive slaves to disloyal or loyal Masters, by military or other authority. The chief information I have recd on this point has been through the press. I have often spoken with him on this subject and expressed the opinion that to return a fugitive slave by Military authority would involve the exercise of judicial powers that we did not possess, in which view I *always understood him as fully concurring*. Genl Stone has devoted himself to the Service with more zeal and energy than is usually found in or out of the Army, and relying upon a consciousness of his own rectitude, he has, to the annoyance of some of his friends, invariably refused to allow his officers to defend him and place him right before the country.

No one will be more highly gratified than myself if the Genl in Chief will order him in command of the division again.

I have the honor to be
Genl your obdt Servt
W. A. Gorman
Brig Genl Comdg
Division

(on the reverse appeared)
This letter was endorsed "private" on the envelope. I now think it only fit to send it to the Sec of State.
Hd Qtrs Army   Geo B McClellan
Feby 10 1862   Maj Genl Cdg[46]

Immediately upon his arrest, General Stone wrote a letter to the Adjutant General requesting a list of the charges that had caused his arrest. Under military law this list of charges was to be given to an officer before his arrest and subsequent trial by court martial. Stone received neither a list of the charges that had caused his arrest nor a trial by court martial.[47]

A few hours after his arrest and just before leaving Washington for Fort Lafayette, Stone gave his "Parole of Honor" not to escape.

Hd Qtrs City Guard
Provost Marshal Office
Washington D. C.

I, Charles P. Stone, Brig. General US Vol Service, do give my "Parole of Honor" as an officer and Gentleman, that I will accompany the officer in whose charge I am placed, to Fort Lafayette, N. York Harbor, and that I will not attempt, or connive, at any attempt to escape from his custody en route to that point.

Chas P. Stone
Brig Genl Vol

witnessed: Geo Sykes
Brig Genl Vols
Jas. A. Snyder
Lieut & A.A.D.C.[48]

Upon his arrival at Fort Layafette (Fort Lafayette was originally started as an artificial island in New York harbor, east of the main shipping channel, in 1812. At first it was named Fort Diamond but the name changed in 1823. It occupies 30.76 acres of artificially created surface and served as part of the harbor defenses of New York City),[49] the lieutenant in charge of General Stone handed to the commander of Fort Lafayette the following order:

Hd Qrts of the Army
Washington, Feby 8, 1862

Lt. Col M. Burke
Comdg at Fort Lafayette
Sir:

This will be handed you by the officer in charge of Brig. Genl. C. P. Stone, U.S. Volunteers, who is under close arrest. You will please confine him in Fort Lafayette, giving him the comforts due his rank, but allowing him no communication with anyone by letter or otherwise except under the usual supervision.

Very respectfully
Geo B. McClellan
Maj Genl Comdg U.S.A.[50]

While imprisoned at Fort Lafayette, General Stone wrote McClellan's Adjutant General requesting a list of the charges under which he had been arrested and sent to Fort Lafayette. Once again General Stone never received a reply.[51] While imprisoned at Fort Lafayette, General Stone was placed in solitary confinement under continuous guard, his outgoing and incoming mail was heavily censored, he was not allowed outside his cell for fresh air and exercise, nor was his wife allowed to join him.[52] At the end of his fifty-four days of solitary confinement at Fort Lafayette, General Stone was transferred to Fort Hamilton on orders of the post surgeon.[53]

Following his transfer from Fort Lafayette, the officer who had charge of General Stone wrote the following reports:

Fort Lafayette
N.Y. Harbor
April 9th, 1862

Colonel:
In obedience to your request, I have the honor

to make the following statement as to the treatment of Brig. Genl. Charles P. Stone U.S. Army while confined at this post.

On his arrival he was immediately placed in one of the most comfortable rooms of the quarters, and supplied with everything it was possible to give him in the way of furniture, such as iron bedstead, mattresses, pillows, linens, blankets, towels, tables, chairs, wash stand and ewer, looking glass, lamp, lamp-oil, water buckets, etc, etc. and a soldier detailed to wait upon him.

He was furnished with a private water closet to which he had the key. A sentinel was placed outside his door upon the porch, and he was not allowed out of the room except to go to the water closet, situated outside the walls of the fort, at which times he was accompanied by one of the Guard, as have been all prisoners confined at the post, but to make it as little annoying to him as possible, and not oblige him to have communication with the Officers of the Guard at such times, he only had to leave his room, and the sentinel at his door accompanied him. The troops of this command were specially charged that they must show him the respect due his rank, and no instances of disrespect ever came to my knowledge. After his limits were extended for exercise inside the Fort, he was always accompanied by Lieut Quincy or myself at such times as he desired to avail himself of the privileges.

His meals were furnished from the mess at Fort Hamilton and brought to the post by the boats of the command.

I am Colonel
Very Respectfully
Your obt Servt
Chas O. Wood
1st Lieut, 9th Infty
Commdg. Post[54]

Fort Lafayette, N.Y.H.
April 11th '62

Colonel

I would respectfully submit the following as a supplement to my report dated the 9th Inst. in regard to the treatment of Brig. Genl. Charles P. Stone U.S. Army while confined at this Post, having omitted these facts in that report.

He was required to deposit his money with me, I giving a receipt for it and holding it subject to his order.

Fort Lafayette in New York harbor where Gen. Stone was held without a list of the charges or a trial by court martial. Illustration from Harper's Weekly, *Sept. 7, 1861.*

All his letters were examined by Lieut Penney or myself both going and coming.

The room in which he was confined was in the men's quarters, the last adjoining the battery, the only available one.

I am Colonel, Very Respectfully
Your most Obt Servt.
Chas. O. Wood, 1st Lt. 9th Infy
Commanding Post[55]

Arriving at Fort Hamilton (The original site of Fort Hamilton had been a Dutch blockhouse which later became a British fort. The fort was named after Alexander Hamilton with the cornerstone being laid in 1825. From 1841-48, Robert E. Lee was the Post Engineer. Stonewall Jackson served there in 1849 as did Abner Doubleday. At the outbreak of the Civil War it was garrisoned by eight men. After Stone's leaving it, it became a depot for invalid companies in 1862)[56] in late March, General Stone started at once on a program of fresh air exercise to regain his health and also renewed his request from the authorities in Washington, for a list of the charges against him.[57] General Stone did not receive any reply from the authorities in Washington.[58] During his confinement at Fort Hamilton, General Stone repeatedly requested that the authorities in Washington either supply him with a list of charges against him or let him fight in the campaign in Virginia. The following examples of some of these telegrams will make evident General Stone's attempts to serve his country and to seek an answer as to the cause of his arrest.

General L. Thomas   Fort Hamilton
Adjt General U.S. Army   March 31, 1862
General:

I respectfully request that, unless it be deemed incompatible with the Public Interest, my wife may be permitted to come to this post and remain during my detention here, under such restrictions as may be deemed proper.

Chas. P. Stone
Brig. Genl. U.S. Vols.[59]

Lt. Col. Martin Burke U.S.A.   War Department
Comdg. Fort Hamilton   Adj. Gen. Office
New York   Wash. April 7th, 1862
Sir:

I have respectfully to inform you that the Secretary of War declines to grant the request of Brig. Genl Stone to have his wife with him.

I am, Sir, etc.
E.D. Townsend
Ast. Adjt. General[60]

Fort Hamilton
N.Y. Harbour, April 7, 1862
Lt. Col. Martin Burke
3rd Regt U.S. Army
Sir:

Having been in confinement under your custody more than eight weeks, I respectfully request that you will furnish me with a copy of the written charges, which, under the 80th Article of War, should have been delivered to you at the time of your receiving me into custody.

Very respectfully, I am, Sir,
Your most obdt servt
Chas. P. Stone Brig. Genl[61]

Fort Hamilton
New York Harbor
April 7, 1862
Brigadier General L. Thomas
Adjutant General of the Army
Washington, D. C.
Sir

Enclosed you will receive the request made by Brigadier Genl. Stone now in my custody at this Post. As a matter of course I could not act upon this request even if I had any charges against him without the authority of the War Department.

Major General McClellan's order is the voucher I have for his confinement. I would be glad if you would inform me whether the parole I gave to Genl. Stone of which I sent you a copy is approved or whether you wish any modification of the same. As I stated in my accompanying letter I have only two modes to pursue to give him that parole or to post a sentry on front and rear of his casement.

Very respectfully
Your obedient servant
Martin Burke
Lieut Col 3d Artillery[62]

Brig Gen L. Thomas   Apl 13, 1862
Adjt Gen U.S.A.   Fort Hamilton
Sir

Being in arrest awaiting charges I respectfully request that the arrest may be suspended and I be permitted to serve in some capacity before Yorktown. Provided such course shall be approved by the Hon. Secy of War and Maj Genl McClellan

Chas. P. Stone
Brig Genl[63]

To the Chairman of the   Fort Hamilton
Joint Com. of Senate and   N.Y. Harbour
H.R. "On the conduct of   May 3d, 1862
the War" Capitol
Washington, D. C.
Sir:

I have observed in the official report of a debate in the Senate April 22d unto that the "Chairman of the Committee on the Conduct of the War" stated positively that *"every word"* of the testimony before that committee against General Stone "was reported to him."

This statement before the Senate greatly surprises me, as I am quite unaware of ever having read, heard, or having seen any portion of the record of any part of the testimony of any person ever examined before the Committee.

Not only this, but I have never yet seen or heard or read any portion of the record of my own testimony before the committee although I repeatedly asked that it might be read over to me, and was told that such opportunity would be afforded.

> Very respectfully, I am
> Sir, Your most obt servt
> Chars. P. Stone, Brig Genl[64]

L. Thomas   May 27, 1862
Adj. U.S.A.   Fort Hamilton, NY
&
Lt. Col. Martin Burke 3rd Arty.
Col.

I wish at this time when large bodies of National troops are again being assembled to renew my application for suspension of arrest and opportunity of service. I will be obliged if this can be communicated to Washington by telegraph at my expense.

> Very Respectfully
> Chas. P. Stone, Brig Genl
> Respectfully forwarded to the Adjt. General
> Martin Burke
> Lt Col 3d Arty[65]

To The President   July 4, 1862
Commander in Chief   Fort Hamilton, N. Y.
of the Army

On this day the anniversary of the Nations Independence I find myself a prisoner under the folds of the flag of the Union, the same flag under which I have so often exposed my life in the service of the country. Last year on this anniversary my face was fanned by the rush of rebel bullets and the brave troops under my command drove the rebellion 10 miles up the length of the Potomac freeing thousands of loyal citizens from the yoke of that rebellion. I am utterly unaware of any act, word or design of mine which should make me today less eligible to an honorable place among the soldiers of the Union than I was on that day or any other day of my past life and I deem it my duty to state this now when the Country seems to need the services of its every willing soldier.

> Very respectfully, I am your
> Excellency, Most obt servant
> Chas. P. Stone, Brig Gen.
> Respectfully forwarded to Adj. Gen. L. Thomas[66]

As can be seen General Stone had been unsuccessfully trying since the time of his arrest to have himself restored to army service and to have a list of the charges under which he had been arrested. By himself General Stone was not successful. He was, however, lucky enough to have excellent aid from personal friends both in and out of Congress. Just eight days after General Stone's arrest his close friend and legal counsel, Joseph Bradley, wrote him offering his help. Stanton intercepted the letter and refused to forward it or let Bradley meet with Stone. A copy of Stanton's letter to Bradley is as follows:

> War Department, Washington
> City, D. C.
> February 20, 1862

Sir:

The Secretary of War directs me to acknowledge your letter of the sixteenth instant with the inclosure for General Stone, and to say in reply that he deems your letter an improper one to be sent to General Stone and will therefore withhold it. Further that your request to be permitted to visit General Stone can not at present be complied with.

> Very respectfully,
> your obedient servant
> P. H. Watson
> Assistant Secretary of War[67]

However, General Stone also received assistance from his brother-in-law as herewith recounted in his 1866 letter to Benson Lossing:

> My brother-in-law, the late Henry Melville Parker of Boston went promptly to Washington, stopping in New York to consult with General Scott, and you will pardon me if I appear egotistical in repeating the indignant words of the old Chief. "Colonel Stone a traitor!" said he to Mr. Parker. "Why if he is a traitor I am a traitor, and we are all traitors. While holding Washington last year, he was my right hand, and I do not hesitate to say that I could not have held the place without him." These words were brought to me in my prison, and this mark of his appreciation of my earnest and humble efforts for the preservation of the Government, greatly as he exaggerated my service, was most cheering. A prisoner in Fort Lafayette in 1862 needed cheering. After that I could read with calmness and smiles the daily outpourings of the *Tribune*.
>
> Mr. Parker remained for weeks in Washington but could not get a court order or a word as that were the charges or allegations against me.[68]

Besides trying to work directly with government officials in Washington, Parker and Bradley tried the indirect method of approach through the citizens of Stone's home state of Massachusetts. There petitions were circulated (as below) calling on the President to have General Stone brought to justice through an immediate trial:

> To His Excellency the President of the United States of America, and Commander-in-Chief of the Army.
>
> The undersigned, citizens of the United States and residents in Massachusetts, respectfully represent,
>
> That Brigadier General CHARLES P. STONE, a native of Massachusetts, an Officer in Army of the United States, and subject to the Articles of War, has been for many weeks in close confinement, without any known accusation against him, and without any known accuser.
>
> Civilians as we are, we yet feel it to be our right and duty to invoke your authority to secure to General Stone the full benefit of the Articles of War (as they have heretofore been uniformly interpreted), and an IMMEDIATE TRIAL.
> March, 1862.[69]

Meanwhile, activities for the release of General Stone were going on directly in Congress as follows:

> On the 24th of March, Senators Latham and McDougall of California, . . . with Aaron W. Sargent, representative from the same State . . . united in an energetic memorial to Secretary Stanton, on behalf of General Stone as a citizen of California. They stated that "the long arrest of General Stone without military trial or inquiry has led to complaints from many quarters. . . . Having known General Stone for years, and never having had cause to doubt his loyalty, we feel it our duty to inquire of the government through you for some explanation of a proceeding which seems to us most extraordinary." To this memorial no reply was made, and after waiting nearly three weeks Mr. McDougall introduced in the Senate a very searching resolution of inquiry, requesting the Secretary of War to state upon whose authority the arrest was made, and upon whose complaint; why General Stone had been denied his rights under the articles of war; why no charges and specifications of his offense had been made; whether General Stone had not frequently asked to be informed of the charges against him; and finally upon what pretense he was still kept in prison. Mr. McDougall spoke in the Senate on the 15th of April in support of his resolution. . . .[70]

As can be seen, the main proponent of General Stone in Congress was Senator McDougall of California. McDougall was born in New York in 1817 and admitted to the Bar in 1837 in Illinois. He was Attorney General of Illinois from 1842-46. He later moved to California where he also became Attorney General, 1850-51. He served in the U.S. House of Representatives from 1853-55 and in the U.S. Senate from 1861-67.[71] Even though he was a close friend of Stone's from their California days and the strongest defender of Stone in the Congress, McDougall was, unfortunately, an alcoholic.[72] This factor would hinder his defense of Stone.[73]

On 20 April, Henry Parker wrote to the Adjutant General of the Army the following letter:

> Willards Hotel
> Wash, April 20, 1862
> Brig Genl L. Thomas
> Adj Gen of the Army of the U.S.
> Sir:
>
> I have the honor to state that I have direct and positive information from Fort Hamilton, N. Y. that the telegram addressed to you on the 13th inst. by Brigadier General Stone, applying for a suspension of arrest and permission to serve before Yorktown, was written and handed to Lt. Col. Burke, and received by him officially; that it was approved by Col Burke, who sent with it a letter to the telegraph operator directing him to forward the application to you. I submit that everything has been regularly done on General Stone's part in making this application.
>
> Yr. most obdt servt
> Henry M. Parker[74]

Meanwhile, in the U.S. Congress, Senator McDougall attacked the Radical Republicans for their handling of the Stone case. He called upon the Secretary of War to explain his involvement in the case. He stated that Stone's treatment was what a prisoner in Russia or Turkey would expect. McDougall then found himself attacked by Senator Wade, leader of the Radicals in the Senate and in the Joint Committee on the Conduct of the War. These attacks and counterattacks in the Senate over General Stone's case continued throughout the month of April. Wade went so far as to title his speech against McDougall, "Traitors and Their Sympathizers." Unfortunately for General Stone, Senator McDougall was so drunk that he presented no serious defense against the attacks of Senator Wade.[75] One positive result of Senator McDougall's efforts was a resolution by the Senate requesting information relevant to the arrest of General Stone.[76] Secretary of War Stanton's response to this resolution was dated 22 April 1862:

> War Department
> Washington City, D. C.
> April 22, 1862
>
> Hamlin, Honorable Hannibal
> President of the Senate
> Sir:
>
> In answer to the Resolution of the Senate passed the 21st instant, I respectfully state that Brigadier

Senator McDougall of California, the primary defender of Gen. Stone in Congress. Courtesy National Archives.

Congressman John Covode, an ardent radical Republican from Pennsylvania who belonged to the Joint Committee. Courtesy National Archives.

General Charles Stone was arrested upon evidence which in my judgment required that he should be arrested and be brought to trial for grave offenses. He has not yet been tried because the officers required to constitute a proper court and the witnesses could not be withdrawn from their commands without serious injury to the service. There will be no unnecessary delay in bringing him to trial, copies of charges will in due season be furnished him and full opportunity will be afforded for his defence. During his imprisonment every proper indulgence has been and will continue to be extended towards him.

Very Respectfully, Your obt Servt
Edwin M. Stanton, Secretary of War[77]

Toward the end of April, James Bradley was finally able to meet with President Lincoln concerning the case of General Stone. Lincoln informed Bradley that as far as he knew Stone had been presented with all the charges against him. Furthermore, Lincoln told Bradley that his doubts about Stone came not from the Joint Committee's hearing or other politicians, but rather from a letter written about General Stone. (It turned out that this letter, amongst others, was stolen and possibly tampered with, from General Stone while he was in Washington on Army business.) Lincoln then referred Bradley to Stanton for further clarification on the matter. Bradley, however, declined to see Stanton since he felt that Stanton would link him with Senator McDougall's verbal attack upon the Secretary of the floor of the Senate.[78] After the meeting with President Lincoln, Parker wrote Bradley this letter on 30 April:

Jos H. Bradley, Esq. New York
  April 30, 1862
Dear Sir:

Your letter of the twenty-sixth overshot me, went to Boston, and is received here only this morning. I have made what speed I can to provide you materials for answering what you wish to answer—as promptly as possible, after conference with the General. I have no copies of what I send to you.

We are much impressed by your wise management of yourself and your business with the President, and don't doubt that you will have a telling interview with the Secretary when you present "A. Lincoln's."

The General desires his warmest thanks and regards to you for all your acts, purposes, and good wishes, and wise endeavours in his behalf.

Yours very truly and respectfully,
Henry M. Parker.

P.S. Who began to employ detectives on General Stone? and when first? Does not their use imply a precedent, (hidden) motive, and desire?[79]

Because of the visit by Joseph Bradley in late April, on 1 May, Lincoln requested a copy of the Senate resolution concerning the arrest of General Stone.[80] After receiving the Senate's resolution President Lincoln wrote the Senate in May:

In answer to the resolution of the Senate in relation to Brigadier General Stone, I have the honor to state that he was arrested and imprisoned under my general authority, and upon evidence which, whether he be guilty or innocent, required, as appears to me, such proceedings to be had against him for the public safety. I deem it incompatible with the public interest, as also, perhaps unjust to General Stone, to make a more particular statement of the evidence.[81]

Such was not to be as the case of General Stone continued to languish in limbo throughout May and June. However, because of the efforts of such men as McDougall, Parker, and Bradley the Congress on 16 July passed a bill forbidding the confinement of any member of the armed forces of the United States for longer than thirty days without having charges brought against them.[82] Because of this law, Charles Pomeroy Stone walked out of Fort Hamilton a free man on 16 August 1862.[83]

However, General Stone's release was stated in such a way as to leave serious doubts about his innocence:

The necessities of the service not permitting the trial, within the time required by law, of Brigadier General Charles P. Stone, now in confinement in Fort Lafayette awaiting trial, the Secretary of War directs that he be released.[84]

A release of this nature neither cleared Stone of the charges against him nor did it answer his supporter's charges of malfeasance against the government for keeping Stone locked up for 189 days without either preferring charges against him or bringing him to trial. It would now be up to General Stone to clear himself of claims against him of treason.[85]

VII

Captains and Kings Depart

Upon being freed, General Stone would soon find out that events had changed the spirit of the northern war effort. In the far west Confederate forces had met defeat at Glorietta Pass in their attempt to take over the southwestern territories. Along the Mississippi River Valley great Union victories had been won at New Madrid, Island No. 10, Memphis, New Orleans, and now Vicksburg was under attack. A new general by the name of Ulysses S. Grant had won victories at Fort Henry, Fort Donelson, and Shiloh. Other Union forces had occupied the first Confederate state capital of Nashville, Tennessee. Along the southeastern coast of the United States Union victories had been achieved at Roanoke Island, New Berne, and Fort Pulaski.

In the eastern theater the *Monitor* had fought its historic duel with the *Virginia;* McClellan had campaigned on the Peninsula and fought the Seven Day's Battles; Stonewall Jackson had marched/fought circles around various Union generals in the Shenandoah Valley; and the Second Bull Run Campaign was well under way with Union General John Pope commanding his newly christened Army of Virginia against Stonewall Jackson and Robert E. Lee. On the political front McClellan had been relieved as Commander-in-Chief of all Union armies on 11 March; the Homestead Act had been passed in May; June had found slavery abolished in all territories of the United States; July saw the Federal Income Tax become law, Land Grant Schools started, and the passing by Congress of the Second Confiscation Act concerning the freeing of the slaves. This latter bill, combined with President Lincoln's first draft of his Emancipation Proclamation, spelled the beginning of the death knell of slavery.[1]

In his letter to Benson Lossing, Stone recounted his release and experiences in Washington through the end of 1862 trying to clear his name:

> Finally, on the 16th of August, Colonel Burke with a smiling face handed me a telegram from the Adjutant General, by order of the Secretary of War directing my release from arrest on the ground stated that a court could not be convened within the time prescribed by law!
>
> Mark—up to this time I had never been served with a charge or allegation, had never been permitted to set an order of arrest which the law requires that an officer ordering an arrest must give a statement in writing, signed with his name, stating the offense within 24 hours.
>
> A copy of this order was handed me. I immediately telegraphed that I had received it, and asked for orders. After waiting 24 hours for a reply I went to New York and there awaited orders for two days—none came. I then returned to Washington, my residence, and reported at the Adjutant General's office. There were no orders for me. I had the records of the office searched to find the order of arrest. There was none. I had those of the War Dept examined. There were none found.
>
> I applied for information at the office of General Halleck then General-in-Chief. He had no orders, or information concerning my arrest, I was told. After some delay I sought an interview with the President. He received me very cordially, said the arrest was made under his general authority but not by him, and that he could never have been made to believe that General Stone was a traitor. He referred me by his card to General Halleck.
>
> So I bandied about from one authority to another, never succeeding in getting official information as to the source of my arrest, until I abandoned its pursuit, and quietly awaited. I could not resign without a clearing up of the mystery, and was forced to remain inactive while the troops I had

After General Stone was freed from imprisonment on August 16, 1862, he traveled to Washington to clear his name. He searched in vain for an acceptable explanation for his arrest. Photographs of General Stone and the Washington Monument, courtesy National Archives.

commanded were fighting in field after field—always gaining the credit of fully performing their duty. I evidently had not instilled them with treason. But all this time the Division was being thinned by battle, and witnesses to my cause while in command are disappearing. So passed the fall of 1862 and the winter of 1863.²

An example of General Stone's efforts to clear his name through official channels in Washington is shown by his letter to the Adjutant General on 25 September 1862:

Brig Genl L. Thomas   Washington, D.C.
Adjt Genl U.S. Army   Sept 25th, 1862
General:

    I have the honor to submit the following for the consideration of the General in Chief.

    On the 8th February 1862 about the hour of midnight I was arrested by an armed guard commanded by Brig. Genl. Geo Sykes and placed in close confinement under guard in the quarters of the officers of the Provost Marshal's Guard.

    At the time of the arrest I asked of General Sykes the cause, but was informed that he was perfectly ignorant of it.

    Early on the morning of the 9th February I addressed the following letter to the Head Quarters of the Army of the Potomac.
viz:

Brig Genl. L. Williams   Washington D.C.
Asst Adjt Genl   Feb 9, 1862
Hd Qrs Army of the Potomac
General:

    This morning about one o'clock I was arrested by Brig Genl Sykes Commanding City Guard, and made a close prisoner, by order, as I was informed, of the Major General, Commander-in-Chief.

    Conscious of being and having been at all times a faithful soldier of the United States, I most respectfully request that I may be furnished at as early a moment as practicable, with a copy of whatever charges may have been preferred against me, and the opportunity of promptly meeting them.

         Very respectfully, I am,
         General, Your most obt servant,
         Chas P. Stone, Brig Gen Vols

    The above letter was carried by Genl Sykes to Genl Williams early in the morning of the 9th February. No answer has ever been received by me.

    During the night of Feby 9th I was conveyed in charge of a Lieutenant and two police officers to Fort Hamilton N.Y. Harbour, and turned over to the custody of Lt. Col. Martin Burke 3rd Artillery who immediately sent me in charge of a guard to Fort Lafayette, where I was delivered to Lieut Wood 9th Infantry.

    At Fort Lafayette the money was taken from my pockets, and I was placed in solitary confinement in a room ordinarily used as enlisted men's quarters, where I was kept forty-nine days, no letter being allowed to reach or to leave me without inspection.

    During this confinement I applied at different times through the proper channels for speedy trial, for charges, for change of locality, and access to the records of my office and Head Quarters to enable me to prepare for trial, etc—but never received any response to any of my communications.

    After forty-nine days I was transferred to Fort Hamilton and allowed opportunities of obtaining air and exercise, but the same restrictions were continued on my correspondence.

    I applied for a copy of the order placing me in confinement, but could not obtain it.

    I applied to my custodian to learn what crime was alleged against me, and he informed me that he knew nothing of it.

    After thus awaiting charges more than two months, I applied for suspension of arrest and opportunity to serve before Yorktown but received no reply.

    Again, on the occasion of the retreat of our forces from the Shenandoah Valley I applied for suspension of arrest and opportunity to serve, but received no reply.

    On the 5th of July I again applied, but received no reply.

    I applied for an extension of limits, but received only the reply that the Secretary of War was absent and no extension could be given until his return.

    Finally, on the 16th August 1862, after 189 days of confinement, I was fully released from arrest without any order as to what to do.

    I immediately reported myself for duty.

    I would respectfully represent that the law requires, peremptorily, that when an officer is placed in arrest, it shall be the duty of the officer who ordered the arrest to see that the officer arrested is furnished within eight days, with a copy of the charges against him.

    Two hundred and twenty eight (228) days have now elapsed since my arrest, and not only have no charges been furnished me, but no allegation of crime to justify arrest has been made to me or to those who had me in custody.

    I now respectfully apply again to the General-in-Chief for a copy of any charges or allegations which may have been made against me, and the opportunity of promptly meeting them.

    And in case trial cannot be had, I would respectfully ask that at least the charges may be furnished, so that I may know what falsehoods require refutation and witnesses I shall require to accomplish the refutation.

    It is perhaps superfluous for me to call attention to the fact that those who have served under my orders and therefore must be witnesses of my conduct in Service have been falling in battle and by disease by hundreds and thousands since the date of my arrest.

    So great have been the casualties that the

General Joseph Hooker who requested Stone for his Chief of Staff in January, 1863. However, pressure from his radical Republican friends caused Hooker to withdraw his offer. Courtesy National Archives.

command from which I was taken is now reduced more than one half.

> Very respectfully, I am
> General
> Your most obt servt
> Chas P. Stone, Brig Genl[3]

In January of 1863, two significant events occurred in General Stone's status. He was recalled to active duty to sit on a court martial board in Washington (an indication that he was being gradually brought back to service with the Army), but sat only part of one day and then was relieved from sitting on the board by a message from the War Department. Following that episode, at the end of January General Joseph Hooker, new commander of the Army of the Potomac, requested Stone for his Chief of Staff. Stone accepted this appointment. However, the War Department disapproved of this appointment stating that it was "not considered for the interest of the service."[4] Bruce Catton described this latter incident as follows:

Hooker found new men for the vacant places, and in the process he did a strange and seemingly an uncharacteristic thing. For the all-important job of his chief of staff he asked the War Department to assign to him Brigadier General Charles P. Stone.

Stone was a man out of the past, deeply buried in disgrace. A brigadier without a command, a soldier without a visible future, he was a ruined living symbol of the fact that the hatred which General Burnside had failed to find among the fighting men had sprouted and flourished mightily among the stout civilians who controlled the destinies of the fighting men. This hatred, mixed with fear and grown old and gray and venomous, Abraham Lincoln greatly lacked, but it seemed that nearly every one else in Washington had a share in it, most notably the very men to whom General Hooker had made his gestures and his overtures as he scrambled toward the top of the heap. General Stone had been its first sacrificial victim.

In the fall of 1861 General Stone had commanded troops along the upper Potomac. In a misguided moment he had thrust a brigade across the river to reconnoiter near Leesburg, and the brigade had blundered into trouble at Ball's Bluff and had been butchered. Butchered among many less notable had been its commander, Colonel

Edward D. Baker, the Illinois-born Californian who had helped save Oregon for anti-slavery Republicanism and who was intimate with the leading men of the party which stood for all-out war. The war party wanted to punish someone for this disaster, and to do that job it had organized the Joint Committee on the Conduct of the War.

Looking into things, the committee had decided that General Stone was at fault and must be punished. It made no formal accusations and it took no direct action against him; it simply received and published accusations against his loyalty, turning him presently into an untouchable, a man who could not be defended, so that he was removed from his command and was even imprisoned for a time, although he had never been charged with any crime. The radical Republicans who had done this had nothing in particular against General Stone. They were simply using him to perfect the new technique which they had accidentally stumbled on. As an object lesson Stone had been extremely effective.

And it was this man whom Joe Hooker was now asking the War Department to send to him to become chief of staff of the Army of the Potomac.

Nothing came of it, to be sure. Stone had to remain on the shelf until Grant came along with a prestige that could overawe even the radical Republicans, and in the end Hooker took for his chief of staff Brigadier General Dan Butterfield.... And yet Hooker's act in asking for General Stone is one of the most interesting things he ever did.

It was completely out of character, or perhaps it proved that Hooker's character was not the open-and-shut case which on the surface it appears to have been. Hooker had schemed and calculated until it had seemed that there was no conceivable thing that he would not do to make political capital with the radicals. Yet now, untested in his perilous new job, he laid schemes and calculations aside and for one brief moment stood up as a straightforward soldier who would defy politics and politicians. He never bothered to explain what made him do it, and it seems that a passion for self-analysis may have been one of the few passions he lacked. He simply did it, leaving the fact that he had done it as a testimonial to something real in his strange, complex soul. It is a point to remember, because to speak up for General Stone took moral courage, a quality which Joe Hooker is rarely accused of possessing.[5]

Meanwhile, the Joint Committee on the Conduct of the War had held no sessions from early July through early December. This is not to say that they were not downcast with the defeat of their favorite, John Pope, at Second Bull Run and were not elated with the dismissal of McClellan in November. After the defeat of their new favorite, Ambrose Burnside, at Fredericksburg in December, Senators Wade and Chandler visited the Army of the Potomac. They returned to report to the Joint Committee that the fault for the loss at Fredericksburg lay with General Franklin, who had commanded a Grand Division there, and not with General Burnside.[6]

Finally, in February of 1863, the Joint Committee, feeling the pressure from Stone's political friends in Washington, from his civilian friends in Massachusetts and California, and from his friends in the Army itself, held a third hearing with General Stone concerning the events surrounding the Battle of Ball's Bluff and General Stone's subsequent arrest. These hearings started on 27 February.[7]

In these hearings, lasting from 27 February through 2 March, both Generals Stone and McClellan gave testimony. General Stone's testimony concerned five major areas: the movements of General McCall, the charges against General Stone, McClellan's knowledge of Stone's crossings, and Stone's arrest. General McClellan centered his testimony around four major points: the crossings of Union troops near Leesburg, the movements of General McCall, the investigation of General Stone and the importance of capturing Leesburg.[8]

In testifying about the movements of General McCall's division, General Stone stated that he was under the impression that McCall was advancing westward along the Leesburg Turnpike to aid in the capturing of Leesburg. Not until after the battles of Ball's Bluff and Edwards Ferry did Stone learn that McCall had withdrawn from Dranesville back to his camps at Langley. Stone then elaborated on his testimony by stating that had he known that McCall had withdrawn he would have accompanied Colonel Devens—and his battalion of the 15th—in a hit-and-run raid to destroy the Confederate camp.[9]

As to the charges brought against him, Stone demolished each one in his testimony. He had left troops ashore in Virginia at Edwards Ferry because he thought General McCall was marching toward Leesburg and would link up with his forces at Edwards Ferry. Packages, letters, and people were allowed to cross the Potomac only after examination and the people only with written approval of the War Department in Washington. Unauthorized crossing of women civilians took place under the eyes of Colonel Tompkins and Captain DeCourcey—two officers who had appeared in front of the committee blaming Stone of their misdeeds. The so-called Confederate fortifications built near Edwards Ferry were in reality those thrown up by Union forces on 21 and 22 October. Furthermore, he never misused his artillery, but at one point left a gun in charge of a veteran senior noncommissioned officer due to the illness of the officer of that battery. The two slaves captured during the crossing at Ball's Bluff had been detained in order that they would not talk about the

Union crossing. Stone had then attempted to return them to their families after the battle, but the Confederate pickets had refused to let the slaves back into Virginia. As far as being too easy on the pro-southern farmers near Poolesville, Stone told the committee that not only did he depend upon them for food for his soldiers, but that he was not there to make war on civilians, especially those whom he hoped to retain in the Union.[10]

The members of the Joint Committee then asked Stone why he had not told them this before now. For two reasons, Stone replied. First, the committee had previously asked only general questions to which only general replies could be given. Also, Stone had not been allowed to either examine the previous testimony against him nor know who had falsely testified against him as in the cases of Tompkins and DeCourcey. The second reason that he had not gone into specifics in his two previous testimonies in front of the committee was that he had been told by McClellan's staff not to do so until they told him otherwise. It seems that he had visited McClellan's headquarters prior to his earlier hearings at which time he was told not to say anything concerning military plans either present or future. Being a good soldier, Stone had obeyed his military commander's request to the dismay of the members of the committee who thought that his reticence was due to his hiding not only his mistakes but possibly also his treason.[11]

The committee asked General Stone if McClellan had approved of his crossings of the Potomac. Stone informed the committee that he had notified McClellan of the Potomac crossings and had received back a telegram of congratulations. However, McClellan was apparently thinking of only the Edwards Ferry area since he had been informed earlier by Stone that he could cross 250 men there every ten minutes. The boat details of men and the boats themselves did not exist at Ball's Bluff for crossing such large bodies of troops in such short a span of time. Stone further elaborated upon his testimony by informing the committee that he had not requested a Court of Inquiry after the Battle of Ball's Bluff because of General McClellan. It seems that upon hearing of the disaster there, McClellan had ridden to the Edwards Ferry/Ball's Bluff area. After making a personal inspection and talking to numerous officers he had telegraphed President Lincoln that Stone was not at fault for the defeat at Ball's Bluff. This was sufficient for Stone not to ask for a Court of Inquiry.[12]

Getting to the heart of General Stone's arrest and detention the Joint Committee wanted to know by whose orders General Stone had been arrested. Stone replied that when General Sykes had arrested him and been questioned as to under whose orders he was acting, Sykes told him those of General McClellan. Stone then asked McClellan's Assistant Adjutant General for a copy of these orders, but never received them. When Stone arrived at Fort Lafayette he asked the commanding officer there by whose orders he was brought there, and that officer replied by order of General McClellan. In further answer to the committee's questions, Stone informed them that written orders were necessary in a military arrest. Those orders were requested from McClellan's Assistant Adjutant General, from the commanding officers of Fort Lafayette and Fort Hamilton, and from the War Department itself. Never once did Stone ever receive the written orders under which he had been arrested. Stone then proceeded to tell the committee of all of the officials that he had seen in Washington and of the run-around that he had been given by them in regards to who had authorized his arrest and who had a written copy of his arrest orders and the charges against him.[12]

The historian T. Harry Williams has this to say concerning General Stone's final hearing in front of the Joint Committee:

> On February 27, 1863, Stone met the inquisitors for the third time. His final appearance was a triumphant acquittal. He had now seen a copy of the testimony and the charges against him, and could answer each accusation specifically. He easily demolished the Committee's previous jaundiced indictment.
>
> This was as close as Stone ever came to any official exoneration. He was never able to secure the formal trial to which he was entitled.[14]

On 6 March, General Stone sent to the committee ten documents bearing on his case. These documents were as follows: arrest order by Stanton signed 28 January 1862; arrest order signed by McClellan on 8 February 1862; transportation order to Fort Lafayette signed by McClellan on 8 February 1862; Stone's letter to McClellan of 9 February 1862, asking why the arrest; Stone's letter to the commanding officer of Fort Hamilton dated 5 April 1862, asking by whose authority he was being confined; McClellan's letter to Stanton stating that since Stone had been released *I will not consider him for active duty until I hear from you*; Halleck's letter of 30 September 1862, to Stone telling him that he was no longer under arrest but that no orders were available for him; Stone's letter to McClellan of 1 December 1862, stating that General Sykes told him that he acted under *your orders in arresting me—please give me a list of the charges under which I was arrested*; McClellan's letter to Stone dated 5

Secretary of War Stanton replaced Seward with the help of friends in Congress. Stanton shared a common desire with the radical Republicans to weaken General McClellan. As a result he cooperated with the Joint Committee in the questionable prosecution of Stone. Courtesy National Archives.

December 1862, informing Stone that Stanton had ordered his arrest at the solicitation of the Joint Committee on the Conduct of the War. McClellan elaborated by stating that Stone's arrest had come about because on 28 January information against Stone had been given by a refugee just arrived from Loudoun County which collaborated earlier negative information against Stone. McClellan closed his letter by informing Stone that he had requested a trial for him but that Stanton had turned him down; Stone's letter to McClellan requesting the name of this refugee only to receive a reply from McClellan's Aide-de-Camp informing him that the refugee's name could not be found.[15]

The final witness that appeared before the Joint Committee concerning Ball's Bluff was General McClellan. The questions and answers of General McClellan's first hearing in front of the committee on 28 February centered on four major areas: the movements of General McCall, the crossing of the Potomac by General Stone, McClellan's investigation of Stone's actions, and the ability of the Union Army to take and hold Leesburg.[16]

Regarding General McCall and his movement to Dranesville, General McClellan stated that this had been done for two reasons. First, to map the territory around Dranesville for future military operations, and second, to see if this movement would force the Confederates to retreat from Leesburg as had happened on a prior occasion. McClellan stated that he had telegraphed Stone that McCall was being pulled back from Dranesville. (However, General Stone always strongly denied that he had received such a telegram. Such a mix-up in military communications is not uncommon.) Even if McCall had advanced further toward Leesburg along the turnpike, McClellan did not think him capable of aiding Stone or Baker because of the distance of McCall's march and the fact that such a march would have made McCall's left flank open to Confederate attack from Centreville.[17]

Concerning Stone's crossing of the Potomac at Edwards Ferry and Ball's Bluff, General McClellan never expected or desired Stone to cross the river. Rather, McClellan had wanted and thought that Stone would demonstrate along the Maryland shoreline of the Potomac. Once Stone had crossed at Ball's Bluff, he should have personally reconnoitered the Virginia shoreline before giving Baker discretionary orders to cross. (On the face of it, this is a perfectly logical thought. However, Stone had personally reconnoitered the crossing at Smarts Mill Ford where he had planned and thought that the major Union crossing was taking place. When he received word about the action at Ball's Bluff, he was personally supervising the demonstration at Edwards Ferry thereby being forced to give Baker discretionary orders since he could not be at two places at the same time.) McClellan stated that it was not possible to have reinforced Baker with Union soldiers from Edwards Ferry due to a Confederate "masked battery" blocking their advance.[18]

Who did General McClellan think was responsible for the disaster at Ball's Bluff? McClellan answered that according to Stone's report it was Baker. McClellan stated that he had talked to numerous officers while at Edwards Ferry on 22 October, and that their conclusion was that it was Baker's fault. McClellan also told the committee that he had telegraphed both the President and the Secretary of War from Edwards Ferry on 22 October, telling them that he had investigated the battle and found no fault with Stone's conduct. Not only did McClellan accept Stone's report, but he understood that it had been accepted by the then Secretary of War, Mr. Seward. In addition, McClellan had heard that shortly after the battle General Stone had presented his report in person to the President and Seward and that both were satisfied with Stone's report.[19]

The final question of McClellan's first session with the Joint Committee was; would McClellan have taken Leesburg if the Confederates there had retreated? General McClellan replied in the affirmative. However, he went on to state that he would have done so only on a temporary basis since Leesburg could not be permanently held by the Union armies without their also capturing Harper's Ferry.[20] (If Leesburg were not to be held permanently for the Union, then why cross the Potomac and sacrifice those soldiers for nothing, Senator Wade had asked at an earlier hearing.) In Wade's mind and that of the other committee members, it could only be to deliberately sacrifice Union soldiers and cause another Union defeat.[21] However, an explanation of military theory of the time offers a more correct explanation:

> What bothered the Committee was that the generals did not seem to want to fight. And the Committee was right in this judgement of many of the generals in the first years of the war. George B. McClellan and other officers like him were in many ways competent commanders. But they shrank from seeking the ultimate and awful decision of Battle. The Committee sensed this fatal hesitation but ascribed it to the wrong reason. The Radical members thought that the generals had a secret sympathy for the South and slavery. They believed that the generals had been indoctrinated with pro-Southern propaganda when they were students at West Point.
>
> Thus Wade and his colleagues explained the failure of Northern commanders to smash the Southern armies. The suspicion had no basis in fact. The supercaution of the generals was the result not of any sympathy for the enemy but of their military

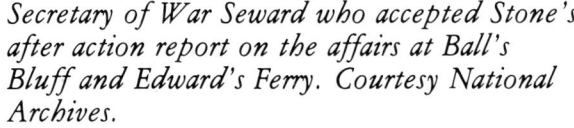
Secretary of War Seward who accepted Stone's after action report on the affairs at Ball's Bluff and Edward's Ferry. Courtesy National Archives.

education. They had been educated in eighteenth-century ways of warfare. They thought of war as bloodless strategy. They believed that wars were won by maneuvering, as on a gigantic chessboard, and that hardly ever did armies come to combat. They viewed war as a kind of game. It was played by professionals and it had no relation to the society that supported the war. Generals fought battles when the conditions were exactly right. They did not fight because civil authorities wanted a battle to sustain popular morale. In short, many of the generals were unfit to command in a modern political war like the Civil War.[22]

On 2 March 1863, General McClellan returned for his final session in front of the committee and what turned out to be the final hearing the Joint Committee held concerning General Stone and the Battle of Ball's Bluff. The committee asked McClellan's knowledge of Stone's arrest. McClellan replied that he received the arrest order from Secretary of War Stanton who told McClellan that it was being issued at the solicitation of the Joint Committee. That event had taken place on 28 January 1862. McClellan held the arrest order for ten days until a refugee from Virginia appeared at McClellan's headquarters with information that corroborated earlier testimony against General Stone. No longer able to delay arresting Stone, McClellan gave the order to do so on 8 February. The lack of a trial for Stone was repeatedly called to Stanton's attention by McClellan. Stanton always informed McClellan that the Joint Committee was not yet ready for a trial. McClellan closed this session by stating that it was his understanding from the Secretary of War that the Joint Committee was still collecting evidence and was therefore not yet ready to go to trial.[23] That trial was never held.

What happened to the cast of personalities, both civilian and military, Confederate and Union, who appeared in the events surrounding the Battle of Ball's Bluff?

For his command of the Seventh Brigade at Ball's Bluff and Edward's Ferry on 21 and 22 October, Colonel Nathan G. "Shanks" Evans was promoted to the rank of Brigadier General to rank from the date of the battle.[24] He returned to his native South Carolina on detached service and served against Federal raiding parties until recalled for active duty with the Army of Northern Virginia during the Second Manassas Campaign. Toward the end of it he had a serious confrontation with General John Bell Hood. Evans then fought at South Mountain and Sharpsburg. He next served in the Vicksburg Campaign and then again in the Carolinas until the end of the war. After the war he served as a high school principal in Alabama dying in 1868 due to severe injuries received in 1864 in a carriage accident.[25]

Lieutenant Colonel William H. Jennifer was promoted to Colonel in January of 1862 and made commanding officer of the 8th Virginia Cavalry Regiment. However, during the reorganization of the Confederate Army in the Spring of 1862 he was voted out of his command.[26] He later served as an Inspector General in the Confederate Cavalry assigned to the defenses of Mobile, Alabama.[27] Little else is known about this Marylander except that he died on the anniversary of Appomattox in 1878.[28]

Following his brilliant performance at Ball's Bluff, Colonel Eppa Hunton found his career temporarily halted due to poor health. He rejoined the Confederate Army in front of Richmond in the late Spring of 1862 and took over Pickett's Brigade after Pickett was wounded. Hunton commanded the 8th Virginia at Sharpsburg and participated gallantly in Pickett's Charge at Gettysburg during which he was wounded. While recovering from his wound he received his commission as Brigadier General. He commanded his brigade at Spotsylvania Court House, Cold Harbor and Petersburg. During the retreat to Appomattox he was captured at Saylor's Creek.[29] After the war Hunton resumed his law practice at Warrenton, Virginia. From 1873-1881 he served in the United States House of Representatives and from 1892-1895 in the United States Senate. In 1877 he served as the only southern member of the electoral commission to settle the presidential election dispute between Tilden and Hayes. He died in 1908.[30]

Because of his courageous and outstanding service as a volunteer aide at Ball's Bluff, Elijah White was given a commission as a Captain in the Provisional Army of the Confederate States and ordered to raise a company of cavalry from Loudoun County. This company formed the nucleus of White's command, militarily known as the 35th Battalion, Virginia Cavalry, but more commonly called 'The Commanches'.[31] They served as scouts on the Peninsula in 1862 and later returned to partisan cavalry activities in Loudoun County. At Chancellorsville they served under the immortal Stonewall Jackson and then fought at Brandy Station. In June they led the Confederate advance into Pennsylvania and then fought many rear guard actions during its retreat to Virginia. White continued his outstanding cavalry career throughout 1864. When the end came in April of 1865 he was commanding the famous Laurel Brigade. Rather than formally surrender his command he dispersed them.[32] He himself was not paroled until May 8 at Winchester. After the war Elijah White entered the banking and farming business in Loudoun County eventually becoming its sheriff. He died in 1907 and is buried in Union Cemetery, Leesburg.[33]

Edwin McMasters Stanton continued as Lincoln's hard-working Secretary of War throughout the Lincoln Administration and into that of his successor, Andrew Johnson. Stanton's reoganization of the War Department was extremely beneficial to the overall Union war effort. He kept in close contact with the Radical Republicans both in the Congress and on the Joint Committee. He handled the trial of the Lincoln conspirators and the tracking down of John Wilkes Booth. Because of serious disagreement over the reconstruction policies of President Johnson, Stanton was asked to resign in August of 1867. He refused to do so and bitterly fought resignation until May of 1868, when the bill to impeach President Johnson failed. Soon after that, Stanton declined in health and died on 20 December 1869.[34]

Senator Benjamin Franklin Wade continued in the Senate and in the Joint Committee throughout the war. An example of his serious disagreement with President Lincoln over policies was the Wade-Davis Bill and then later the Wade-Davis Manifesto. He initially supported Salmon P. Chase for President in 1864, and did nothing for Lincoln's reelection until the end of the campaign. His serious disagreements over presidential policy toward the South continued into the administration of Andrew Johnson. On 2 March 1867, he was elected president *pro tempore* of the Senate and held that position throughout the impeachment trial of Andrew Johnson. He retired from the Senate in 1869 and resumed his law practice, dying in 1878.[35]

Zachariah Chandler remained in the U.S. Senate until 1876. He was a member of the Joint Committee throughout its existence and was Chairman of the Senate Committee on Commerce during his entire career. During the war he was in favor of a national bank, the issuance of greenback currency, and generally approved the Reconstruction Acts though he maintained that some were too soft. After the war he served as Chairman of the Republican Congressional Committee for the elections of 1868 and 1876, but lost his own Senate seat in the election of 1874. He served as Secretary of the Interior from 1875-79, the year he died.[36]

Congressman George Washington Julian continued as a member of the Joint Committee throughout its existence until it closed in 1865. He was Chairman of the Committee on Public Lands and supported Lincoln's renomination and election in 1864. In 1867, he assisted in the preparation of articles of impeachment against President Andrew Johnson. Though he failed in his bid for reelection in 1870, he remained active in national politics. In 1885, he was appointed surveyor of the New Mexico Territory, a position that he held until 1889. He died ten years later.[37]

Daniel Webster Gooch, Congressman from Massachusetts, served throughout the war years in Congress as a member of the Joint Committee on the Conduct of the War. He resigned his seat in Congress in September of 1865, and was appointed the Navy agent for the port of Boston. In 1866, President Johnson removed him from that position. Gooch was reelected to Congress for the term of 1873-75, and then failed for reelection. He served as a pension agent for Union veterans and resumed his law practice. He died in 1891.[38]

Congressman John Covode was one of the members of the Joint Committee who did not serve the entire time of the committee's existence. He resigned from his congressional seat and from the Joint Committee in 1863. In 1865, the U.S. Government sent him to investigate Reconstruction policies in the lower Mississippi valley. President Johnson refused to accept his report and thus made an enemy. Covode was then reelected to Congress and it was he who introduced the resolution in the House of Representatives calling for the impeachment of Andrew Johnson. He died in 1871.[39]

The Democratic member of the Joint Committee was Representative Moses Fowler Odell of Brooklyn. He was a member of both the House of Representatives and the Joint Committee until he resigned in March of 1865. Thereafter he served as Navy agent for New York City until his death the following year.[40]

The one member of the Joint Committee who advanced his political position was Senator Andrew Johnson of Tennessee. In March of 1862, President Lincoln appointed him as War Governor of his home state of Tennessee. This took Johnson out of the U.S. Congress and off of the Joint Committee. Because of his service as War Governor of Tennessee, Johnson became Lincoln's Vice President in 1864 and upon Lincoln's death in April of 1865, President of the United States. He put into effect Lincoln's Reconstruction Plan, thus bringing upon himself the hatred of his former colleagues on the Joint Committee. Their attempt to impeach him in 1868 failed by one vote. His administration ended in March of 1869, and he retired to Tennessee. He returned to Congress as U.S. Senator from Tennessee in 1875, but due to ill health died later the same year.[41]

Though he had a number of friends in Congress, General Stone's most ardent supporter was Senator James Alexander McDougall of California. Senator McDougall served his complete term in the Senate, all the while maintaining his close support for his friend, Charles P. Stone. He declined to run for reelection in 1867 and died the same year.[42]

General George Archibald McCall continued in the U.S. Army until 1863. After his involvement in the Ball's Bluff campaign, he returned again to Dranesville in December and defeated a Confederate foraging expedition under General J.E.B. Stuart. He participated in the Peninsula Campaign in the spring of 1862, and fought a solid battle at Mechanicsville on 25 June. He was taken prisoner on 30 June during the Battle of Glendale. In August he was exchanged and remained on sick leave until his resignation in March of 1863. He died in 1866.[43]

In March of 1862, George Brinton McClellan was stripped of his position as Commander-in-Chief of the Armies of the United States. Retaining his appointment as Commander of the Army of the Potomac, he fought in the Peninsula Campaign against Joe Johnston and the Seven Days' Battles against Robert E. Lee. Returning to Washington at the end of August, he was reappointed Commander of the Union forces to repel Lee's invasion of Maryland. He successfully did so first at South Mountain and then at Antietam. Relieved by President Lincoln in November, he was never again on active duty. In 1864, McClellan campaigned against Lincoln for the presidency and lost. Following the war, he wrote his memoirs. Later, he was elected governor of his home state of New Jersey from 1878-81. He died in 1885.[44]

Colonel Charles Devens, commander of the 15th Massachusetts Infantry Regiment at Ball's Bluff, was promoted on April 15 of 1862 to the rank of Brigadier General. In May of 1862 he was wounded at the battle of Seven Pines (Fair Oaks). He went on to fight at Fredericksburg and Chancellorsville where he was again wounded. For his conduct at the latter battle he was promoted to the rank of Brevet Major General. In 1864 and 1865 he served in the Army of the James. Returning to his law practice in Massachusetts he became a judge of the superior court and then in 1873 a justice of the supreme court of Massachusetts. President Rutherford B. Hayes appointed him Attorney General of the United States in 1877. He died in 1891.[45]

Following the completion of the Joint Committee hearings on Ball's Bluff in March, General Stone waited for orders in Washington. On 13 April, he wrote the following letter to the Adjutant General:

Brig. Gen L. Thomas   Washington, D. C.
Adjt General U.S. Army   April 13, 1863
General:

It would appear from the recently published report of the Congressional Committee "on the conduct of the present war" that the immediate cause of my arrest and imprisonment on the 8th of February 1862 was a document submitted to the Hon the Secretary of War by Major General George B. McClellan, then General-in-Chief of the Army, by him described as "the written result of the examination of a Leesburg refugee."

I have made application to Major General McClellan for a copy of that document and for the name of the refugee but have been informed in writing that he did not recollect the name of the refugee, and that the last time he saw the document was just previous to my arrest, in the War Office.

I respectfully request, as a matter of justice to myself, that I may be furnished from the War Department with a copy of the statement of this refugee, which seems to have produced such important impressions on the mind of Major General McClellan.

Very respectfully, I am,
General, Your most obt servt
Chas. P. Stone, Brig Genl.[46]

General Stone received no reply to this letter.[47] However, less than two weeks later General Nathaniel P. Banks requested the War Department to send General Stone to assist him in his first Red River Campaign:

HQ, Dept of the Gulf
19th Army Corps
Opelousas, April 25, 1863
Sir,

In view of the pressing need for General Officers of rank and experience in this Department, I most respectfully but earnestly request that Brigadier General **Charles P. Stone** may be ordered to report to me immediately for assignment to duty. His services are greatly needed, and, having entire confidence in his zeal and ability, I will hold myself responsible to the Government for his conduct in the future.

Very respectfully,
Your mo. obt. servt.
N. P. Banks
Major General Comdg.

Major General H. W. Halleck
General-in-Chief
Washington, D. C.[48]

In May of 1863, General Stone joined General Banks just as the first Red River Campaign was ending. The historian of the 19th Corps wrote about General Stone as follows:

On the 7th day of May Halleck issued the orders asked for, and in the last days of the month Stone reported for duty before Port Hudson. At first Banks was rather embarrassed by the gift he had solicited, for he saw that he himself was falling into disfavor at Washington; the moment was critical; and it was easy to perceive how disaster, or even the slightest check, might be magnified in the shadows of Ball's Bluff and Fort Lafayette. Moreover, Stone was equally unknown to and unknown by the troops of the Nineteenth Army Corps. Instead, therefore, of giving him the command of Sherman's division, for which his rank indicated him, Banks kept Stone at headquarters without special assignment, and made every use of his activity, as well as of his special knowledge and ready skill in all matters relating to ordnance and gunnery.[49]

Stone served in the seige of Port Hudson in such an outstanding manner that Banks chose him to be one of the commissioners to receive the Confederate surrender on 9 July 1863.[50] This campaign cost the Confederates control of their last stronghold on the Mississippi River.[51] Continuing in Bank's command as his Chief of Staff, General Stone participated in the campaign of Bayou Teche in October of 1863.[52]

In February of 1864, Stone made one final appeal for justice to President Lincoln:

To the President   New Orleans, La.
Your Excellency: February 1st, 1864

As a soldier, I make to you my last appeal for justice.

This will be the last letter which I shall address to you for justice during my life, or to justify myself in history.

There is no modesty in my using that word; for alongside other and more distinguished and fortunate names, mine must go into the history of our country for the past three years.

The records of the War Department will show that I was the first soldier mustered into the service of the United States for the present war; and that the first sixteen companies mustered into the Service, were troops of my own training and under my own command.

It is now more than two years since I was suddenly taken from the command of one of the largest and finest divisions of the Army, and incarcerated in a prison set aside for traitors and subverters of the Government.

I entered that prison house as true a soldier of the United States as then served in her armies.

I remained in prison one hundred and eighty-nine days, as true a soldier of the United States as remained in her armies.

I left that prison, as true and faithful a soldier of the United States as could be found in her armies.

I will not recall the frequent appeals which I made during those 189 days—appeals for appearance of accusers, appeals for statement of accusations, appeals for hearings, appeals for opportunity of service.

It is sufficient that none were ever regarded, and that I was discharged without ever having seen accusation or the name of the accuser, without an acknowledgement of the receipt of an appeal.

After six months of imprisonment and nine months of forced inactivity following it, I was suddenly ordered, at the commencement of the sickly season of 1863, to order for duty in the Department of the Gulf.

In two days, I was on my way, and on the 1st of June, 1863, I reported for duty before Port Hudson.

My further services were rendered in the operations which resulted gloriously in the opening of the Mississippi River.

From the 1st of June 1863 to the present day I have been daily and nightly on duty without one day of intermission, and whoever also may not know it, I know that my duties have been performed with a single eye to the service of the country's cause, and fidelity to the Commander at whose request I was recalled to duty.

A new campaign is now about to open. It may be the last of many which I have had the fortune to participate in. It will perhaps be fortunate for all concerned that it should be so. That campaign will probably open before you can see this letter.

I respectfully ask, for the sake of the Service which I have loved and never dishonored, and for the sake of my name in history to be read by my descendants, that some act, some word, some order, may issue from the Executive which shall place my name clear of reproach, as I know it should be.

If it shall meet your needs to accede to my request, I shall be rejoiced.

If on the contrary, this like my previous appeals shall be fruitless, I shall appeal no more, but shall continue to perform the duties of a soldier wherever I may find myself placed, so long as the Government of my country needs a soldier's services, and I live to perform them.

I am,
Your excellency
Your obt servt

Chas. P. Stone
Brig Genl (Chief of Staff)

Respectfully approved and
forwarded to the President
N. P. Banks
M.G.C.[53]

During the second Red River Campaign of March-May, 1864, Stone participated in the battles of Sabine Crossroads, Louisiana (8 April) and Pleasant Hill (9 April).[54] However, on 4 April the War Department had mustered him out of the service in the grade of Brigadier General of Volunteers. This left Stone as a Regular Army Colonel without a command.[55]

Stone then left Bank's command and proceeded up the Mississippi to Cairo, Illinois, where he awaited orders from Washington during the months of April until August.[56] During that time period he sent the following two telegrams and one letter to the War Department in Washington:

```
Cairo, Ill                                      2:00 P.M.
Via Chicago                                  June 29, 1864
Adjt Genl Army
```
If my services are not desired in the field I respectfully tender the resignation of my commission to take effect July first.

C. P. Stone
Col, 14th Infy[57]

```
Adjt Gen of the Army                          Cairo, Ills.
Washington, D. C.                          July 11th, 1864
General:
```
Unless my services are desired with my regiment in the field during the present campaign, I respectfully tender the resignation of my commission, to take effect on the 15th inst.

I tendered my resignation by telegram on the 28th ulto to take effect on the 1st inst., but having received no reply, presume the telegram was not received.

I would further request that in case of acceptance, such acceptance be immediately telegraphed to me, at my expense if necessary, for the reason that I desire to remove my sick wife from this climate, without a delay which would probably cost her life; and she is already so reduced that I fear to have her take a long journey without my personal escort.

I regret the necessity of this introducing my private affairs into official correspondence, but duty

The Statue of Liberty stands on a pedestal engineered by Stone as the ocean liner Queen Mary passes through New York harbor. Courtesy National Archives.

Stone in later life. After 13 years in the service of the Khedive of Egypt, Stone became the chief engineer for the construction of the pedestal for the Statue of Liberty. From Harper's Weekly, *November 6, 1886.*

to my family requires it.

Should my resignation not be immediately accepted, I would request that permission be telegraphed to me to accompany my wife to Massachusetts, whence I would be ready to report at any point which might be deemed desirable.

Very respectfully, I am,
General, Your most obt servt
Chas P. Stone
Col 14th U.S. Inf[58]

Cairo via Chicago   9:00, July 13, 1864
Adjt Genl USA

Observing the news from Washington (ed. note—Early's Raid) I respectfully withdraw my resignation and solicit active service.

C. P. Stone
Col 14th Infy[59]

In August of 1864, Stone reported back to the Army of the Potomac then engaged in beseiging Richmond and Petersburg. He commanded the First Brigade, Second Division, Fifth Corps, from 21 August until 10 September.[60] On his application to resign from the Army his commanding officer had written:

Col Stone has been diligent and zealous in the performance of all the duties which have developed upon him since joining the command on the 21st ulto.—but as he necessarily must judge and decide for himself of the condition of things which lead to the belief stated within, I though, with regret at the loss of his able services, approve of this application. He is authorized to present his application (resignation) at Corps Headquarters in person.[61]

Retiring from the service he loved so well, Charles Stone took no further part in the Civil War. Following the war he headed the Dover Mining Company in Goochland County (just northwest of Richmond), Virginia from 1865-69. In 1870, he joined the service of the Khedive of Egypt serving for thirteen years, achieving the position of Chief of Staff and the rank of Lieutenant General. For his outstanding services in Egypt he was made the Grand Officer of the Order of the Medjidieh by the Egyptian Government and a Commander of the Order of the Crown of Italy by the Italian Government.[62]

Stone returned to the United States in 1883 and became the engineer in charge of the Florida Ship Canal and Transit Company.[63] On April 3, 1886,[64] Stone was appointed "Engineer-in-Chief" of the American Commitee of the Statue of Liberty.[65] He first constructed the huge pedestal for the Statue and then proceeded to erect the Statue of Liberty.[66] On October 28, 1886[67] the Statue of Liberty was dedicated with General Charles P. Stone acting as Grand Marshal.[68] All of this was done by Stone while he was in sight of his former prison at Fort Lafayette where he had lost his liberty. Charles Pomeroy Stone, first soldier of the Republic in 1861, martyr for freedom in 1862, builder of the Statue of Liberty in 1886, died on January 24, 1887.[69]

Regiments Meet Again

In one of the ironies that seems to personify the Civil War, the same regiments that fought against each other at Ball's Bluff later fought against each other on three other battlefields—Antietam, Fredericksburg and Gettysburg.

On the following pages brief explanations, quotations, illustrations and maps will enable the reader to more fully understand these three other battles. In addition, since all of these sites are now within the National Park Service, a point of contact is given for those who wish to follow up these engagements.

Antietam

It is the late morning of September 17, 1862 and the mists have faded from Antietam Creek. A titanic struggle has been waged since early dawn by the Union Army of the Potomac under General George B. McClellan against the Confederate Army of Northern Virginia under General Robert E. Lee. The earlier struggle in Miller's cornfield has ended with a follow-up advance of Sedgwick's Union division. This division was once known as "The Corps of Observation" when it was under General Stone in 1861.

Unknown to the Union soldiers they are advancing into an unplanned Confederate ambush in the West Woods. Part of the Confederate forces attacking them are their old enemies from Ball's Bluff, Barksdale's Mississippi Brigade consisting of the 13th, 17th and 18th Mississippi Regiments.

The regimental history of the 20th Massachussetts regiment gives the following account of this dreadful slaughter:

> As our first line stopped when the fire commenced, the lines crowded very closely together. No one in the second or third line could fire a shot. The men and some of the officers commenced smoking. We had remained in this position some minutes—the most advanced one reached—watching the line in front firing and falling, when suddenly the cry was raised, "The enemy is behind us!" There they were, not twenty rods from us, coming in on the left flank, and the regiments there were breaking. Howard's brigade went first and very quickly, while other regiments held their ground or ran away according to their courage and discipline. The Twentieth faced about, but was so crowded in the centre of the division that only a few could fire without killing men on our own side.

For further information you should contact:
Antietam National Battlefield Park
P.O. Box 158
Sharpsburg, Maryland 21782
301-432-5124

Fredericksburg

Following the bloodiest day of the war at Antietam Creek the armies returned to the 'sacred soil' of Virginia. Soon thereafter General Ambrose Burnside took command of the Union Army and decided to lead it to Richmond via the old colonial town of Fredericksburg. Upon arriving there, General Burnside had to force a crossing of the Rappahannock River in order to establish a bridgehead on the south bank of the river. Among the Union regiments that participated in this amphibious assault on December 11, 1862, were the 7th Michigan, 19th and 20th Massachusetts. Opposed to them were their old foes—Barksdale's Mississippi Brigade.

A member of the 19th Massachusetts left this account of the river crossing:

> The instant the batteries ceased firing, the men of the Seventh Michigan and the Nineteenth Massachusetts took to the boats, twenty in each and poled across the river under a heavy musketry fire from the enemy. Crack! Crack! Crack! from a hundred lurking places went the rebel shots at the brave fellows, who, stooping low in the boats, sought to avoid the fire. The murderous work was well done. Lustily the men pushed on the poles, however, and presently, having passed the middle of

Shell-shattered Fredericksburg as it looked in the winter of 1862-1863. William Barksdale's Mississippi brigade defended the city from dugout positions in and around the basements of the structures along the river's edge. Their foes from Ball's Bluff, the 19th and 20th Massachusetts, crossed the Rappahannock under heavy fire to rout them from their positions. Matthew Brady photo, courtesy National Archives. The button, a Mississippi infantry specimen, was found on the streets of Fredericksburg on December 13, 1862 by a Union soldier and taken home as a war trophy. Courtesy Loyal Legion Museum, Philadelphia, PA.

the stream, the boats, and their gallant frieght came under the cover of the opposite banks.

For further information you should contact:
   Fredericksburg and Spotsylvania National
      Battlefield Parks
   120 Chatham Lane
   Fredericksburg, Virginia 22405
   703-373-4461

Gettysburg

After Chancellorsville the armies headed north to meet at a small Pennsylvania farm village called Gettysburg. There the fate of the Union and the Confederacy hung in the balance as both the Blue and the Gray fought with overwhelming valor. But it is now July 3, 1863, and the Confederate General Robert E. Lee has decided to launch Pickett's Charge against the Union center on Cemetery Ridge. Among the Virginians of Pickett's immortal division are the men who fought so gallantly at Ball's Bluff, the 8th Virginia Infantry Regiment from Loudoun and Fairfax counties. Opposing them will be their old enemies, the Tammany Regiment, the 15th, the 19th and 20th Massachusetts Regiments, and the 71st (1st California) Pennsylvania Regiment.

The immortal charge of Pickett's Division is described by an eyewitness as follows:

> None on that crest now need be told that the enemy is advancing. Every eye could see his legions, an overwhelming resistless tide of an ocean of armed men sweeping upon us! Regiment after regiment and Brigade after Brigade move from the woods and repaidly take their places in the lines forming the assault. Pickett's proud division, with some additional troops, hold their right, Pettigrews's their left. The first line at short interval is followed by a second, and that a third succeeds; and columns between support the lines. More than a half a mile their front extends; more than a thousand yards the long gray lines deploy, man touching man, rank pressing rank, and line supporting line. The red flags wave, their horsemen gallop up and down; the arms of twelve thousand men, barrel and bayonet, gleam in the sun, a sloping forest of flashing steel. Right on they move, as with one should, in perfect order, without impediment of ditch, or wall or stream, over ridge and slope, through orchard and meadow, and cornfield, magnificent, grim, irresistible.

For further information you should contact:
   Gettysburg National Military Park
   P.O. Box 1080
   Gettysburg, Pennsylvania 17325
   (717) 334-1124.

Battlefield Chronicle

On 22 October 1861, the day after the Battle of Ball's Bluff, Colonel Hinks, commanding the 19th Massachusetts Infantry Regiment then stationed on Harrison's Island, ordered Captain Vaughn to proceed under a flag of truce back to Ball's Bluff to bury the Federal dead. Overcoming both military and personal problems, Captain Vaughn's party was able to inter 47 corpses before nightfall ended his work. In reporting to Colonel Hinks he reported that these 47 dead were approximately 2/3 of the total. The remainder were buried in shallow unmarked graves by the Confederates.[1]

In the Spring of 1862 the Governor of Pennsylvania sent his military agent to remove the bodies of the Pennsylvania soldiers who fell at Ball's Bluff. That report, with map, is as follows:

Battlefield at Balls Bluff, Virginia
April 18th, 1862
Surgeon General H. H. Smith:

Sir - In obedience to your order dated April 18th I proceeded with the party assigned me to this place; arriving here early this morning; and at once commenced making the examination necessary to determine the expediency of removing the bodies of Pennsylvania volunteers who fell in the battle at this place on the 21st of October 1861 to the soil of their own State for burial.

The advanced stage of decomposition in which I found the bodies utterly precluded any attempt at their removal.

I found the bodies of our killed in that engagement deposited in various places—some in isolated graves, all of which are in good condition—but most of them had been promiscuously placed in sluices or washes formed by recent water currents on the declivities of the battleground. These had been but superficially covered with earth, and some of the bodies were exposed. Some had been mutilated. (Ed. note—these bodies had been disturbed by animals.)

Being unable in many cases to determine the State to which the bodies had belonged; and finding that the condition of them all admitted of no recognition of their identity, I concluded that my proper course was to leave those which were undisturbed in the places where I found them; to re-inter the detached portions of bodies in the places from which they had been removed; to cover them properly with earth and stones; and guard so far as could be done against their future exposures. I deem it proper to state that this course received the unqualified approbation of those members of my party who had kindred among those slain and buried here.

Having procured a party of laborers from Leesburg, I proceeded to carry out this determination. A mound of earth of sufficient thickness was thrown over each of the five distinct places of promiscuous burial. These were flagged with stones and again covered with earth. A large stone was placed at each extremity of the several lines of graves, distinctly marking their position. Trenches were dug around them so as to protect them from future washing and so far as possible the water courses were changed by digging new channels. Grass seed was sown upon the mounds, and much pains were taken to give them a neat appearance. No enclosure could be erected for want of materials. A reliable man was engaged to attend to keeping all things about these graves in their present condition.

The owner of the land on which these graves are situated is now absent in the Rebel army, and no overseer or agent could be found. Satisfactory assurances were given me by loyal citizens of Leesburg that this burial place of our soldiers shall in the future, be properly respected. They have kindly cooperated with me in carrying out the objects which

I have sought to accomplish.

Accompanying this I transmit a map of the ground showing the situation of all the graves upon the field.

Very Respectfully
Your Obedient Servant
I. B. Crawford
Assistant Surgeon[2]
P.V.

In the fall of 1865 a Union examination team visited the sites of various small battles throughout Northern Virginia. Their report to the Quartermaster General was dated 8 December 1865 and stated in part:

> The remains of those who fell here rest in various places near the bluff without a single mark to designate their graves except the tall blue grass, nature's unmistakable indication of those interred near the surface.
>
> No kindly feeling seems to have actuated those living in the vicinity to care for the dead, and after they were permitted to lie for days exposed to the ravages of animals, were only covered with earth, when the air became fouled with the odor from the bodies.
>
> I would respectfully recommend that these remains be disinterred and removed to a suitable site on the bluff; and their graves be marked Unknown United States Soldiers, killed Oct 21 - 1861; and enclosed by a neat paling fence. The tablets to be similar to those used by the Government.
>
> (Sgd) Jas M. Moore
Bvt Lieut Col and Asst QM Ma U.S.A.[3]

In remarking upon this report the Quartermaster General of the United States Army, Major General Montgomery C. Meigs, wrote:

> Gov Swann gives the site if it proves to be on his land. Let deeds be prepared and let him be requested to execute them; and then let this be reported to the Secretary of War, with recommendations that his action be suitably acknowledged.
>
> (Sgd) M.C.M.[4]

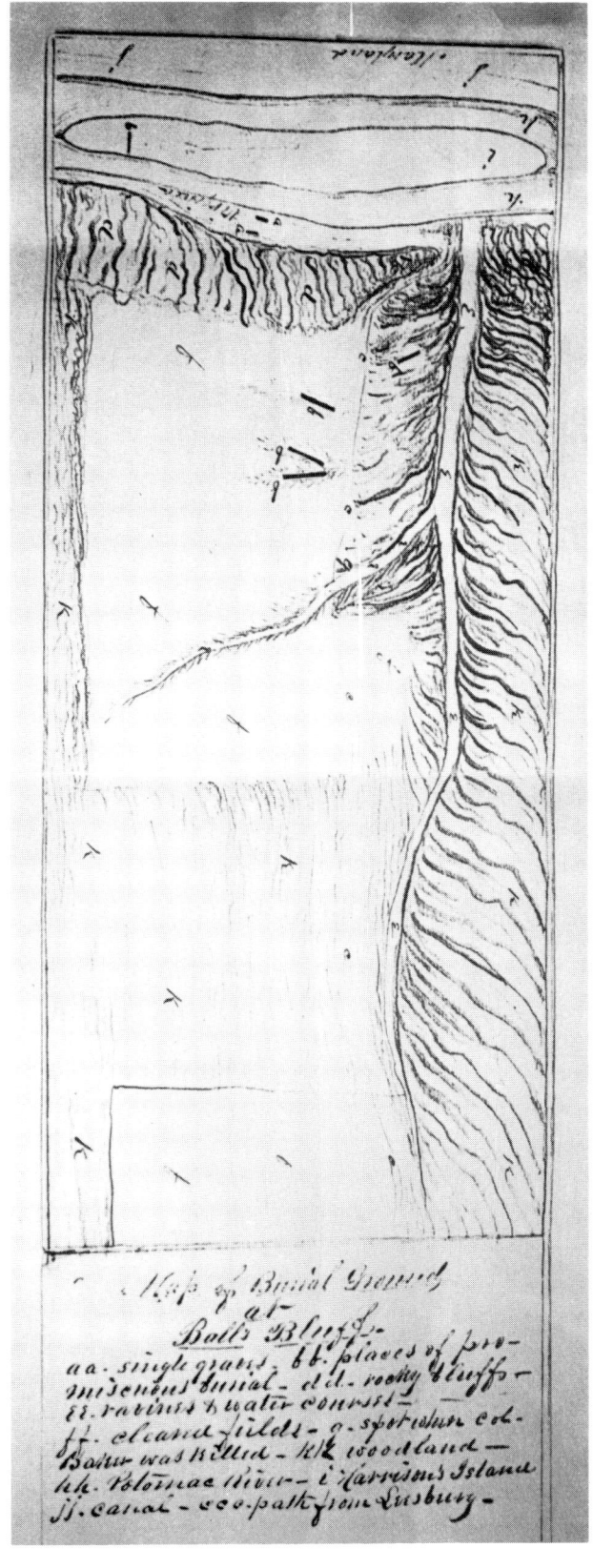

This crude map was drawn in the Spring of 1862 after the Rebels withdrew to the Rappahannock River. The Governor of Pennsylvania sent his military agents to the Ball's Bluff battle site to locate and remove the remains of state soldiers. However, the advanced state of decay rendered identification impossible. The Governor's agents mapped the location of the remains before reburial. Courtesy Richard Saveos, Pa. Flag Pres. Off.

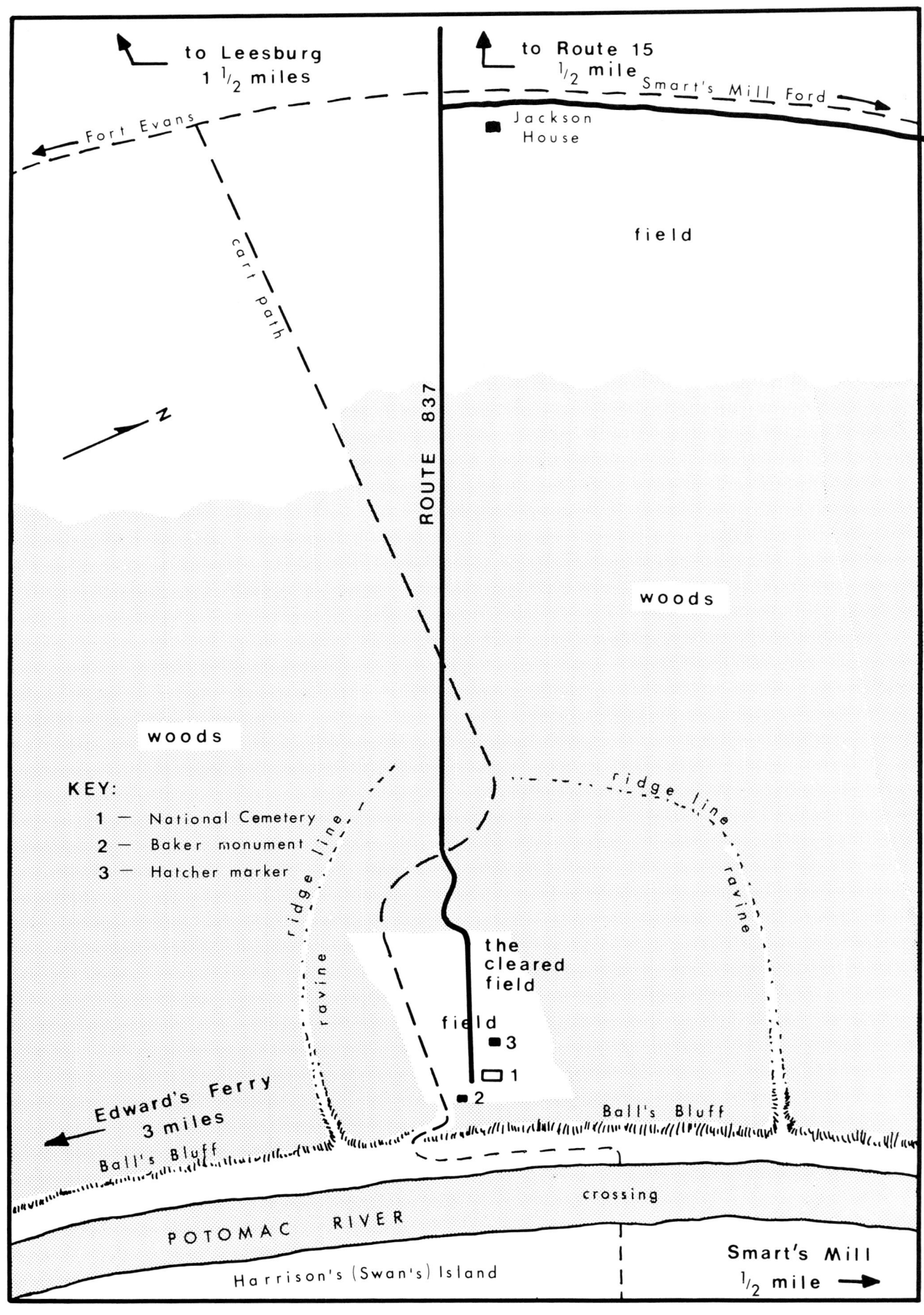

The official report from the Secretary of War to Congress in 1872 concerning National Cemeteries had this to say about the Ball's Bluff National Cemetery:

> This little cemetery is situated about two miles from Leesburg, on the Ball's Bluff battlefields. There is no direct road to it, and the approach is by a roundabout way over a very bad private road.
>
> The lot is a square of sixteen yards, and is enclosed by a red sandstone wall recently built; coping not yet put on. The entrance is in the south side and is closed by a light iron gate. An Osage orange hedge has been planted around the lot, three feet inside the wall. The plants have not grown vigorously.
>
> There are twenty-five graves arranged on an arc of a circle, leaving a vacant space in front of the entrance, perhaps one-fourth of the circumference. The graves are leveled and grassed over and have rose bushes growing over them. They are said to contain the remains of fifty-four Union soldiers who fell in the action at this place. All but one are unknown; that is, the remains could not be identified, although the names of all who fell are known.
>
> The place is in charge of a citizen who lives near by. It is in pretty good order. The wall is high and the gate is kept locked so there is very little danger of molestation or damage.
>
> The expenditures amount to $820 up to August 31, 1871.[5]

In reply to an inquiry submitted to the Pennsylvania Department of Public Works in 1884, the Adjutant General of the United States Army noted that:

> From a careful examination of the records and papers pertaining to the National Cemetery at Ball's Bluff, Va, it does not appear that the ground has ever been legally conveyed to the United States. A survey was made and a plat and draft of deed thereto were transmitted to Governor Swann, the owner of the land in Nov 1871, but no further action seems to have been had as appears from copy of a letter to him from the Quartermaster General, dated April 28th 1874, requesting return of the papers. Neither is it known that the ground occupied by the Cemetery includes the spot where Col Baker fell.[6]

The matter of the legal transfer of the property upon which the Ball's Bluff National Cemetery rests

Built by the U.S. Army in 1907 this narrow road provides the only easy access to the Ball's Bluff battlefield. It parallels the old cart path used by the soldiers and terminates at the small Federal cemetery.

was settled in 1904 when the twelve heirs of Governor Swann signed Quitclaim deeds with the United States Government for a dollar each for the 4.63 acres.[7] This initial legal transfer of property rights was followed on 7 March 1907 by a deed between Rachel A. Paxton and the United States Government for a road right-of-way.[8] This is the current road upon which you travel to the Ball's Bluff National Cemetery from Route 15.

The official report of the Inspector General's Office, Department of the Army, for the biennial inspection of 1908 noted that the caretaker was Mr. Joseph Waters, a veteran of Company K of the 5th Massachusetts Cavalry Regiment. Mr. Waters was paid $60.00 per year and had one hand lawn mower, one rake and one wheelbarrow as his equipment. Under "remarks," the inspecting officer—Major L. S. McCormick noted that the flag was not raised when he visited and that weeds were starting to grow along the government road from Route 15 to the National Cemetery.[9]

By 1915 the Inspector General was reporting the condition of Ball's Bluff National Cemetery as follows:

> Item (1) Grass not trimmed and weeds growing in enclosure.
>
> Item (2) The Depot Quartermaster reports that it has been found that the present caretaker, F. W. Smale, has been derelict in his duty and steps have been taken to obtain another caretaker who will attend to the necessary duties in a proper manner.
>
> Item (3) Flagstaff badly rotted at base, and defaced with pencil markings. The expenditure of $25 has been authorized for having the rotten portion of the flagstaff removed and the entire flagstaff repainted. The Depot Quartermaster reports that it is impossible to avoid the marking up of the flagstaff with lead pencil by visitors, who are in the habit of writing their names on convenient places.
>
> Item (4) Hole in bronze gate inscription plate made by bullet. It is reported that the bullet hole in this bronze plate cannot be repaired, but the question of providing a new one will be considered.
>
> Paragraph 6 of the report. Recommendation that the cemetery be abandoned. This office does not concur in the recommendation that the cemetery be abandoned at this time. Efforts will be made to have the cemetery kept in proper condition.[10]

The U.S. Army inspectors continued to visit Ball's Bluff every two years and send in their reports. The Great War came and ended as did the 1920's; then came the Depression. In 1933 the Washington Evening Star published a report on the battlefield by W. K. Wimsatt, Jr., entitled: "An Almost Forgotten Battlefield Near Washington—Ball's Bluff, Along Potomac, Where Federals Suffered Heavy Loss." The first three paragraphs gave an excellent impression of Ball's Bluff battlefield in 1933:

> Within 30 miles of Washington lies a Civil War battlefield of unusual interest because it has remained almost unchanged in appearance since the time of the war. Ball's Bluff on the Potomac, a few miles from Leesburg, presents today very much the same wild features as on the day nearly a thousand Union soldiers met death at its edge as a result of a strategic blunder that put Washington in a furor for months and provoked a Senate investigation, ending in the imprisonment of a general of the United States Army.
>
> This has never yet been a sight-seer battlefield. It is back in the country, on the edge of a woods, approachable by a dirt road. There has been no effort to make it into a park. The State of Virginia has called attention to its location by a sign on the Point of Rocks road about a mile north of Leesburg. On the actual site there is a little National Cemetery, with its flagpole, enclosed by a low wall of red brick. Four years after the battle the skeletons of 54 men were collected from the rocky and overgrown declivities of the spot and buried in this cemetery—all but one unknown soldier.
>
> Otherwise, the battlefield remains the same in its landscape features as it was on the day it served as a death trap for a small army. The place itself tells the story of the men who crept up the bluff at midnight, to be met the next day by a withering Confederate fire that sent them back stumbling through the thick woods and down the rocky, tangled face of the bluff to the swirling river. The people living in the neighborhood know the story and still speak of the "poor Yankee soldiers who went over the bluff," and exclaim, "Wasn't it a pity!" with as much feeling as if the battle had been fought in the past week. Where the turf is worn away by the edge of the road the fortunate visitor may pick up one of the big lead "minie" balls, smooth and creamy with oxide, which at other battlefields are made into watch fobs.[11]

In its biennial report for 1938 the Office of the Inspector General, Department of the Army, noted the following:

> The entire right-of-way fence has been completed to include a small area west of the cemetery wall and north of the right-of-way. A walk gate was placed near the cemetery to permit access to Ball's Bluff and a picnic ground north of the cemetery. Two farm gates were placed to permit access to property on both sides of the right-of-way and two openings for jumps were constructed for the use by hunters of the Loudoun Hunt Club.
>
> A permanent caretaker has been appointed, Mr. Andrew F. Athey, who lives near the cemetery

The southern exposure of the enclosed cemetery as it appears today from the Baker monument (foreground). This was the site of the field during the battle, a picnic ground at the turn of the century, now largely overgrown with trees.

and who has taken excellent care of the cemetery, grounds, fence, and roadway.

Also in 1938 a lease was signed between the United States of America and Joseph S. Whitmore/Horace C. Littlejohn for a period of twenty years to permit the turning of vehicles at the edge of the National Cemetery for those individuals visiting the site in their automobile. This lease was made for the sum of $1.00 per year.

Then came World War II and the battlefield/National Cemetery at Ball's Bluff was all but forgotten as America fought for freedom around the globe. A 1947 report erroneously noted that: "Colonel Baker's grave is located on private property situated 66 feet south of the cemetery. It is marked with a Headstone and this grave is on the property of Mr. F. S. Whitmore. The grave of a Confederate soldier, Clinton Hatcher, is located 103 feet from the northwest corner of the cemetery." The report did note correctly that: "This battle was of high political and military significance."[13]

Then in 1950 came war in Korea as the United States once again found itself fighting for freedom on a distant battlefield. With the end of the war in Korea and the approach of the Civil War Centennial, interest was once again renewed in Ball's Bluff National Cemetery and battlefield.

Then in 1957 a serious problem developed when, in a budget cutting move, the Department of the Army decided to remove the Union dead from the National Cemetery. The *Loudoun Times-Mirror* had this to say in its editorial of 3 April 1958:

This Hallowed Ground

A little way northeast of Leesburg, overlooking the Potomac, is a spot of hallowed ground. This is Ball's Bluff, a walled enclosure with a flag-pole centered against a semi-circle of graves where brave men lie buried. More than 50 Union soldiers who gave their lives for their country have slept peacefully there at Ball's Bluff for nearly one hundred years.

And now to save a paltry $500 a year, the Army

wants to dig them up. Men who ought to consider these Ball's Bluff soldiers as brothers in arms want to tear up the site, take what is left of the bones, and move them willy-nilly to a new, strange grave 60 miles away.

It makes us wonder what is going to happen to the graves of equally brave Americans who have died in later wars. When the parents and wives and children of our World War II dead are no longer around to protest, will these men, too, be dug up and "consolidated" somewhere to save a little money? Will the Tomb of the Unknown Soldier be torn down when the last World War I veteran has died?

Ball's Bluff may not have been a big battle; it was a very important one. It started General George B. McClellan on his way down. It brought on a Senate investigation of the conduct of the war. It resulted in a censorship fight which filled the newspapers ... it remains—to military men—a classic example of how not to cross a river under fire.

Ball's Bluff needs more attention, not less. Let the Army save its money from the vast waste of its military operations, not from the petty cash it takes to maintain the graves of honored American dead. Let those 54 Union soldiers continue to sleep in peace and let Ball's Bluff remain a shrine.[14]

Then on 21 October 1961 came the Centennial celebration of the Battle of Ball's Bluff. Due to severe rain the ceremony was held at Leesburg Elementary School. The main address was given by noted historian Walter Lord. Colonel John Eisenhower represented Pennsylvania, White House Aide Arthur Schlesinger, Jr., represented Massachusetts, Mrs. L. W. Austin represented Mississippi, Mr. Kenneth Bartlett—Vice President of Syracuse University represented New York, former Congressman A. W. Lafferty represented Oregon and Mr. Charles Pickett of Fairfax, great-nephew of Major General George Pickett, represented the 8th Virginia Infantry Regiment. Mrs. W. C. Crane of Leesburg placed a wreath on the grave of James Allen of Massachusetts and Mr. Thomas Hatcher, great-great-nephew of Clinton Hatcher placed a wreath at

Trees have grown over the position where the two Federal howitzers had stood. It was a field in 1861. Photo, Mike O'Donnell.

A lone tree now commands the ridge where Captain Philbrick had stood when he spied the large "Confederate camp" in the valley below. This error proved disastrous to the Yankees. Photo, Mike O'Donnell.

the Hatcher memorial marker. In addition to the services held in Leesburg, the town of Poolesville, Maryland (headquarters for General Stone and his Corps of Observation) along with Montgomery County Historical Society held their programs to commemorate the Centennial of the Battle of Ball's Bluff.[15]

Following the end of the Centennial, Ball's Bluff was remembered by a battle reenactment in 1968 hosted by the Grand Army of the Reunion and then in 1975 by another battle commemoration, this time hosted by The First North-South Brigade.[16]

By the early 1980's the growth of the greater Washington Metropolitan area reached the battlefield of Ball's Bluff. This led to private and public concern over the future of the Ball's Bluff National Cemetery and the Ball's Bluff battlefield. An example of the drive to save the National Cemetery and the battlefield was the all-night vigil held at Ball's Bluff on October 17-18, 1981 by Mr. Hugh Harmon of Leesburg.[17] The Loudoun County Board of Supervisors next met with concerned organizations and individual citizens concerning the future of Ball's Bluff. On 18 August, 1984 a magnificent ceremony was held on the courthouse grounds to honor Ball's Bluff Battlefield and National Cemetery being named a NATIONAL HISTORIC LANDMARK by the National Park Service of the Department of the Interior. The plaque designating this was presented by Russell Dickerson, Director of the National Park Service to Loudoun County Supervisor James F. Brownell. The keynote address was given by the Honorable Endicott Peabody, former governor of Massachusetts. Two officials who worked strongly behind the scenes to save Ball's Bluff were Loudoun Supervisor Frank Raflo and the Honorable John B. Hannum, senior judge of the Eastern Pennsylvania Federal District Court.[18]

Tour Guide

This appendix serves as your historical tour guide to the Ball's Bluff Battlefield, the town of Leesburg, the county of Loudoun, Montgomery County in Maryland and the C & O Canal that runs along the north bank of the Potomac River. Each of these areas of interest is covered with a basic introduction, relevant Civil War highlights, pertinent publications, points of contact and a basic map for guidance.

A fine overall guide to the history, current happenings, shops and restaurants of this region may be found in the brochure entitled POTOMAC VALLEY REVUE. This outstanding regional information brochure is distributed free by the various Chambers of Commerce of the area and by the businesses who advertise in it. For further information you should contact: Bayer Enterprise, Inc., Publisher; 1712 Preston Road, P.O. Box 2032, Hagerstown, Maryland 21742 or call 301-790-1789.

A Maryland State Highway map may be obtained by contacting the Maryland Office of Tourist Development, Department of Economic and Commercial Development, 45 Calvert Street, Annapolis, Maryland 21401 or phone 301-269-2686. A Virginia State Highway map may be obtained by contacting the Virginia Division of Tourism, 202 North 9th Street, Richmond, Virginia 23219 or phone 804-786-2051.

Leesburg

An outstanding blend of history, culture, beauty, recreation and fine Virginia hospitality greet the visitor to Leesburg, Virginia. Your initial point of contact is the Loudoun Museum and Visitors Center, 16 West Loudoun Street, Leesburg, Virginia 22075; phone 703-777-0519 or from the Metro D. C. area phone 471-6093.

Your first stop should be at the abovementioned Museum and Visitors Center (marked with a star on the accompanying map) where there is a basic orientation slide program, small museum (with something for everyone) and convenient parking. A highlight of events is the August Court House Days blending Virginia hospitality with many family events, Colonial Americana, Civil War Living History and a great parade.

In planning a walking tour of Leesburg you and your family should have a copy of "A Walk Around Leesburg" by the Honorable Frank Faflo, member of the Loudoun County Board of Supervisors from Leesburg. Those stops that have a connection with the Civil War are #5 (Ball House - owned by a member of Mosby's Rangers), #18 (site of personal combat), #25 (Confederate Soldier Monument), #31 (tunnel built to this house during the war), #32 (John Janney Home - Lee stayed here on way to battle of Antietam), #33 (law offices of John Janney), #40 (post war house of local Confederate hero Colonel Elijah White), #44 (ante-bellum split of this Methodist Church presaged that of the Civil War). In addition you will want to visit the large cemetery on the north edge of town that includes many Civil War sites. Please note: many of these historic homes are now private homes/offices and one should conduct oneself accordingly.

Loudoun County

Beautiful and historic Loudoun County was the scene of a great amount of Civil War activity. In addition to fighting at Ball's Bluff the Confederate Army passed through here on its way to the battle of Antietam in September of 1862. In June of 1863 the Union Army marched through Loudoun on its way to a little Pennsylvania farm village called Gettysburg. Confederate General Jubal Early traveled through here twice going and coming from his famous raid on Washington in July of 1864. In addition, Route 50 saw major cavalry battles at Aldie, Middleburg and Upperville. Also there were cavalry fights at Waterford, and many battles/raids by the famous Grey Ghost, Colonel John S. Mosby.

Two ante-bellum mansions in Loudoun, which are close to Ball's Bluff, are Oatlands Plantation (run by the National Trust for Historic Preservation) and Morven Park Plantation (run by the Westmoreland Davis Memorial Foundation of New York City). At

A bronze Confederate soldier stands guard in front of the historic courthouse in downtown Leesburg. This rustic town was the goal of the Federal troops who were defeated at Ball's Bluff and Edward's Ferry. Now it attracts visitors from around the world. Photo by author.

Oatlands Mosby's Men purchased for their renowned commander a spirited horse with money they had captured in their famous Greenback Raid. Oatlands is opened from mid-April to mid-November and may be contacted by writing/phoning Oatlands, Route 2, Box 352, Leesburg, Virginia 22075: 703-777-3174. Morven Park is a magnificent house in the grand tradition. Morven Park Plantation is open Tuesday-Sunday, Memorial Day weekend to Labor Day weekend and may be contacted by writing/phoning: Morven Park, Route 3, Box 50, Leesburg, Virginia 22075: 703-777-2414.

Excellent booklets/pamphlets abound on Loudoun. A small brochure entitled *Virginia's Hunt Country: Loudoun County* has recently become available. This may be obtained from the Loudoun Museum and Information Center as noted earlier. You should also ask for a copy of *Loudoun Events* which is published quarterly. This handy booklet gives you current information as to people and events taking place in Loudoun. In 1984 a new publication entitled *Loudoun County Handbook* became available. This is a free, indepth guide to all aspects of life in Loudoun, both current and historical. It may be obtained from the County of Loudoun, Office of the County Administrator, 18 North King Street, Leesburg, Virginia 22075 (phone 703-777-0200, Metro Phone is 471-0200).

Ball's Bluff Battlefield

As mentioned in my author's foreword the Ball's Bluff Battlefield is *not* a battlefield park and is therefore basically unmarked. On the accompanying map you will note the roads that lead to the battlefield. The intersection of Virginia Route 837 (the 1908 U.S. Army road back to the battlefield) and U.S. Route 15 is a *dangerous* crossroads—please cross here with extreme caution.

As you drive down Route 837 the ridge on your left is where the initial skirmish occurred, the two lone trees on the right ridge line is the approximate location where Captain Philbrick looked down upon the non-existing Confederate camp. When you reach the ridge top the dirt road to your left leads to the general location of Smartt's Mill Ford. Because of the extremely poor condition of this road do not attempt to drive it without a four-wheel drive vehicle. The white house on top of the ridge on your left is the Jackson House around which the second phase of the morning battle took place. This is a *private residence*—please do not trespass.

Proceeding straight down the dirt road you will eventually come to the end of it and the Ball's Bluff National Cemetery. There are 53 unknown American soldiers buried here along with the only known one—James Allen. Unfortunately, because of the heavy vandalism the American Flag, flagpole and ornate cemetery gate are no longer standing. This cemetery marks the approximate location of the 12 pounder James Rifle during the battle.

The small stone marker on your left just before you arrive at the cemetery is to the memory of Private Clinton Hatcher, color bearer of the 8th Virginia Infantry, who was killed at this location just prior to the final Confederate victory charge. Just after the turn of the century a group of Massachusetts veterans of the battle returned to visit the scene of their baptism of fire. They were guided by local Confederate veteran of the battle Colonel Elijah White. He told them about Clinton Hatcher. After the veterans returned to Massachusetts they kindly sent this marker stone of Massachusetts granite to honor the memory of Clinton Hatcher. It was in such spirit that the reunification of America took place after the Civil War.

The Baker Stone just south of the National Cemetery marks the location of the death of Colonel Edward Baker, Lincoln's close friend. This is known because of the original drawing that appeared in Colonel Wistar's autobiography in 1914.

There are two paths to take after you park at the cemetery. The path at the side of the cemetery wall will lead you upriver behind the main Union battleline to a magnificent overlook of the bluff, Potomac River and Harrison's Island. However, because there are no guardrails here do not under any circumstances allow children to run about as a fall

Pewter U.S. military button (circa 1795) worn by the Wayne Legion and found in the vicinity of Fort Evans. Courtesy Chuck Thompson.

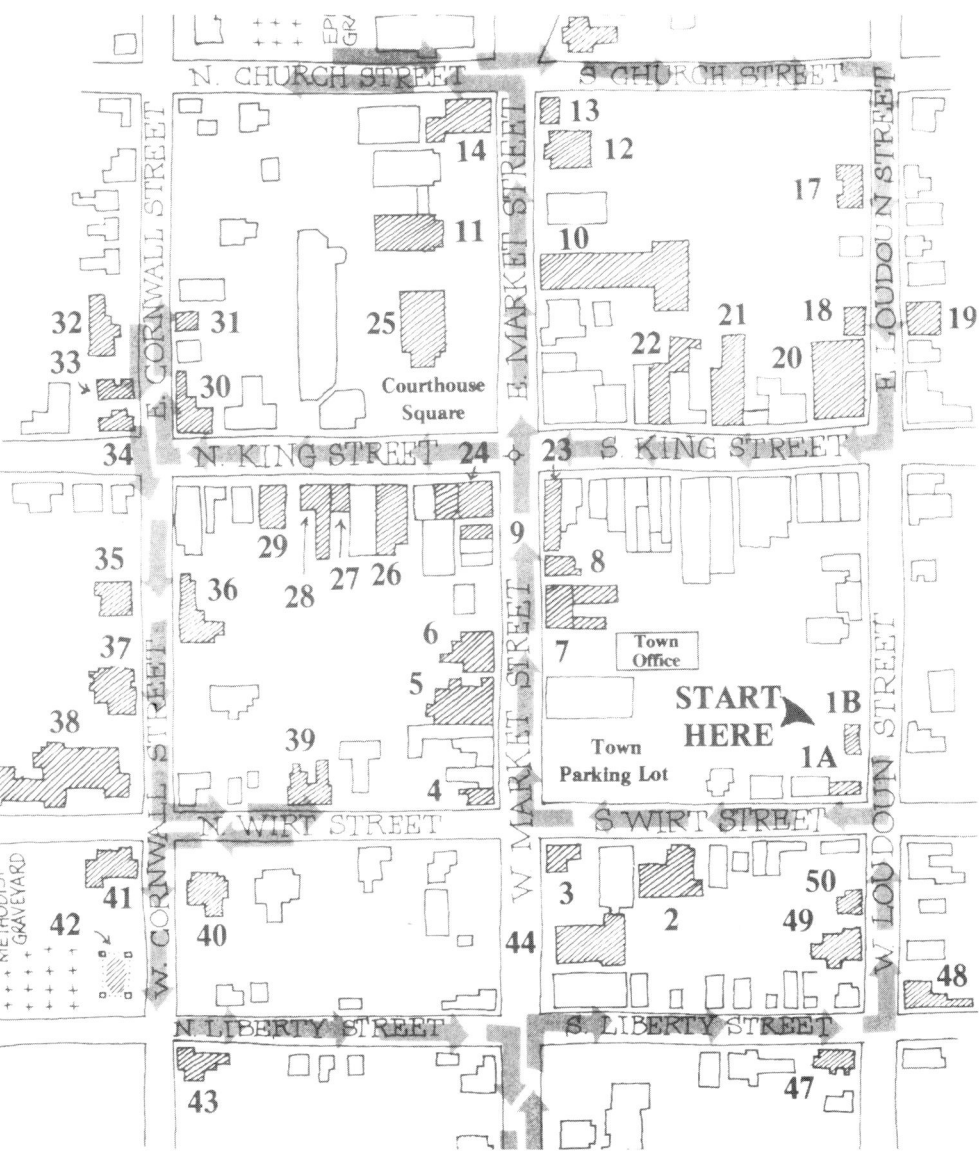

The Loudoun Museum, above, overlaid with a tour guide to the historic section of Leesburg. The shaded-in buildings predate the Civil War; many stood during the Revolution.

The Ball's Bluff National Cemetery contains the remains of 54 Federal soldiers. The wall which encloses it was made of stone quarried from the bluff adjacent to the cemetery. Photo, Mike O'Donnell.

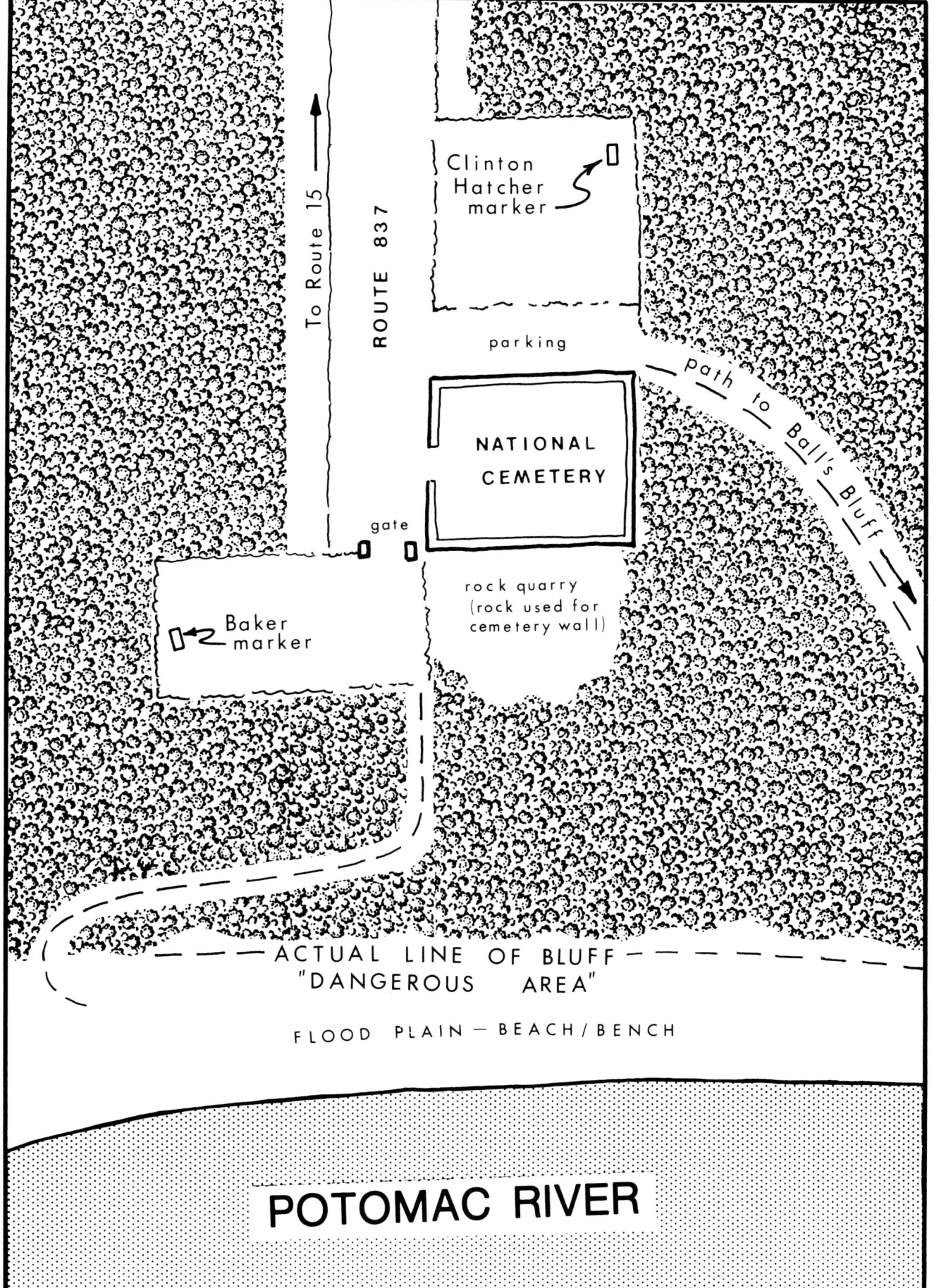

Author Kim Holien, right, discusses the events of October 21, 1861 with two local enthusiasts visiting the battle site. Standing at left is Welby Kenny, postmaster of Upperville, Va. In the center is Ralph Gheen whose grandfather fought at Ball's Bluff with the 8th Virginia and was later captured during Pickett's Charge. Photo, M. O'Donnell.

down the bluff would be dangerous in the extreme. The old barbed wire fence located at the end of this path marks the northern edge of the famous cleared field. Proceed back to the parking area and take the path leading down to the river from in front of the cemetery gate. Again, be extremely careful with children as this path also skirts the dangerous edge of the Bluff. Also please note that it is very difficult for elderly people and handicapped individuals.

Ball's Bluff battlefield is, during warm months, the home to many poisonous copperhead snakes. You should at all times be careful and watch where you walk. In addition, stinging insects, ticks, and small wild animals are also to be guarded against here at this site. If you have an emergency there is a modern hospital in the northwest corner of Leesburg.

It is to be hoped that by the time of the 125th Anniversary of the battle in October of 1986 a proper battlefield park will have been established in time for ceremonies to mark the anniversary of the battle and to commemorate the valor of those who fought here so nobly for the Blue and the Gray.

Montgomery County, Maryland

During the Ball's Bluff Campaign and Battle, Montgomery County (located in south central Maryland) was the Union campground and drill field with General Stone having his headquarters at Poolesville. In addition many Civil War events happened in and personalities criss-crossed the county during the four years of war.

The best way to travel to the Civil War sites in Montgomery County is by first purchasing for $3.00 (plus postage and Maryland tax) the "Civil War Guide to Montgomery County, MD" by Mr. Charles T. Jacobs. Civil War sites mentioned in this booklet that are pertinent to Ball's Bluff are Darnestown (pages 8-9), Edward's Ferry (pages 11-12), Harrison's Island (pages 13-14), Poolesville (pages 17-19) and Rockville (pages 20-22). This outstanding local history is available from either the Montgomery County Historical Society, 103 West Montgomery Avenue, Rockville, Maryland 20850, phone 301-762-1492 or 301-340-9853: 12-4 p.m., Tuesday - Saturday or from the Montgomery County Civil War Round Table, c/o Ms Vicki Heilig, 11843 Summer Oak Drive, Germantown, MD 20874; phone 301-972-3496.

In addition to the Ball's Bluff Campaign of 1861 the county saw both Union and Confederate armies pass through it for the Antietam, Gettysburg and Washington Campaigns of 1862-1864 and cavalry raids and battles by such Confederate wizards of the saddle as Jeb Stuart, John S. Mosby and local hero Colonel Elijah White. A small museum exists in Poolesville which houses—on the second story—large displays of artifacts from the camps of the Union regiments that fought at Ball's Bluff. You may contact the John Poole Museum at Poolesville, Md. 20837. Phone: (301) 972-8635.

The Chesapeake and Ohio Canal

The magnificent Chesapeake and Ohio Canal runs 184½ miles from Georgetown in western Washington, D. C. along the north bank of the Potomac River, to Cumberland, Maryland, In its route it marks the entire border of Montgomery County with the Potomac River.

From Seneca Creek to the Monocacy, a distance of 19 miles, this strategic commercial and military waterway was picketed by men of General Stone's 'Corps of Observation'.

Today this beautifully historic river route has been preserved for Americans under the auspices of the National Park Service. You should start your tour at the Great Falls Visitor Center in Maryland, phone 301-299-3613, Metro Phone 299-3613. Here is a museum, a mid-19th century canal boat ride, and an excellent introduction to the canal. In addition while you are there you may wish to purchase an excellent guidebook entitled "Towpath Guide to the C & O Canal" by Captain Thomas Hahn. This is the finest historical guide to the Canal as well as being an outstanding practical guide for visitors and hikers. Its cost is $10.00 plus postage and Maryland tax. In addition you may wish to purchase a superb portfolio of maps by the Interstate Commission on the Potomac River Basin. This portfolio packet is entitled "The Potomac River and the C & O Canal: Five Colorful Strip Maps, Georgetown to Antietam Creek" and costs $4.50 plus Maryland tax and postage. Both of these outstanding publications may be obtained by visiting the Maryland Great Falls Visitor Center or by writing to the Superintendent, C & O Canal National Historical Park, Box 4, Sharpsburg, Maryland 21782. Enjoy your American Heritage and in so doing thank your National Park Service for its years of dedicated service to America's Heritage.

Scenic Harper's Ferry situated at the confluence of the Shenandoah and Potomac rivers several miles from Leesburg and Ball's Bluff. Photo, D. Tabler. Courtesy Moss Publications.

Bibliography

Manuscripts

Manuscript Division, Library of Congress
Nathaniel P. Banks Papers
Thomas Bayard Papers
P.G.T. Beauregard Papers
Simon Cameron Papers
Joseph Holt Papers
Joshua R. Giddings/George W. Julian Papers
Phillip Kearny Papers
Frederick W. Lander Papers
Abraham Lincoln Papers
John MacEwen Papers
George B. McClellan, Sr., Papers
Isaac M. Somers Papers
Edwin M. Stanton Papers

Frederick Wight Papers

University of Rocherster Library
William H. Seward Papers

Rutgers University
Washington A. Roebling Papers

State Historical Society of Wisconsin
General Horatio G. Gibson papers

University of Michigan
James S. Schoff Collection

National Archives

Washington, D. C. National Archives. Military Service Branch. Record Group 94. Charles P. Stone; Appointments, Commissions and Promotions File.
Washington, D. C. National Archives, Military Service Branch. Record Group 15. Charles P. Stone; Staff Officer File.
Washington, D. C. National Archives. Military Service Branch. Record Group 94. Letters Received, Adjutant General's Office, File 336 B, 1862.
Washington, D. C. National Archives. Navy and Old Army Branch. Record Group 107. Reports to Congress from the Secretary of War. Records of the Office of the Secretary of War.

Other Government Agencies

Washington, D. C. Veterans Administration, Cemetery Services Office. Ball's Bluff National Cemetery File.

Newspapers

Baltimore Sun, 20 October 1957.
Boston Evening Transcript, 22 October 1861.
Boston Evening Transcript, 23 October 1861.
Boston Evening Transcript, 24 October 1861.
Boston Evening Transcript, 25 October 1861.
Boston-Evening Transcript, 26 October 1861.
Loudoun Times-Mirror, 5 September 1957.
Loudoun Times-Mirror, 24 October 1957.
Loudoun Times-Mirror, 3 April 1958.
Loudoun Times-Mirror, 9 April 1959.
Loudoun Times-Mirror, 23 April 1959.
Loudoun Times-Mirror, 30 April 1959.
Loudoun Times-Mirror, 28 May 1959.
Loudoun Times-Mirror, 17 April 1980.
Loudoun Times-Mirror, 7 June 1980.

Loudoun-Times Mirror, 9 October 1980.
New York Times, January 25, 1887.
San Francisco Sunday Examiner & Chronicle, 15 July 1979.
Washington Daily News, 8 October 1958.
Washington Daily News, 5 May 1961.
Washington Daily News, 21 October 1961.
Washington Evening Star, 10 September 1933.
Washington Evening Star, 21 October 1961.
Washington Post, 1 April 1958.
Washington Post, 8 October 1958.
Washington Post, 12 October 1969.
Washington Post, 23 November 1967.
Washington Post, 23 October 1980.
Washington Post, 5 October 1981.
West Virginia Hillbilly, 30 January 1982.

Published Primary Sources

Austin, Aurelia. ed. "A Georgia Boy with Stonewall Jackson: The Letters of James Thomas Thompson." *The Virginia Magazine of History and Biography* 70 #3 (July 1962) 317-318.
Beale, Howard K., ed. *The Diary of Edward Bates.* Washington, D. C. United States Government, 1933.
Blackford, Susan L. compiler. *Letters from Lee's Army.* New York: Charles Scribner Sons, 1947.
Blaine, James G. *Twenty Years of Congress.* Norwich, Conn.: The Henry Bell Publishing Company, 1884.
Buel, Clarence C., and Johnson, Robert U., eds. *Battles and Leaders of the Civil War.* Vol. 1 and 2. New York: The Century Company, 1884-1887.

Caffey, Thomas E., *Battlefields of the South.* New York: John Bradburn, 1864.

Dennett, Tyler, ed. *Lincoln and the Civil War in the Diaries and Letters of John Hay.* New York: Dodd, Mead and Company, 1939.

Dwight, Wilder. *Life and Letters of Wilder Dwight.* Boston: Ticknor and Fields, 1868.

Fontaine, Lamar. *My Life and Lectures.* New York: The Neale Publishing Company, 1908.

Gibbs, George A. "A Mississippi Private at 1st Bull Run and Ball's Bluff." *Civil War Times Illustrated,* April 1965, pp. 27-42.

Gonan, Gilbert and Livingwood, James W. eds. *The Memoirs of John Haskell, the Personal Narrative of a Confederate Officer.* New York: G. P. Putnam's Sons, 1960.

Goree V, Langston J. ed. *The Thomas Jewett Goree Letters, Vol. I, The Civil War Letters.* Bryan, Texas: Family History Foundation, 1981.

Hamilton, J.G.D.R., ed. *The Papers of Randolph Albott Shotwell.* Vol. 1. Raleigh: The North Carolina Historical Commission, 1929.

Hammond, Harold E. ed. *Diary of a Union Lady: 1861-65.* New York: Funk and Wagnalls, 1962.

Harris, Lt. William C. *Prison Life in the Tobacco Warehouse at Richmond.* Philadelphia: George W. Childs, 1862.

Hay, John. "Colonel Baker." Harpers New Monthly Magazine 24 #139 (December, 1861): 105-110.

Hay, John, and Nicolay, John. *Abraham Lincoln:* A History. Vol. 3 and 4. New York: The Century Company, 1890.

Hendricks, Thurman Earl: *History of Thurman Earl Hendricks and 20 Others in the Service of the Confederate States of America.* Vol. 1. Little Rock, Arkansas: General T. J. Churchill Chapter No. 1373, United Daughters of the Confederacy, 1931.

Howe, Mark D., ed. *Touched With Fire: The Civil War Letters of Oliver Wendell Holmes.* Cambridge: Harvard University Press, 1946.

Jones, John B. *A Rebel War Clerk's Diary, Vol. 1.* Philadelphia: J. B. Lippincott & Co., 1866.

Julian, George W. *Political Recollections, 1840-1872.* Chicago: McClury and Company, 1884.

Major General George B. McClellan from August 1st, 1861 to August 1st, 1862. New York: H. Derter, 1862.

McCarthy, Carlton, ed. *Contributions to a History of the Richmond Howitzer Battalion,* Pamphlet No. 4, Section III. "Extracts from an old 'Order Book' of the First Company Richmond Howitzers." Richmond: J. W. Randolph and English, 1886.

McClellan, George B. *McClellan's Own Story.* New York: Charles L. Webster and Company, 1887.

McGuire, Mrs. Judith W. *Diary of a Southern Refugee during the War.* Richmond, Virginia: J. W. Randolph and English, 1889.

Meade, Lt. Col. George G. *The Life and Letters of George Gordon Meade,* Vol. 1. New York: Charles Scribner Sons, 1913.

Mearns, David C., ed. *The Lincoln Papers.* Vol. 2. Garden City, New York: Doubleday and Company, Inc., 1948.

Mitgang, Herbert, ed. *Washington in Lincoln's Time* by Noah Brooks. New York: Rhinehart and Company, 1958.

Morse, Charles F. *Letters Written During the Civil War.* Boston: Privately Printed, 1898.

Morton, Lt. G. Nash. "The Richmond Howitzers and the Battle of Ball's Bluff." *Confederate Veteran,* January 1924, pp. 13-15.

Nevins, Allan, ed. *The Diary of General George T. Strong, The Civil War, 1860-1865.* New York: The MacMillan Company, 1962.

Paciulli, Orlo C. compiler. "The Capture and Escape of Capt. J. Owens Berry." *The Historical Society of Fairfax County* 15 (1978-1979): 1-12.

Palfrey, Francis W. *Memoir of William Francis Bartlett.* Boston Houghton, Osgood and Company, 1878.

Patch, Major General Joseph D. *The Battle of Ball's Bluff.* Leesburg: Potomac Press, 1958.

Pierce, Edward L. *Memoir and Letters of Charles Sumner.* Vol. 4. Boston: Roberts Brothers, 1893.

Pierson, Charles L. *Ball's Bluff: A Monograph.* Salem: The Salem Press, 1913.

Pinkerton, Allan. *The Spy of the Rebellion.* New York: G. W. Carleton and Company, 1885.

Quint, Alonzo. *The Potomac and the Rapidan, Army Notes, 1861-1863.* Boston: Crosby and Nichols, 1864.

Reichardt, Theodore. *Diary of Battery A, First Regiment Rhode Island Light Artillery.* Providence, Rhode Island: N. Bangs Williams, 1865.

Silver, James W., ed. "Robert A. Moore: The Diary of a Confederate Private." *The Louisiana Historical Quarterly* 39, No. 3. (July 1956): 235-374.

Sparks, David S., ed. *Inside Lincoln's Army: The Diary of Marsena Rudolph Patrick, Provost Marshal General of the Army of the Potomac.* New York: Thomas Yoseloff, 1964.

Stone, Charles P. "A Dinner With General Scott." *Magazine of American History,* 1884, pp. 528-532.

"Washington in March and April, 1861." *Magazine of American History,* July 1885, pp. 1-24.

Silver, James W. ed. "Robert A. Moore: The Diary of a Confederate Private." *The Louisiana Historical Quarterly* 39, No. 3 (July 1956): 235-374.

Stowe, Sergeant Jonothan P. "Life with the 15th Massachusetts." *Civil War Times Illustrated,* August 1972, pp. 4-11 and 48-54.

United States Government. *Official Records of the War of the Rebellion.* Washington, D. C.: U.S. Government Printing Office, 1894.

Report of the Committee on the Conduct of the War, Part Two. Washington, D. C.: U.S. Government Printing Office, 1863.

White, Colonel E. V. *History of the Battle of Ball's Bluff.* Leesburg: The Washingtonian Print, 1904.

Wistar, Isaac J. *Half a Century in War and Peace: An Autobiography* New York: Harper and Brothers, 1937.

Wolf, Hazel C., ed. "Campaigning with the First Minnesota: A Civil War Diary." *Minnesota Historical Society* 25 (1944): 11-35.

Wood, Lindsay L., ed. *Leaves from an old Washington Diary, 1854-1863.* Mount Vernon, New York: The Golden Eagle Press, 1943.

Secondary Sources

Adams, Captain John G.B. *Reminiscences of the Nineteenth Massachusetts Regiment.* Boston: Wright and Potter Printing Company, 1889

American Historical Society, *The Cyclopedia of American Biography*, n.p. 1918, pp. 215-216.

Andrews, J. Cutler. *The North Reports the Civil War.* Pittsburgh: The University of Pittsburgh Press, 1955.

Angle, Paul M. *A Pictorial History of the Civil War Years.* Garden City, New York: Doubleday and Company, Inc., 1967.

Bailey, Ronald H. *The Civil War: Forward to Richmond.* Alexandria, Virginia: Time-Life Books, 1983.

Baltz, John D. *Honorable Edward D. Baker: U.S. Senator from Oregon.* Lancaster: Inquirer Printing Company, 1888.

Banes, Charles H. *History of the Philadelphia Brigade.* Philadelphia: J. B. Lippincott and Company, 1876.

Benjamin, Marcus, ed. *Washington During War Time.* Washington, D. C. The National Tribune Company, 1904.

Blair, Harry C., and Tarshis, Rebecca. *Colonel Edward D. Baker: Lincoln's Constant Ally.* Portland: Oregon Historical Society, 1960.

Board of Commissioners. *Minnesota in the Civil and Indian Wars, 1861-1865.* St. Paul, Minnesota: The Pioneer Press, 1890.

Boatner, Colonel Mark M. III. *The Civil War Dictionary.* New York: David McKay Company, 1959.

Botterud, Keith A. "The Joint Committee on the Conduct of the War." M. A. thesis, Georgetown University, 1949.

Bowen, Catherine D. *Yankee from Olympus.* Boston: Little, Brown and Company, 1944.

Bowers, Claude G. *The Tragic Era: The Revolution After Lincoln.* Cambridge: Houghton Mifflin, 1929.

Bradley, Erwin S. *Simon Cameron, Lincoln's Secretary of War: A Political Biography.* Philadelphia: University of Pennsylvania Press, 1966.

Bruce, Lieutenant Colonel George A. *The Twentieth Regiment of Massachusetts Volunteer Infantry.* Boston: Houghton, Mifflin and Company, 1966.

Carroll, J. M. compiler. *List of Staff Officers of the Confederate Army, 1861-1865.* Mattituck, New York: J. M. Carroll and Company.

Catton, Bruce. *Glory Road.* Garden City, New York: Doubleday and Company, Inc., 1954.

Mr. Lincoln's Army. Garden City, New York: Doubleday and Company, 1951.

Terrible Swift Sword. Garden City, New York: Doubleday and Company, 1963.

The Hallowed Ground. Garden City, New York: Doubleday and Company, Inc., 1956.

Commonwealth of Massachusetts. *A Record of the Dedication of the Statue of Major General William Francis Bartlett.* Boston: Wright and Potter Printing Company, 1905.

Conrad, James L. "From Glory to Contention: The Sad History of 'Shanks' Evans." *Civil War Times Illustrated*, September 1983, pp. 32-38.

Cooling, Dr. B. Franklin. *Symbol, Sword and Shield.* Hamden, Conn.: The Shoe String Press 1975.

Crouch, Howard. *Relic Hunter.* Falls Church, Virginia: Howard Crouch, 1976.

Cullem, George W. *Biographical Register of the Officers and Graduates of the United States Military Academy*, 2 Volumes. Boston: Houghton Mifflin Co., 1891.

Davis, William C. *The Deep Waters of the Proud.* Garden City, New York: Doubleday and Company, Inc., 1982.

Divine, John et al. *Loudoun County and the Civil War.* Leesburg: Loudoun County Civil War Centennial Commission, 1961.

8th Virginia Infantry. Lynchburg, Virginia: H. E. Howard, Inc., 1983.

Donald, David. *Charles Sumner and the Coming of the Civil War.* New York: Alfred A. Knopf, 1960.

Charles Sumner and the Rights of Man. New York: Alfred A. Knopf, 1970.

Dornbusch, C. E. *Military Bibliography of the Civil War.* New York: The New York Public Library and Readex Books, 1975.

Dupuy, Colonels R. Ernest and Trevor N. *The Encyclopedia of Military History.* New York: Harper and Row, 1977.

Dyer, F. H. *A Compendium of the War of the Rebellion.* Dayton, Ohio: Moringside Bookshop, 1978.

Elliott, Charles W. *Winfield Scott: The Soldier and the Man.* New York: The MacMillan Company, 1937.

Flynn, Kevin C., ed. *The Potomac River and the C&O Canal: Five Colorful Strip Maps, Georgetown to Antietam Creek.* Rockville, Maryland: Interstate Commission on the Potomac River, n.d.

Ford, Andrew E. *The Story of the Fifteenth Regiment Massachusetts Volunteer Infantry.* Clinton: W. J. Coulter, 1898.

Gordon, George H. *History of the Second Massachusetts Regiment of Infantry.* Boston: Alfred Mudge and Sons, 1874.

Hahn, Thomas F. *Towpath Guide to the C&O Canal.* Shepherdstown, West Virginia: American Canal and Transportation Center, 1983.

Harrington, Fred H. *Fighting Politician: Major General N. P. Banks.* Philadelphia: University of Pennsylvania Press, 1948.

Haskin, Brevet Major William L. *The History of the First Regiment of Artillery from its Organization in 1821, to January 1st, 1876.* Portland, Maine: B. Thurston and Company, 1879.

Heitman, Francis B. *Historical Register and Dictionary of the United States Army,* 2 Volumes. Washington, Government Printing, 1903.

Hesseltime, William B., and Wolf, Hazel C., *The Blue and the Gray on the Nile.* Chicago: The University of Chicago Press, 1961.

Holmbrick, R. I. *History of the First Minnesota Volunteer Infantry, 1861-1864.* Stillwater, Minnesota: Easton and Masterman Printers, 1916.

Howe, Mark D., ed. *Holmes-Pollack Letters: The Correspondence of Mr. Justice Holmes and Sir Frederick Pollack, 1874-1932.* Volume 1. Cambridge: Harvard University Press, 1944.

Hurlburt, William H. *General McClellan and the Conduct of the War.* New York: Sheldon and Company, 1864.

Hyman, Harold M., and Thomas, Benjamin P. Stanton: *The Life and Times of Lincoln's Secretary of War.* New York: Alfred A. Knopf, 1962.

Hynd, Alan. *Arrival 12:30 - The Baltimore Plot Against Lincoln.* Camden: Thomas Nelson and Sons, 1967.

Ianni, Juan B. "The Despot's Heel: Federal Military Policy in Maryland During the Opening Months of the Civil War, Including a Comparison with the Policies Pursued in Missouri and Kentucky." M.A. thesis, George Mason University, 1977.

Irwin, Richard B. *History of the Nineteenth Army Corps.* New York: G. P. Putnam's Sons, 1892.

Jacques, John W. *Three Years' Campaign of the Ninth, N.Y.S.M.* New York: Hilton and Company, 1865.

Jacobs, Charles. *Civil War Guide to Montgomery County.* Rockville, Maryland: Pacemaker Press, Inc., 1983.

Johnson, Ludwell. *The Red River Campaign.* Baltimore: the Johns Hopkins Press, 1958.

Jones, Virgil Carrington. *Gray Ghosts and Rebel Raiders.* New York: Henry Holt and Company, 1959.

Jordon, David M. *Roscoe Conkling of New York, Voice in the Senate.* Ithaca, New York: Cornell University Press, 1971.

Kennedy, Elijah R. *The Conquest for California in 1861.* Boston: Houghton Mifflin and Company, 1912.

Klein, Dr. Frederic S. "Thaddeus Stevens - A Personality Profile." *Civil War Times Illustrated,* February 1964, pp. 18-23.

Krick, Robert E. *Lee's Colonels.* Dayton, Ohio: Moringside Bookshop, 1979.

Leech, Margaret, *Reveille In Washington.* New York: Harper and Brothers, 1941.

Long, E. B. *The Civil War Day by Day.* Garden City, New York: Doubleday and Company, Inc., 1971

Longacre, Edward G. "Charles P. Stone and the Crime of Unlucky Generals." *Civil War Times Illustrated,* November 1974, pp. 4-9, and 38-41.

Lookwood, Allison. "Disaster at Ball's Bluff." *American History Illustrated,* February 1982, pp. 36-41.

Lossing, Benson J. *Pictorial History of the Civil War.* Vol. 2. Hartford: T. Belknap, 1868.

Magdol, Edward. *Owen Lovejoy: Abolitionist in Congress.* New Brunswick, New Jersey: Rutgers University Press, 1967.

McDermott, Adjutant Anthony W. *A Brief History of the 69th Regiment Pennsylvania Veteran Volunteers.* Philadelphia: D. J. Gallagher and Co., 1889.

Mitchell, Maryl. *Divided Town: A Study of Washington, D. C. During the Civil War.* Barre, Massachusetts: Barre Publishing, 1968.

Moore, Frank, ed. *Heroes and Martyrs: Notable Men of the Time.* New York: G. P. Putnam, 1861.

The Rebellion Record, Volume 4. York: Arno Press, 1977.

Nevins, Allan. *The War for the Union: War Becomes Revolution,* Volume 7. Austin, Texas: Shoal Creek Publishers, 1971.

Newman, Ralph, ed. *Lincoln for the Ages.* New York: Doubleday and Company, 1960.

Nielson, Jon M. "Debacle at Ball's Bluff." *Civil War Times Illustrated,* January 1976, pp. 25-36.

Pearson, Henry G. *The Life of John A. Andrew: Governor of Massachusetts, 1861-1865.* Volume 1. Boston: Houghton Mifflin and Company, 1904.

Peterson, Harold L. "The Illinois Soldier and the Belgian Musket." *Military Collector and Historian* 2, No. 1 (March, 1950)

Peterson, Linda, ed. "She's A Grand Old Lady." *Correspondent* (November/December 1984): 1-6.

Pierson, William W. "The Committee on the Conduct of the Civil War." *American Historical Review* 23 (April 1918): 550-576.

Poland, Charles P., Jr. *From Frontier to Suburbia.* Marceline, Missouri: Walsworth Publishing Company, 1976.

Potter, John M. *Thirteen Desperate Days.* New York: Ivan Obolensky, Inc., 1964.

Randall, J. G. *The Civil War and Reconstruction.* Boston: D. C. Heath and Company, 1953.

Ratchford, J. W. *Some Reminiscences of Persons and Incidents of the Civil War,* Austin, Texas: Shoal Creek Publishers, 1971.

Rhodes, John H. *The History of Battery B, First Regiment Rhode Island Light Artillery in the War to Preserve the Union, 1861-1865.* Providence, Rhode Island: Snow and Farnham, 1894.

Riddleberger, Patrick. *George Washington Julian: Radical Republican.* Indianapolis: Indiana Historical Bureau, 1966.

Sandburg, Carl. *Abraham Lincoln, The War Years.* New York: Harcourt, Brace and World, Inc., 1939.

Sedgwick, Paul, ed. *Study in Patriotism.* Washington, D. C.: District of Columbia Civil War Centennial Commission, 1965.

Sypher, Josiah R. *History of the Pennsylvania Reserve Corps.* Lancaster, Pennsylvania: Elias Barr and Co., 1865.
Thompson, Colonel Magnus S. *From the Ranks to Brigadier General: The Service Record of Col. Elijah V. White, 1861-1865.*
Trefousse, Hans L. *Benjamin Franklin Wade: Radical Republican from Ohio.* New York: Twayne Publishers, Inc., 1963.
"The Joint Committee on the Conduct of the War: A Reassessment." *Civil War History* 10 (March 1964): 5-19.
The Radical Republicans: Lincoln's Vanguard for Racial Justice. New York: Alfred A. Knopf, 1969.
U.S. Government. *Biographical Directory of the American Congress, 1774-1971.* Washington, D. C.: U.S. Government Printing Office, 1971.
Waitt, Ernest C. *History of the Nineteenth Regiment Massachusetts Volunteer Infantry.* Salem: Salem Press, 1906.
Ward, Joseph R.C. *History of the One Hundred and Sixth Pennsylvania* Philadelphia: F. McManus, Jr., and Company, 1906.
Warner, Ezra J. *Generals in Blue.* Baton Rouge, Louisiana: Louisiana State University Press, 1964.
Generals in Gray, Baton Rouge, Louisiana: Louisiana State University Press, 1959.
Westwood, Howard C. "The Joint Committee on the Conduct of the War, An Agency of the Radical Faction?" Paper read before the D. C. Civil War Round Table, September 1972. Transcript copy.
White, John I. *American Vignettes: A Collection of Footnotes to History.* Convent Station, New Jersey: Travel Vision, 1976.
Williams, Harrison. *Legends of Loudoun.* Richmond: Garrett and Massie Inc., 1938.
Williams, T. Harry. "Investigation: 1862." *American Heritage Magazine,* December 1954, pp. 16-21.
Lincoln and the Radicals. Madison: The University of Wisconsin Press, 1941.
"The Committee on the Conduct of the War." *American Military Institute,* Fall 1939, pp. 139-156.
Woodward, C. Vann ed. *Mary Chestnut's Civil War.* New Haven, Connecticut: Yale University Press, 1981.
Woodward, Major E. M. *History of the Third Pennsylvania Reserve.* Trenton, New Jersey: MacCrellish & Quigley, 1883.
Yoder, Sandra, "Charles P. Stone and the Battle of Ball's Bluff." M.A. thesis, College of William and Mary, 1975.
Younger, Edward. ed. *Inside the Confederate Government.* New York: Oxford University Press, 1957.

Pamphlets

Bayer, Samuel W. *Potomac Valley Review,* Hagerstown, Maryland: Bayer Enterprises, 1984.
Loudoun County Handbook, Leesburg, Virginia: Hart Associates, 1984.
Raflo, Frank. *Loudoun Events.* Leesburg, Virginia: Frank Raflo, 1984.
A Walk Around Leesburg. Leesburg, Virginia: n.p., n.d.
The Town of Leesburg in Virginia. n.p., 1984.
Virginia's Hunt Country. n.p., 1984.

Footnotes

CHAPTER I

[1] George McClellan, *McClellan's Own Story* (New York: Charles L. Webster and Company, 1887), pp. 66-70.

[2] Warren W. Hassler, Jr, *General George B. McClellan: Shield of the Union* (Baton Rouge: Louisiana State University Press, 1957), p. 19.

[3] McClellan, *McClellan's Own Story*, pp. 66-67.

[4] Ibid, p. 68.

[5] Ibid, p. 68.

[6] George McClellan, *General McClellan's Reports and Campaigns* (New York: Sheldon and Company, 1864), p. 449.

[7] Ibid, p. 450.

[8] Ezra Warner, *Generals in Blue* (Baton Rouge: Louisiana State University Press, 1964), p. 480.

[9] Ibid, p. 480.

[10] Report of the Adjutant General prepared for the Committee on Invalid Pensions, U.S. House of Representatives, 15 February 1888, Charles P. Stone—Appointments, Commissions and Promotion File, Military Service Records Branch, Record Group 94, National Archives and Records Service, Washington, D. C.

[11] Warner, *Generals in Blue*, p. 480.

[12] Clarence C. Buel and Robert U. Johnson, eds., *Battles and Leaders of the Civil War* (New York: The Century Company, 1884-87), 1:9.

[13] Ibid., p. 13.

[14] Ibid., pp. 11-17.

[15] Ibid, pp. 11-17.

[16] Charles P. Stone, "A Dinner with General Scott in 1861," *Magazine of American History*, 1884, p. 528.

[17] John Hay and John Nicolay, *Abraham Lincoln: A History* (New York: The Century Company, 1890), 3:138.

[18] Charles W. Elliot, *Winfield Scott: The Soldier and the Man* (New York: The McMillan Company, 1937), p. 693.

[19] Buel and Johnson, *Battles and Leaders of the Civil War*, Vol. I, p. 24.

[20] Ibid., pp. 21-25.

[21] Ibid., pp. 24-25.

[22] Charles P. Stone, "Washington in March and April, 1861," *Magazine of American History*, July 1885, p. 4.

[23] Ibid., pp. 4-6.

[24] Ibid., p. 6.

[25] Ibid., pp. 10-23.

[26] Margaret Leech, *Reveille in Washington* (New York: Harper and Brothers, 1949), pp. 79-81.

[27] Report of the Adjutant General prepared for the Committee on Invalid Pensions, U.S. House of Representatives, 15 February 1888, Charles P. Stone—Appointments, Commissions and Promotion File, Military Service Records Branch, Record Group 94, National Archives and Records Service, Washington, D. C.

[28] Ibid.

[29] Ibid.

[30] Ibid.

[31] Warner, *Generals in Blue*, p. 480.

CHAPTER II

[1] John Q. Imholte, *The First Volunteers: History of the First Minnesota Volunteer Regiment, 1861-1865*, (Minneapolis: Ross and Haines, Inc., 1963), p. 82.

[2] Major General George B. McClellan, *General McClellan's Reports and Campaigns*, (New York: Shelden and Company, 1864), p. 450.

[3] R. I. Holcombe, *History of the First Regiment Minnesota Volunteer Infantry 1861-1864*, (Stillwater, Minnesota: Easton and Masterman, 1916), p. 62.

[4] The Board of Commissioners, *Minnesota in the Civil and Indian Wars, 1861-1865*, (St. Paul: The Pioneer Press Company, 1890), p. 16.

[5] McClellan, *General McClellan's Reports and Campaigns*, p. 454.

[6] William F. Amann, *Personnel of the Civil War*, (New York: Thomas Yoseloff, 1968), p. 209.

[7] McClellan, *General McClellan's Reports and Campaigns*, p. 454.

[8] John Divine, *Loudoun County and the Civil War*, (Leesburg, Virginia: Potomac Press of Leesburg, 1961), p. 22.

[9] Ibid., p. 21.

[10] McClellan, *General McClellan's Reports and Campaigns*, p. 454.

[11] Ibid.

[12] Ezra Warner, *Generals in Blue*, (Baton Rouge, Louisiana: Louisiana State University Press, 1964), p. 178-179.

[13] Ibid., p. 16.

[14] McClellan, *General McClellan's Reports and Campaigns*, p. 454.

[15] T. Harry Williams, *Lincoln and the Radicals*, (Madison: The University of Wisconsin Press, 1941), p. 42.

[16] Mary Alice Wills, *The Confederate Blockade of Washington, D. C. 1861-1862*, (Parsons, West Virginia: McClain Printing Company, 1975), p. 63-88.

[17] Joseph Mills Hanson, *Bull Run Remembers* (Manassas, Virginia: National Capitol Publishers, Inc., 1957), p. 38-39.

[18] Divine, *Loudoun County and the Civil War*, p. 22.

[19] Clarence C. Buel and Robert U. Johnson, ed. *Battles and Leaders of the Civil War, Volume II* (New York: The Century Company, 1884-1887), p. 126.

[20] George F. Price, compiler, *Across the Continent with the Fifth Cavalry* (New York: Antiquarian Press Ltd., 1959), p. 339-336.

[21] Lt. Colonel George Meade, Jr., *The Life and Letters of George Gordon Meade* (New York: Charles Scribner's Sons, 1913), p. 224.

[22] General Joseph E. Johnston, *Narrative of Military Operations* (Bloomington, Indiana: Indiana University Press, 1959), p. 77.

[23] Mead, *The Life and Letters of George Gordon Meade*, p. 224.

[24] McClellan, *General McClellan's Reports and Campaigns*, p. 77.

[25] Ibid., p. 78.

[26] Douglas Southall Freeman, *Lee's Lieutenants*, Volume I, (New York: Charles Scribner's Sons, 1942), p. 137-147.

[27] Lt. Colonel George A. Bruce, *The Twentieth Regiment of Massachusetts Volunteer Infantry, 1861-1865* (Boston: Houghton, Mifflin and Company, 1906), p. 33-34.

[28] U.S. Government, *Report of the Joint Committee on the Conduct of the War*, Part II (Washington, D. C. Government Printing Office, 1863), p. 256.

[29] U.S. War Department. *The War of the Rebellion: A Compilation of the Official Records of the Union and Confederate Armies* (Washington, D. C. Government Printing Office, 1880-1901), Series I, Volume V, p. 293.

[30] Andrew E. Ford, *The Story of the Fifteenth Regiment Massachusetts Volunteer Infantry in the Civil War, 1861-1864* (Clinton,

Massachusetts, 1898), p. 59-60.

[31] U.S. War Department, *Official Records*, Series I, Volume V, p. 293.

[32] Ibid., p. 293.

[33] Ibid., p. 293-295.

[34] Ibid., p. 293.

[35] Ibid., p. 293-295.

[36] Ford, *The Story of the 15th Massachusetts*, p. 68.

[37] Ibid., p. 68.

[38] U.S. War Department, *Official Records*, Series I, Volume V, p. 349.

[39] Divine, *Loudoun County and the Civil War*, p. 24.

[40] U.S. War Department, *Official Records*, Series I, Volume V, p. 308.

[41] Ibid., p. 308.

[42] Ibid., p. 308-309.

[43] Ibid., p. 363-364.

[44] Ibid., p. 363-364.

[45] Ibid., p. 309.

[46] Divine, *Loudoun County and the Civil War*, p. 24-25.

[47] U.S. War Department, *Official Records*, Series I, Volume V, p. 295-296, and 302-303.

[48] Ibid., p. 303.

[49] Warner, *Generals in Blue*, p. 16.

[50] U.S. War Department, *Official Records*, Series I, Volume V, p. 294-295.

[51] Holcombe, *History of the First Regiment Minnesota Volunteer Infantry, 1861-1865*, p. 75-76.

[52] U.S. War Department, *Official Records*, Series I, Volume V, p. 349.

[53] Ibid., p. 349.

[54] Ibid., p. 349.

[55] John Divine, *8th Virginia Infantry* (Lynchburg, Virginia: H. E. Howard, Inc., 1983), p. 4.

[56] U.S. War Department, *Official Records*, Series I, Volume V, p. 368-369.

[57] Divine, *8th Virginia Infantry*, p. 4.

CHAPTER III

[1] Divine, *8th Virginia Infantry*, p. 4.

[2] U.S. War Department, *Official Records*, Series I, Volume V, p. 297.

[3] Divine, *Loudoun County and the Civil War*, p. 26.

[4] Ford, *The Story of the Fifteenth Regiment Massachusetts Volunteer Infantry*, p. 78-80.

[5] Lt. Col. George A. Bruce, *The Twentieth Regiment of Massachusetts Volunteer Infantry, 1861-1865*, (Boston: Houghton Mifflin and Company, 1906), p. 44.

[6] John H. Rhodes, *The History of Battery B, First Regiment Rhode Island Light Artillery in the War to Preserve the Union, 1861-1865*, (Providence: Snow and Farnham, 1894), p. 33.

[7] Ibid., p. 33-34.

[8] Divine, *Loudoun County and the Civil War*, p. 26.

[9] U.S. War Department, *Official Records*, Series I, Volume V, p. 303.

[10] Bruce, *The Twentieth Regiment of Massachusetts Volunteer Infantry, 1861-1865*, p. 38-44.

[11] U.S. War Department, *Official Records*, Series I, Volume V, p. 310.

[12] Ibid., p. 310.

[13] Divine, *Loudoun County in the Civil War*, p. 27.

[14] Francis Palfrey, *Memoir of William Francis Bartlett*, (Boston: Houghton, Osgood and Company, 1878), p. 23.

[15] U.S. War Department, *Official Records*, Series I, Volume V, p. 364.

[16] Ibid., p. 320-321.

[17] Colonel E. V. White, *History of the Battle of Ball's Bluff*, (Leesburg: The Washingtonian Press, 1907), p. 10.

[18] U.S. War Department, *Official Records*, Series I, Volume V, p. 294-295.

[19] Ibid., p. 354-355.

[20] Ibid., p. 365.

[21] Palfrey, *Memoir of William Francis Bartlett*, p. 23-24.

[22] U.S. War Department, *Official Records*, Series I, Volume V, p. 297.

[23] Colonel Isaac J. Wistar, *Autobiography of Isaac Jones Wistar*, (New York: Harper and Brothers, 1937), p. 364-365.

[24] Divine, *Loudoun County in the Civil War*, p. 27-28.

[25] Wistar, *Autobiography of Isaac Jones Wistar*, p. 365.

[26] White, *History of the Battle of Ball's Bluff*, p. 10-12.

[27] Divine, *Loudoun County and the Civil War*, p. 32.

[28] Ibid., p. 28.

[29] George A. Gibbs, "A Mississippi Private at 1st Bull Run and Ball's Bluff," *Civil War Times Illustrated* 4:1 (April, 1965): 46-7.

[30] Divine, *Loudoun County in the Civil War*, p. 29.

[31] Lamar Fontaine, *My Life and My Lectures* (New York: The Neale Publishing Company, 1908), p. 84-85.

[32] U.S. War Department, *Official Records*, Series I, Volume V, p. 358.

[33] U.S. War Department, *Official Records*, Series I, Volume LI, p. 47-48.

[34] Divine, *Loudoun County and the Civil War*, p. 29.

[35] Palfray, *Memoir of William Francis Bartlett*, p. 24.

[36] U.S. War Department, *Official Records*, Series I, Volume V, p. 328.

[37] Divine, *Loudoun County and the Civil War*, p. 29-30.

[38] Ford, *The Story of the Fifteenth Regiment Massachusetts Volunteer Infantry in the Civil War, 1861-1864*, p. 88-89.

[39] Palfray, *Memoir of William Francis Bartlett*, p. 25-26.

[40] J. G. De Roulhac Hamilton, ed., *The Papers of Randolph Abbott Shotwell*, Vol. I (Raleigh: The North Carolina Historical Commission, 1929), p. 118.

[41] Palfray, *Memoir of William Frances Bartlett*, p. 25-26.

[42] U.S. War Department, *Official Records*, Series I, Volume V, p. 322.

[43] Ibid., p. 361.

[44] James W. Silver, ed., *A Life for the Confederacy*, (Jackson, Tennessee: McCowat-Mercer Press, Inc., 1959), p. 69-70.

[45] U.S. War Department, *Official Records*, Series I, Volume V, p. 322.

CHAPTER IV

[1] Ford, *The Story of the Fifteenth Regiment Massachusetts Volunteer Infantry in the Civil War, 1861-1864*, p. 90-91.

[2] Bruce, *The Twentieth Regiment of Massachusetts Volunteer Infantry, 1861-1865*, p. 53-54.

³Palfray, *Memoir of William Francis Bartlett*, p. 27-29.

⁴White, *History of the Battle of Ball's Bluff*, p. 16.

⁵Ibid., p. 16-20.

⁶Ernest L. Waitt, compiler, *History of the Nineteenth Regiment Massachusetts Volunteer Infantry 1861-1865*, (Salem, Massachusetts: The Salem Press, 1906), p. 22-25.

⁷Robert Todd Lincoln Collection of Abraham Lincoln Papers, Manuscript Division, Library of Congress.

⁸War Department, *Official Records*, Series I, Volume V, p. 298-299.

⁹John W. Jaques, *Three Years' Campaign of the Ninth, N.Y.S.M., during the Southern Rebellion* (New York: Hilton and Company, 1865) p. 48-49.

¹⁰Alonzo H. Quint, *The Potomac and the Rapidan, Army Notes, 1861-1863* (Boston: Crosby and Nichols, 1864), p. 37.

¹¹Holcombe, *History of the First Regiment Minnesota Volunteer Infantry 1861-1865*, p. 77.

¹²War Department, *Official Records*, Series I, Volume V, p. 355.

¹³Holcombe, *History of the First Minnesota Volunteer Infantry 1861-1865*, p. 78-79.

¹⁴Divine, *Loudoun County in the Civil War*, p. 31.

¹⁵Bruce, *The Twentieth Regiment of Massachusetts Volunteer Infantry 1861-1865*, p. 64.

CHAPTER V

¹E. B. Long, *The Civil War by Day* Garden City, N. Y.: Doubleday and Company, 1971), p. 148.

²Hans L. Trefousse, "The Joint Committee on the Conduct of the War: A Reassessment," *Civil War History* 10 (March 1964):7.

³Ibid.

⁴Ibid., pp. 7-8.

⁵Keith A. Botterud, "The Joint Committee on the Conduct of the Civil War: A Summary of Its Major Investigations" (M.A. thesis, Georgetown University, 1949), p. 6.

⁶Howard P. Westwood, "The Joint Committee on the Conduct of the War, An Agency of the Radical Faction?," p. 6. Paper presented at the District of Columbia Civil War Round Table, Washington, D. C., 12 September 1972.

⁷Trefousse, "The Joint Committee on the Conduct of the War: A Reassessment," pp. 7-8.

⁸Westwood, "The Joint Committee on the Conduct of the War, An Agency of the Radical Faction?," p. 5.

⁹Hans L. Trefousse, *Benjamin Franklin Wade: Radical Republican from Ohio* (New York: Twayne Publishers, Inc., 1963), p. 157.

¹⁰*Dictionary of American Biography*, 1964 ed., s.v. "Wade, Benjamin Franklin."

¹¹Trefousse, *Benjamin Franklin Wade: Radical Republican from Ohio*, p. 157.

¹²*Dictionary of American Biography*, s.v. "Chandler, Zachariah."

¹³Botterud, "The Joint Committee on the Conduct of the Civil War: A Summary of Its Major Investigations," p. 25.

¹⁴Ibid., pp. 29-30.

¹⁵*Dictionary of American Biography*, s.v. "Johnson, Andrew."

¹⁶Williams, *Lincoln and the Radicals*, p. 69.

¹⁷Botterud, "The Joint Committee on the Conduct of the Civil War: A Summary of Its Major Investigations," p. 36.

¹⁸*Biographical Dictionary of the American Congress, 1774-1971*, 1971 ed., s.v. "Gooch, Daniel Wheelwright."

¹⁹Williams, *Lincoln and the Radicals*, p. 69.

²⁰Botterud, "The Joint Committee on the Conduct of the Civil War: A Summary of Its Major Investigations," p. 22.

²¹*Dictionary of American Biography*, s.v. "Julian, George Washington."

²²Botterud, "The Joint Committee on the Conduct of the Civil War: A Summary of Its Major Investigations," pp. 22-23.

²³*Dictionary of American Biography*, s.v. "Covode, John."

²⁴*Biographical Dictionary of the American Congress, 1774-1971*, s.v. "Odell, Moses Fowler."

²⁵Williams, *Lincoln and the Radicals*, pp. 70-71.

²⁶*Dictionary of American Biography*, s.v. "Stanton, Edwin McMasters."

²⁷Ibid.

²⁸Williams, *Lincoln and the Radicals*, p. 97.

²⁹*Dictionary of American Biography*, s.v. "Baker, Edward Dickinson."

³⁰Warner, *Generals in Blue*, p. 16.

³¹*Dictionary of American Biography*, s.v. "Baker, Edward Dickinson."

³²Harry C. Blair and Rebecca Tarshis, *Colonel Edward D. Baker: Lincoln's Constant Ally* (Portland, Oregon: Abbott, Kerns & Bell Company, 1960), pp. 65, 79, 88, 93-94, 109-114.

³³Leech, *Reveille in Washington*, p. 44.

³⁴Warner, *Generals in Blue*, p. 16.

³⁵*Dictionary of American Biography*, s.v. "Baker, Edward Dickinson."

³⁶Warner, *Generals in Blue*, p. 16.

³⁷McClellan, *General McClellan's Reports and Campaigns*, p. 454.

³⁸Catton, *Mr. Lincoln's Army*, pp. 77-79.

³⁹Williams, *Lincoln and the Radicals*, p. 61.

⁴⁰Letter of Charles P. Stone to Benson J. Lossing, 5 November 1866, James S. Schoff Collection, Clements Library, University of Michigan.

⁴¹Howard K. Beale, ed., *The Diary of Edward Bates: 1859-1866* (Washington, D. C.: U.S. Government Printing Office, 1933), p. 199.

⁴²Hay and Nicolay, *Abraham Lincoln: A History*, pp. 459-60.

⁴³Buel and Johnson, *Battle and Leaders of the Civil War*, Vol. II, p. 132.

⁴⁴Henry G. Pearson, *The Life of John A. Andrew: Governor of Massachusetts, 1861-1865* (Boston: Houghton, Mifflin and Company, 1904), 1:314-15.

⁴⁵Ibid.

⁴⁶Ibid., pp. 315-16.

⁴⁷Ibid.

⁴⁸George F. Hoar, *Charles Sumner: His Complete Works* (New York: Negro University Press, 1969), pp. 8-9.

⁴⁹Buel and Johnson, *Battles and Leaders of the Civil War*, Vol. II, p. 133.

⁵⁰Catton, *Mr. Lincoln's Army*, pp. 82-85.

⁵¹Hassler, *General George B. McClellan: Shield of the Union*, p. 19.

⁵²Williams, *Lincoln and the Radicals*, pp. 16-18, 25-26, 34, 50-51, 56-57.

⁵³Ralph Newman, ed., *Lincoln for the Ages* (New York: Doubleday and Company, 1960), p. 195.

⁵⁴Leech, *Reveille in Washington*, p. 154.

⁵⁵Ibid, p. 149.

⁵⁶William Swinton, *Campaigns of the Army of the Potomac* (New York: Charles B. Richardson, 1866), pp. 73-76.

⁵⁷Catton, *Mr. Lincoln's Army*, pp. 90-91.

⁵⁸Bruce Catton, *This Hallowed Ground: The*

Story of the Union Side of the Civil War (Garden City, N. Y.: Doubleday & Company, Inc., 1956), pp. 82-83.

[59]Swinton, *Campaigns of the Army of the Potomac*, pp. 73-76.

[60]Dr. Benjamin Franklin Cooling, *Symbol, Sword and Shield: Defending Washington During the Civil War* (Hamden, Conn.: The Shoe String Press, 1975), p. 103.

[61]E. B. Long, *The Civil War Day by Day: Almanac, 1861-1865* (Garden City, N. Y.: Doubleday and Company, 1971), pp. 130-53.

[62]Warner, *Generals in Blue*, p. 274.

[63]McClellan, *General McClellan's Reports and Campaigns*, p. 454.

[64]Ibid.

[65]Warner, *Generals in Blue*, p. 274.

[66]U.S. Government, *Report of the Joint Committee on the Conduct of the War*, Part II (Washington, D. C.: U.S. Government Printing Office, 1863), p. 253-57.

[67]Colonel Mark Boatner, *The Civil War Dictionary* (New York: David McKay Company, Inc., 1973), pp. 522-23.

[68]Warner, *Generals in Blue*, p. 289.

[69]McClellan, *General McClellan Reports and Campaigns*, p. 455.

[70]McClellan, *McClellan's Own Story*, pp. 180-81.

[71]Warner, *Generals in Blue*, p. 289.

[72]U.S. Government, *Report of the Joint Committee on the Conduct of the War*, Vol. II, pp. 257-60.

[73]Ibid., p. 261.

[74]Ibid., pp. 261-64.

[75]Warner, *Generals in Blue*, pp. 462-63.

[76]Boatner, *The Civil War Dictionary*, p. 775.

[77]U.S. Government, *Report of the Joint Committee on the Conduct of the War*, Vol. II, pp. 264-65.

[78]Ibid., pp. 253-65.

[79]"The Vindication of General Charles P. Stone," December 1912, an unpublished collection of documents and letters, General Horatio G. Gibson papers, State Historical Society of Wisconsin, Madison, Wisconsin.

[80]U.S. Government, *Joint Committee on the Conduct of the War*, Vol. II, pp. 265-66.

[81]Ibid., p. 266.

[82]Colonel R. Ernest Dupuy and Colonel Trevor N. Dupuy, *The Encyclopedia of Military History: From 3500 B.C. to the Present* (New York: Harper & Brothers, 1977), pp. 62-71, 711-12, 756-59.

[83]U.S. Government, *Joint Committee on the Conduct of the War*, Vol. II, pp. 266-68.

[84]Sandra D. Yoder, "Charles P. Stone and the Battle of Ball's Bluff" (M.A. thesis, The College of William and Mary, 1975), p. 59.

[85]U.S. Government, *Joint Committee on the Conduct of the War*, pp. 268-70.

[86]Ibid., pp. 267-72.

[87]Ibid., p. 270.

[88]Frank Moore, ed., *The Rebellion Record* (New York: Arno Press, 1977): 3:96.

[89]U.S. Government, *Joint Committee on the Conduct of the War*, Vol. II, pp. 270-77.

[90]Bruce Catton, *Terrible Swift Sword* (Garden City, N. Y.: Doubleday and Company, Inc., 1963), pp. 189-90.

[91]U.S. Government, *Joint Committee on the Conduct of the War*, Vol. II, p. 278.

[92]Moore, *The Rebellion Record*, 4:28.

[93]U.S. Government, *Joint Committee on the Conduct of the War*, Vol. II, p. 496.

[94]T. Harry Williams, "The Committee on the Conduct of the War," *American Military Institute* 3 (Fall 1939): 139.

[95]U.S. Government, *Joint Committee on the Conduct of the War*, Vol. II, pp. 278-80.

[96]Yoder, "Charles P. Stone and the Battle of Ball's Bluff," p. 63.

CHAPTER VI

[1]Long, *The Civil War Day by Day: Almanac 1861-1865*, pp. 150-65.

[2]Buel and Johnson, *Battles and Leaders of the Civil War*, Vol. II, p. 120.

[3]Long, *The Civil War Day by Day: Almanac 1861-1865*, pp. 159-60.

[4]Leech, *Reveille in Washington*, pp. 124-25.

[5]Ibid., p. 128.

[6]McClellan, *General McClellan's Reports and Campaigns*, p. 454.

[7]Benjamin F. Wade Papers, Library of Congress, Washington, D. C.

[8]U.S. Government, *Joint Committee on the Conduct of the War*, Vol. II, pp. 283-416.

[9]Robert Todd Lincoln Collection of Abraham Lincoln Papers, Manuscript Division, Library of Congress.

[10]Ibid.

[11]Williams, *Lincoln and the Radicals*, pp. 96-97.

[12]U.S. Government, *Joint Committee on the Conduct of the War*, Vol. II, pp. 331-38.

[13]Ibid., pp. 388-96.

[14]Ibid., pp. 306-18, 403-14.

[15]Ibid., pp. 426-33.

[16]Leech, *Reveille in Washington, pp. 126-27.*

[17]U.S. Government, *Joint Committee on the Conduct of the War*, Vol. II, pp. 428-35, 473-86.

[18]Moore, *The Rebellion Record*, Vol. III, pp. 96-97.

[19]U.S. Government, *Joint Committee on the Conduct of the War*, Vol. II, pp. 435-86.

[20]U.S. Government, *Joint Committee on the Conduct of the War*, Vol. II, pp. 283-426.

[21]Catton, *Mr. Lincoln's Army*, pp. 13-14.

[22]Buel and Johnson, *Battles and Leaders of the Civil War*, Vol. II, pp. 133-34.

[23]Williams, *Lincoln and the Radicals*, p. 99.

[24]Yoder, "Charles P. Stone and the Battle of Ball's Bluff," pp. 56-57, 74.

[25]U.S. Government, *Joint Committee on the Conduct of the War*, Vol. II, p. 433.

[26]Williams, *Lincoln and the Radicals*, p. 101.

[27]Beale, *The Diary of Edward Bates: 1859-1866*, p. 229.

[28]Papers of George Brinton McClellan, Sr., Manuscript Division, Library of Congress, Washington, D. C.

[29]Ibid.

[30]Ibid.

[31]Ibid.

[32]Buel and Johnson, *Battles and Leaders of the Civil War*, Vol. II, p. 134.

[33]Papers of George Brinton McClellan, Sr., Manuscript Division, Library of Congress, Washington, D. C.

[34]Williams, Lincoln and the Radicals, p. 93.

[35]James G. Blaine, *Twenty Years of Congress* (Norwich, Conn.: 1884), 1:385.

[36]James S. Schoff Collection, Clements Library, University of Michigan.

[37]Moore, *The Rebellion Record*, 4:28.

[38]Buel and Johnson, *Battles and Leaders of the Civil War*, Vol. II, p. 133.

[39]Williams, *Lincoln and the Radicals*, p. 101.

⁴⁰Allan Nevins, *The War for the Union: War Becomes Revolution* (New York: Charles Scribner & Sons, 1960), p. 314.

⁴¹Allan Nevins, ed., *The Diary of George Templeton Strong: The Civil War, 1860-1865* (New York: The MacMillan Company, 1962), p. 206.

⁴²David S. Sparks, ed., *Inside Lincoln's Army: The Diary of Marsena R. Patrick, Provost Marshal General, Army of the Potomac* New York: Thomas Yoseloff, 1964), p. 40.

⁴³McClellan, *General McClellan's Reports and Campaigns*, p. 452.

⁴⁴Frederick Wight Papers, Miscellaneous Manuscripts Collection, Manuscript Division, Library of Congress.

⁴⁵Charles P. Stone Appointments, Commissions, and Promotions File, Military Service Branch, Military Archives Division, National Archives and Records Service.

⁴⁶General Charles P. Stone's Appointments, Commissions and Promotion File, Military Service Branch, Military Archives Division, National Archives and Records Service.

⁴⁷U.S. Government, *Report of the Joint Committee on the Conduct of the War*, Vol. II, p. 499.

⁴⁸Letters Received, Adjutant General's Office, File 336 B 1862, Record Group 94, Adjutant General's Office Records, National Archives and Records Service.

⁴⁹Fort Lafayette File, Historical Services Records Branch, Center of Military History, Department of the Army.

⁵⁰Letters Received, Adjutant General's Office, File 336 B 1862, Record Group 94, Adjutant General's Office Records, National Archives and Records Servic e.

⁵¹U.S. Government, *Report of the Joint Committee on the Conduct of the War*, Vol II, p. 499.

⁵²Blaine, *Twenty Years of Congress*, p. 386.

⁵³James C. Schoff Collection, Clements Library, University of Michigan.

⁵⁴Letters Received, Adjutant General's Office, File 336 B 1862, Record Group 94, Adjutant General's Office Records, National Archives and Records Service.

⁵⁵Ibid.

⁵⁶Fort Hamilton File, Historical Services Records Branch, Center of Military History, Department of the Army.

⁵⁷Blaine, *Twenty Years of Congress*, p. 386.

⁵⁸U.S. Government, *Report of the Joint Committee on the Conduct of the War*, Vol. II, pp. 499-500.

⁵⁹Letters Recd, Vol. II, Adj. Gen. Office, File 336 B 1862, Rec Gp 94, Adj. Gen. Off. Rec., National Archives and Records Service.

⁶⁰Ibid.

⁶¹Ibid.

⁶²Ibid.

⁶³Ibid.

⁶⁴Ibid.

⁶⁵Ibid.

⁶⁶Robert Todd Lincoln Collection of Abraham Lincoln Papers, Manuscript Division, Library of Congress.

⁶⁷"The Vindication of General Charles P. Stone," December, 1912, an unpublished collection of documents and letters, General Horatio G. Gibson papers, State Historical Society of Wisconsin, Madison, WI.

⁶⁸Letter of Charles P. Stone to Benson J. Lossing, 5 November 1866, James S. Schoff Collection, Clements Library, University of Michigan.

⁶⁹Abraham Lincoln Papers, Manuscript Division, Library of Congress.

⁷⁰Blaine, *Twenty Years in Congress*, p. 387.

⁷¹*Biographical Directory of the American Congress*, 1774-1971, s.v. "McDougall, James Alexander."

⁷²Botterud, "The Joint Committee on the Conduct of the Civil War: A Summary of Its Major Investigations," p. 51.

⁷³Trefousee, *Benjamin Franklin Wade: Radical Republican from Ohio*, p. 186.

⁷⁴Letters Received, Adjutant General's Office, File 336 B 1862, Record Group 94, Adjutant General's Office Records, National Archives and Records Service.

⁷⁵Trefousse, *Benjamin Franklin Wade: Radical Republican from Ohio*, pp. 185-86.

⁷⁶Docket Cards, Letters Received, Adjutant General's Office, Record Group 94, File 336 B 1862, Adjutant General's Office Records, National Archives and Records Service.

⁷⁷Reports to Congress from the Secretary of War, Record Group 107, Records of the Office of the Secretary of War, National Archives and Records Service.

⁷⁸"The Vindication of General Charles P. Stone," December, 1912, an unpublished collection of documents and letters, General Horatio G. Gibson papers, State Historical Society of Wisconsin, Madison, Wisconsin.

⁷⁹Ibid.

⁸⁰Docket Cards, Letters Received, Adjutant General's Office, Record Group 94, File 336 B 1862, Adjutant General's Office Records, National Archives and Records Service.

⁸¹Yoder, "Charles P. Stone and the Battle of Ball's Bluff," p. 80.

⁸²Ibid.

⁸³U.S. Government, *Joint Committee on the Conduct of the War*, Vol. II, p. 500.

⁸⁴Yoder, "Charles P. Stone and the Battle of Ball's Bluff," p. 80.

⁸⁵Ibid.

CHAPTER VII

¹E. B. Long, *The Civil War Day by Day: An Almanac, 1861-1865* (Garden City, N. Y.: Doubleday and Company, 1971), pp. 168-251.

²Letter of Charles P. Stone to Benson J. Lossing, 5 November 1866, James S. Schoff Collection, Clements Library, University of Michigan.

³Letters Received, Adjutant General's Office, File 336 B 1862, Record Group 94, Adjutant General's Office Records, National Archives and Records Service.

⁴Letters of Charles P. Stone to Benson J. Lossing, 5 November 1866, James S. Schoff Collection, Clements Library, University of Michigan.

⁵Bruce Catton, *Glory Road* (Garden City, N. Y.: Doubleday and Company, Inc., 1954), pp. 164-65.

⁶William Pierson, Jr., "The Committee on the Conduct of the Civil War," *American Historical Review* 23 (April 1918): 570-71.

⁷U.S. Government, *Joint Committee on the Conduct of the War*, Vol. II, p. 486.

⁸Ibid., pp. 486-502.

⁹Ibid., pp. 490-91.

¹⁰Ibid., pp. 486-89, 492-99.

¹¹Ibid., p. 489.

¹²Ibid., pp. 489-92.

¹³Ibid., pp. 499-502.

¹⁴Williams, *Lincoln and the Radicals*, p. 104.

¹⁵U.S. Government, *Joint Committee on the Conduct of the War*, Vol. II, pp. 502-5.

¹⁶Ibid., pp. 506-10.

¹⁷Ibid., pp. 508-9.

¹⁸Ibid., pp. 506-9.

¹⁹Ibid., pp. 507-8.

²⁰Ibid., p. 509.

²¹ Williams, *Lincoln and the Radicals*, p. 96.

²²Ralph Newman, ed., *Lincoln for the Ages*

(New York: Doubleday and Company, 1960), p. 195.

[23]U.S. Government, *Joint Committee on the Conduct of the War,* Vol. II, pp. 509-10.

[24]Ezra Warner, *Generals in Gray* (Baton Rouge: Louisiana State University Press, 1959),pp. 83-84.

[25]Ibid., pp. 83-84.

[26]Robert Krick, *Lee's Colonels* (Dayton, Ohio: Morningside Bookshop, 1979), p. 191.

[27]J. M. Carroll, *List of Staff Officers of the Confederate Army, 1861-1865* (Mattituck, New York: J. M. Carroll and Company), p. 85.

[28]Krick, *Lee's Colonesl,* p. 191.

[29]Colonel Mark Boatner, III. *The Civil War Dictionary* (New York: David McKay, 1959), pp. 419-420.

[30]Warner, *Generals in Blue,* p. 146.

[31]John Divine, *Loudoun County in the Civil War* (Leesburg: Loudoun County Civil War Centennial Commission, 1961), p. 39.

[32]Ibid., p. 49.

[33]Krick, *Lee's Colonels,* pp. 365-366.

[34]*Dictionary of American Biography,* 1964 ed., s.v. "Stanton, Edwin McMasters."

[35]Ibid., "Wade, Benjamin Franklin."

[36]Ibid., "Chandler, Zachariah."

[37]Ibid., "Julian, George Washington."

[38]*Biographical Directory of the American Congress,* 1971 ed., s.v. "Gooch, Daniel Webster."

[39]*Dictionary of American Biography,* 1964 ed., s.v. "Covode, John."

[40]*Biographical Directory of the American Congress,* 1971 ed., s.v. "Odell, Moses Fowler."

[41]*Dictionary of American Biography,* 1964 ed., s.v. "Johnson, Andrew."

[42]*Biographical Directory of the American Congress,* 1971 ed., s.v. "McDougall, James Alexander."

[43]Warner, *Generals in Blue,* pp. 289-90.

[44]Ibid., pp. 290-92.

[45]Ibid., pp. 122-123.

[46]Letters Received, Adjutant General's Office, File 336 B 1862, Record Group 94, Adjutant General's Office Records, National Archives and Records Service.

[47]Docket Cards, Letters Received, Adjutant General's Office, Record Group 94, File 336 B 1862, Adjutant General's Office Records, National Archives and Records Service.

[48]Letters Received, Adjutant General's Office, File 336 B 1862, Record Group 94, Adjutant General's Office Records, National Archives and Records Service.

[49]Lt. Colonel Richard B. Irwin, *History of the Nineteenth Army Corps* (New York: G. P. Putnam & Sons, 1892), p. 220.

[50]Yoder, "Charles P. Stone and the Battle of Ball's Bluff," p. 85.

[51]Boatner, *The Civil War Dictionary,* p. 663.

[52]Charles P. Stone Appointments, Commissions, and Promotions File, Record Group 94, Adjutant General's Office Records, National Archives and Records Service.

[53]Robert Todd Lincoln Collection of Abraham Lincoln Papers, Manuscript Division, Library of Congress.

[54]Charles P. Stone Appointments, Commissions, and Promotions File, Record Group 94, Adjutant General's Office Records, National Archives and Records Service.

[55]Ibid.

[56]Boatner, *The Civil War Dictionary,* p. 800.

[57]Charles P. Stone Appointments, Commissions, and Promotions File, Records Group 94, Adjutant General's Office, National Archives and Records Service.

[58]Ibid.

[59]Ibid.

[60]Boatner, *The Civil War Dictionary,* p. 800.

[61]Charles P. Stone Appointments, Commissions, and Promotions File, Record Group 94, Adjutant General's Office Records, National Archives and Records Service.

[62]Yoder, "Charles P. Stone and the Battle of Ball's Bluff," p. 83.

[63]Ibid., p. 83.

[64]Major General George W. Cullum, *Biographical Register of the Officers and Graduates of the U.S. Military Academy* (Boston: Houghton, Mifflin and Company, 1891), pp. 214-219.

[65]*New York Times,* January 25, 1887.

[66]American Historical Society, *The Cyclopedia of American Biography* (n.p. 1918), pp. 215-216.

[67]Linda Peterson, ed. "She's A Grand Old Lady." *Correspondent,* November/December 1984, pp. 1-6.

[68]Cullum, *Biographical Register of the Officers and Graduates of the U.S. Military Academy,* pp. 214-219.

[69]Ibid., pp. 214-219.

BATTLEFIELD CHRONICLE

[1]History Committee, *History of the 19th Regiment Massachusetts Volunteer Infantry, 1861-1865.* Salem, Massachusetts: Salem Press, 1906, p. 25-29.

[2]Pennsylvania State Archives.

[3]U.S., National Archives and Record Services, Navy and Old Army Branch, Quartermaster General of 1865.

[4]U.S., National Archives and Record Services, Navy and Old Army Branch, Quartermaster General Report of 1884.

[5]U.S., 42nd Congress—2nd Session, Executive Document #79, Letter from the Secretary of War dated 1 May 1872.

[6]U.S., National Archives and Record Services, Navy and Old Army Branch, Inspector General Report of 1884.

[7]U.S., Veterans Administration, Cemetery Services Office, Ball's Bluff National Cemetery File.

[8]U.S., National Archives and Record Services, Navy and Old Army Branch, Inspector General Report of 1908.

[9]U.S., National Archives and Record Services, Navy and Old Army Branch, Inspector General Report of 1908.

[10]U.S., National Archives and Record Services, Navy and Old Army Branch, Inspector General Report of 1916.

[11]"An Almost Forgotten Battlefield Near Washington—Ball's Bluff, Along Potomac, Where Federals Suffered Heavy Loss." *Washington Star,* 10 September 1933, p. unknown.

[12]U.S., National Archives and Record Services, Modern Miliary Branch, Inspector General Report of 1938.

[13]U.S. Veterans Administration, Cemetery Services Office, Ball's Bluff National Cemetery File.

[14]"The Hallowed Ground," *Loudoun Times-Mirror.* 3 April 1958, p. Editorial page.

[15]"Rites Mark Milestone of Ball's Bluff Battle." *Washington Star,* 22 October 1961, p. unknown.

[16] Personal knowledge of the Author.

[17]"Civil War Buff Girds to Fight Second Battle of Ball's Bluff." *The Washington Post,* 5 October 1981, p. B-6.

[18]"Ceremony in Leesburg Marks Ball's Bluff Acceptance as National Landmark." *Loudoun Times-Mirror,* 23 August 1984, p. A-8.

Index

Adams, Charles H., 46
Alexandria, 12, 14, 15, 17, 110
Andrew, John, 95, 96
Aqueduct bridge, 91
Austrian musket, 31

Baker, Edward, 18, 34, 35, 37, 47, 48, 51, 56, 62, 63, 64, 66, 95
Ball, William, 38, 41
Ball's Bluff, 24, 26-35, 47, 48, 51, 63, 70, 72, 85, 95, 98, 102, 148
Ball's Mill, 28, 111
Banks, Nathaniel, 22, 82, 85, 132
Barksdale, William, 54, 83
Bartlett, William F., 55, 66, 69, 75
Bates, Joseph, 78
Beckenbaugh, John, 78
Berkeley, Charles, 76, 77
Bieral, Capt., 66
Big Spring, 28, 30
Bowman, Henry, 40
Bradley, Joseph, 118, 121
Brady, James, 108
Bramhall, 44, 46, 47, 48, 50, 52, 55, 62, 63
Buchanan, President, 10, 11, 92
Burnt Bridge, 27, 41, 42
Burt, Erasmus R., 54, 59, 60, 62

C & O Canal, 24, 47, 83, 153
Cameron, Simon, 92, 104
Campbell, Capt., 38
Capitol building, 7, 13
Cart path, 48, 60, 68
Centennial, 144
Chain Bridge, 13
Chandler, Zachariah, 90, 92, 93, 107, 126, 129, 131
Cogswell, Milton, 44, 50, 58, 63, 64, 66, 82, 110

Commanches, 59, 130
Conkling, Roscoe, 104, 105, 108
Conrad's Ferry, 17, 26, 28, 44, 83
Corps of Observation, 17, 18, 47, 95, 99
Covode, John, 90, 92, 120, 131

Daily house, 54, 58
Derby, Richard, 40
Devens, Charles, 27, 28, 30, 31, 33, 42, 43, 48, 66, 72, 76, 109, 132
Dimmick, J. 104, 108
Dranesville, 21, 22, 23, 24, 27, 100, 101, 128
Duff, William, 28, 31, 37, 38, 50

Eager, Charles H., 72
Eames, Walter A., 72, 74
Eckford, Capt., 86
Edward's Ferry, 17, 23, 24, 27, 35, 52, 54, 66, 79, 83, 86, 99, 102, 128
Evans, Fort, 20, 35, 37, 50, 51, 76
Evans, Nathan B., 21, 22, 23, 27, 37, 41, 51, 52, 54, 55, 130

Featherston, Winfield Scott, 54, 62, 69, 70
Fletcher, Capt., 35
French, Lt., 48, 55, 59
Friction primer, 61

Georgetown, 13, 91
Georgetown Pike, 21
Gooch, Daniel, 90, 92, 94, 131
Goose Creek, 35, 52, 110
Gorman, Willis A., 20, 23, 24, 35, 52, 79, 81, 83, 86, 114
Griffin, T. M., 62
Gum Springs Road, 110

Hamilton, Fort, 115, 117, 124
Harper's Ferry, 17, 153
Harrison's Island, 24, 27, 28, 33, 34, 44, 46, 47, 50, 69, 72, 74, 79, 85, 106, 110
Harvey, Col., 22
Hatcher, Clinton, 68, 69, 148
Hinks, Col., 110, 138
Hooker, Joseph, 125
Howe, Church, 26, 28, 31, 33, 34, 102, 105, 107, 109
Hunton, Eppa, 42, 48, 52, 56, 58, 59, 130

Inauguration, Lincoln's, 7, 8, 10, 14, 82, 95, 104, 121

Jackson house, 30, 31, 33, 42, 43, 44
Jennifer, Col., 37, 38, 41, 42, 50, 64, 130
Johnson, Andrew, 90, 92, 94, 131
Johnson, Fort, 109, 110
Johnston, Joseph E., 21, 23, 24
Joint Congressional Committee on the Conduct of the War, 90, 92, 95, 99, 100, 104, 109, 110, 111, 126, 130
Julian, George Washington, 90, 92, 94, 131

Kephart's Mill, 86

Lafayette, Fort, 109, 112, 114, 115, 116, 124
Lander, Frederick, 18, 88, 99, 101
Langley, Va., 100
Lee, William R., 31, 42, 46, 48, 63, 66, 82, 96, 110
Leesburg, 18, 20-23, 35, 100, 129, 146

165

Leesburg Turnpike, 23, 24, 27, 35, 37, 38, 52
Libby Prison, 108
Lincoln, Abraham, 7, 9, 10, 14, 82, 95, 99, 104, 121
Loudoun County, 146
Loudoun Court House, 147
Loudoun Museum, 146, 149

Manassas, 6, 8, 20, 21, 23, 55, 98, 101
Marshall Hotel, 14
Masked battery, 36, 52, 55, 56, 102, 129
Mason's Island, 28, 111
McCall, George A., 21-24, 27, 100, 128, 132
McClellan, George B., 6, 16, 19, 20, 21, 82, 95, 96, 98, 104, 111, 122, 129, 130, 132
McDougall, Sen., 119, 120, 131
McGriffen, Thomas, 70
McGuirk, John, 69
McPherson, Capt., 50
Meade, George G., 21, 27
Meade, W. W., 38
Mexican War, 6, 95, 100
Mix, Major, 35, 36, 52

National Cemetery, 69, 141, 142, 143, 150
National Park Service, 136
Noland's Ferry, 18

Odell, Moses, 90, 92, 131

Philbrick, Chase, 24, 26, 27, 33, 102, 145
Pinkerton, Allan J., 10, 111, 112
Poolesville, Md., 18, 22, 83, 99, 101
Potomac River, 13, 15, 16, 17, 22, 24, 27, 34, 44, 46, 60, 69, 74, 79, 106

Radical Republicans, 35, 90, 92, 95, 98, 102, 125, 129
Revere, Paul, 44, 110
Rifles, National, 8
Rockville Expedition, 17

Scott, Winfield, 8, 9, 10, 17
Seneca, Md., 18, 37
Seward, Sec. of War, 128, 129
Shorbs, James, 111, 112
Shrapnel, 61
Slave, fugitive, 95, 97, 102, 103
Sloan, Capt., 48
Smart's Mill Ford, 24, 26, 28, 31, 33, 47, 64, 75, 102
Smith, William F., 101
Stanton, Edwin M., 92, 95, 104, 109, 111, 112, 114, 128, 131
Statue of Liberty, 134, 135
Stephen's House, 30
Stewart, Capt., 52, 63
Stone, Charles Pomeroy, 6, 8-13, 17-20, 23, 24, 35, 47, 82, 95, 96, 97, 98, 102, 109, 114, 115, 121, 122, 123, 132, 135
Stuart's Mill, 28, 30
Studley, Capt., 48
Sugar Loaf Mtn., 22
Sumner, Charles, 97, 98
Sykes, George, 112, 113, 124

Telegraph, 12
Trent Affair, 99, 104
Trundle house, 38

United States Military Academy, 6, 100, 107

Van Alen (cavalry), 18, 35, 52, 55, 110, 111
Vaughn, Capt., 138

Wade, Benjamin, 90, 92, 93, 107, 109, 119, 126, 131
Ward, George, 28, 31, 33, 42, 82
Washington, D. C., 7, 8, 9, 17
Washington, Fort, 11
Washington Monument, 123
Welborn, Capt., 38
White, Elija V., 59, 76, 77, 130, 148
Willard's hotel, 10, 11, 112
Wistar, Isaac J., 48, 50, 55, 56, 58, 109
Worthington, Capt., 55

Young, Francis G., 64, 105, 106, 107, 109, 110

Addendum

Above, Colonel Edward D. Baker.

Below, a waist belt picked up by a soldier of the 8th Virginia Infantry from the battlefield of Ball's Bluff the day of the battle. The artifact has been passed down through the soldier's family, who believe it to have belonged to Colonel Baker. Courtesy Dick Hammond.

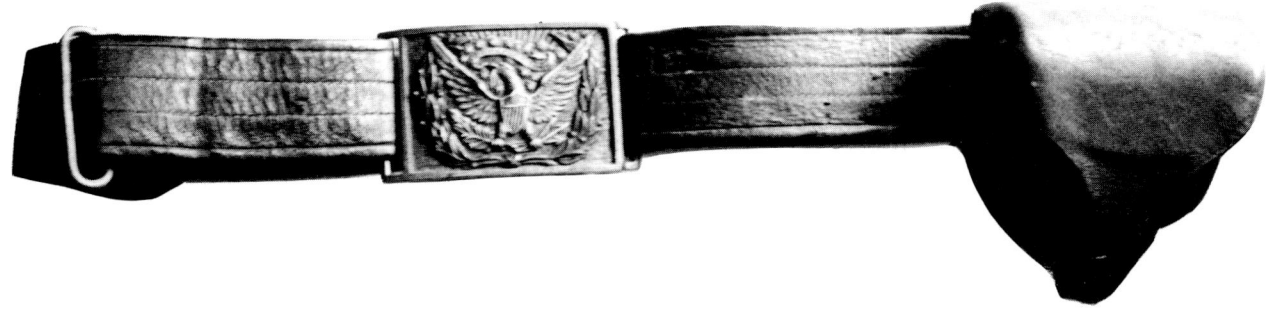

I

Changes and Additions at the Battlefield

The Northern Virginia Regional Park Authority

Ball's Bluff Battlefield is administered by the Northern Virginia Regional Park Authority (5400 Ox Road, Fairfax Station, Virginia 22039). Additional Civil War sites—although not necessarily marked as such—administered by the Park Authority are Upton Hill, Bull Run Marina, Fountainhead Regional, Hemlock Overlook, Washington & Old Dominion Railroad, Carlyle House, Red Rock Regional Park and Bull Run Regional Park.

The Northern Virginia Regional Park Authority was founded in 1959 to acquire parkland for the rapidly developing region of Northern Virginia. This far-sighted move encompassed the governments of Arlington County, Loudoun County, Fairfax County, and the independent cities of Falls Church and Alexandria. As of 1995 the Park Authority had 11,000+ acres that it managed for the citizens of Northern Virginia.

On April 27, 1984, the Veterans Administration and the Beus Corporation formally turned over to the Park Authority those parcels of the Ball's Bluff battlefield that they held. This move was heralded by a major celebration/ceremony at Leesburg, Virginia. Following the ceremony the National Park Service (NPS)—using the author's master's thesis as a basis—developed a 1986 Master Plan for the battlefield to encompass "Long-range Goals on the Potomac." They projected 75,000 visitors per year and expansion of the battlefield to 150.7 acres. They further proposed a fifty-person picnic area and the continuous presence of park staff. Two information gazebos were needed at a cost of $80,000, the "Cleared Field" was to be returned to its battle condition at a cost of $140,000, restoration of the cart path was estimated to be $11,000, and installation of the three missing cannon (albeit reproductions), $62,000. The NPS also recommended hiking trails, which the Park Authority is currently working on, but unfortunately did not see the need for a permanent Visitor Center—something that any battlefield visitor could have told them was a definite plus for understanding the battle.

125th Anniversary Celebration Brings Ball's Bluff to the Nation's Attention

In October 1988, the 125th anniversary reenactment of the Battle of Ball's Bluff was held at Ida

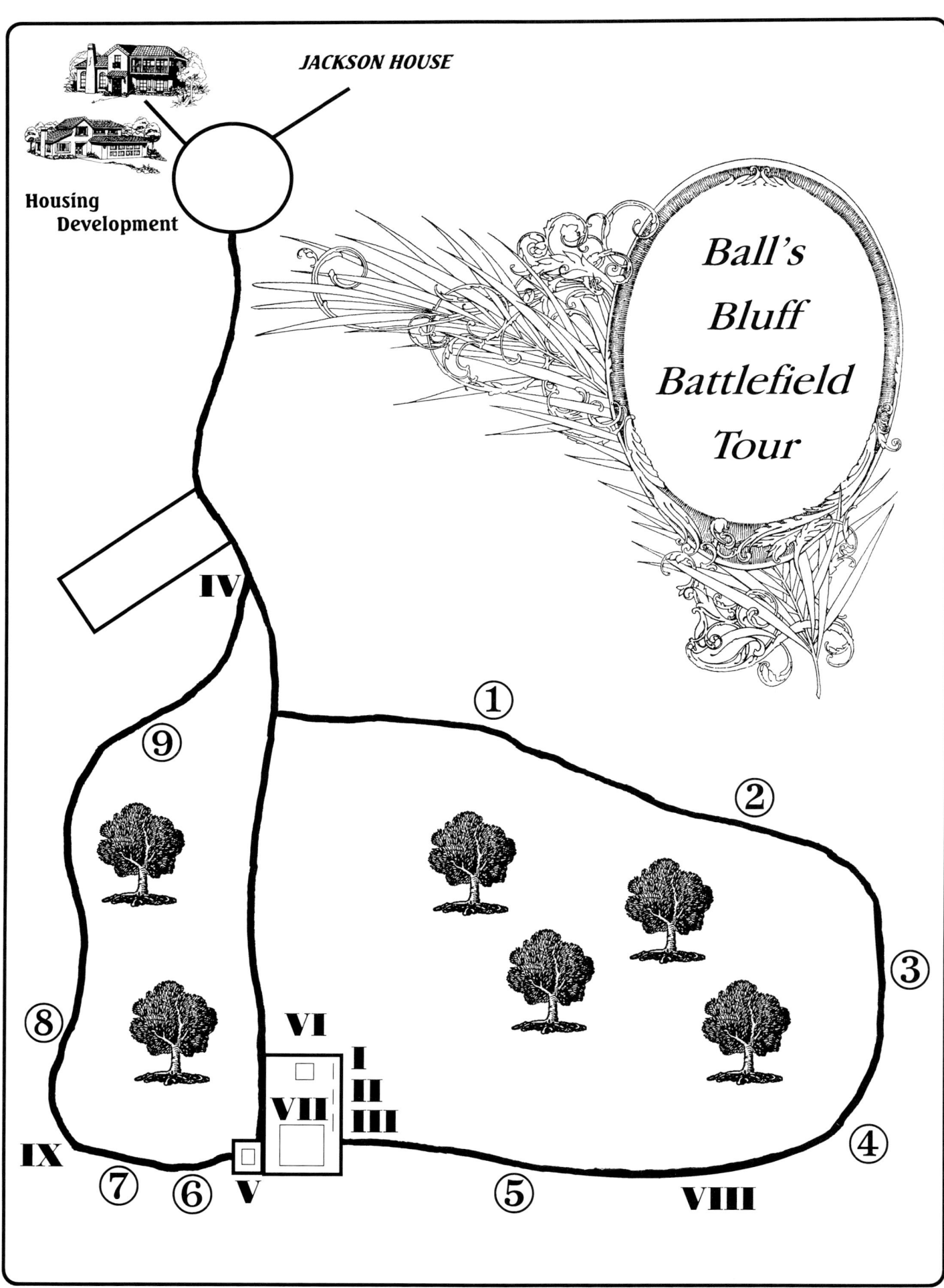

Trail Signs

1. The Battle at Ball's Bluff*
2. 8th Virginia Infantry*
3. Jennifer's Virginia Cavalry*
4. Union Artillery*
5. 20th Massachusetts Infantry*
6. 42nd New York Infantry*
7. 15th Massachusetts Infantry*
8. 18th Mississippi Infantry*
9. 17th Mississippi Infantry*

Interpretive Signs

I   A Divided American, a Divided Loudoun County
II   The Battle at Ball's Bluff
III   Aftermath of Ball's Bluff
IV   Confederate Leaders*
V   Colonel Baker Memorial Stone*
VI   Clinton Hatcher Memorial Stone*
VII   Ball's Bluff National Cemetery*
VIII   Union Leaders*
IX   Attempted Breakout to Edward's Ferry*

* Projected for completion in 1995

New interpretive signs at Ball's Bluff

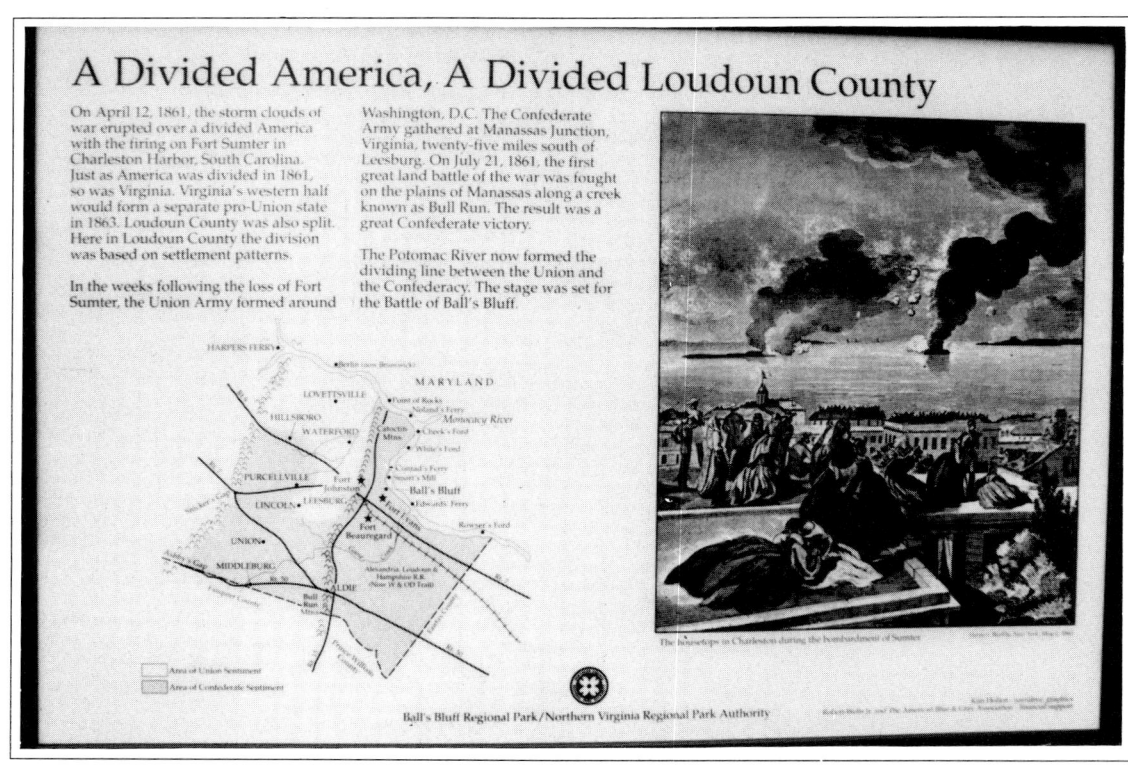

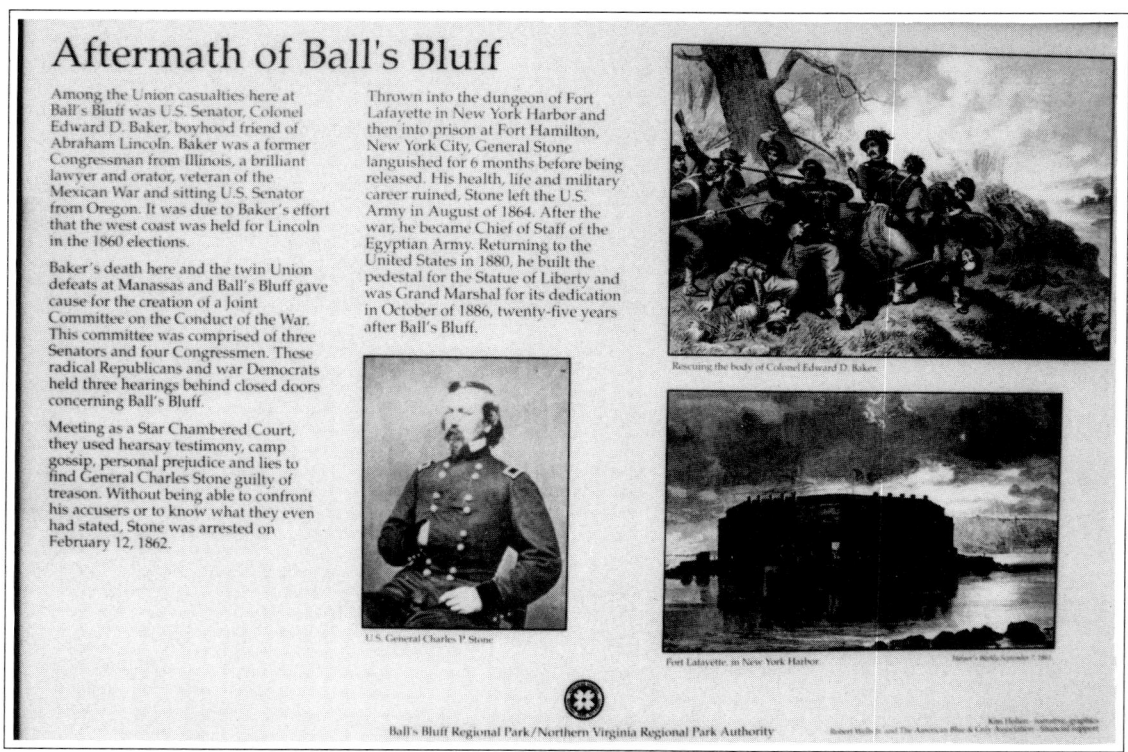

Above, two of the interpretive signs at the cemetery. Text, maps, and illustrations were provided by the author and the construction was paid for by the Blue and Gray Association.

Lee Park outside Leesburg with the ceremonies at the battlefield proper. Some 500 reenactors participated in the battle, which was viewed by some 5,000 spectators. There was even an entire busload of school children from Nantucket, Massachusetts, which had provided a company for the 15th Massachusetts Infantry Regiment. The reenactment was held by Napoleonic Tactics, Inc., and narrated by the author of this book.

Following the event, the National Archives and Records Administration took a serious interest in the Ball's Bluff battlefield. In their master teaching packet entitled *The Civil War: Soldiers and Civilians* (1990), they included Ball's Bluff as their Civil War selection. This valuable teaching aid includes maps of the Ball's Bluff region and five letters by participants in the battle itself.

By 1992 the Northern Virginia Regional Park Authority was moving to historically develop the Ball's Bluff battlefield. They constructed both an upper loop historical trail and a lower loop historical trail. The old road (Virginia Route 837) to the cemetery was closed off and a new parking lot was built. Access to the Ball's Bluff battlefield is now via the newly constructed Battlefield Parkway and Ball's Bluff Road.

Three major interpretative signs were designed and built at the cemetery. The text, maps and illustrations were provided by the author at no cost; the physical construction was paid for by the Blue and Gray Association. These interpretative signs are titled:

(1) "A Divided America, A Divided Loudoun County";
(2) "Battle at Ball's Bluff, October 21, 1861"; and
(3) "Aftermath of Ball's Bluff."

Four small interpretative trail markers were also installed to show the location of various regiments during the battle.

In June 1993, a rededication of the Ball's Bluff Regional Park took place. The featured speaker was the Honorable Frank Wolf, congressman for the 8th US Congressional District of Virginia. Congressman Wolf is known to all Civil War historians as a strong supporter of the preservation of these sacred battlefields. Following Congressman Wolf's words, a significant historical address was given by Mr. John Divine of Leesburg, whose tireless efforts have done so much to preserve Ball's Bluff and the Civil War heritage of Loudoun County in general.

Above, John Divine, whose ancestors include soldiers from both North and South, speaks at the June 19, 1993, rededication of the Ball's Bluff Regional Park. Also speaking that summer day was the Honorable Frank Wolf, staunch preservationist and congressman for the 8th U.S. Congressional District of Virginia.

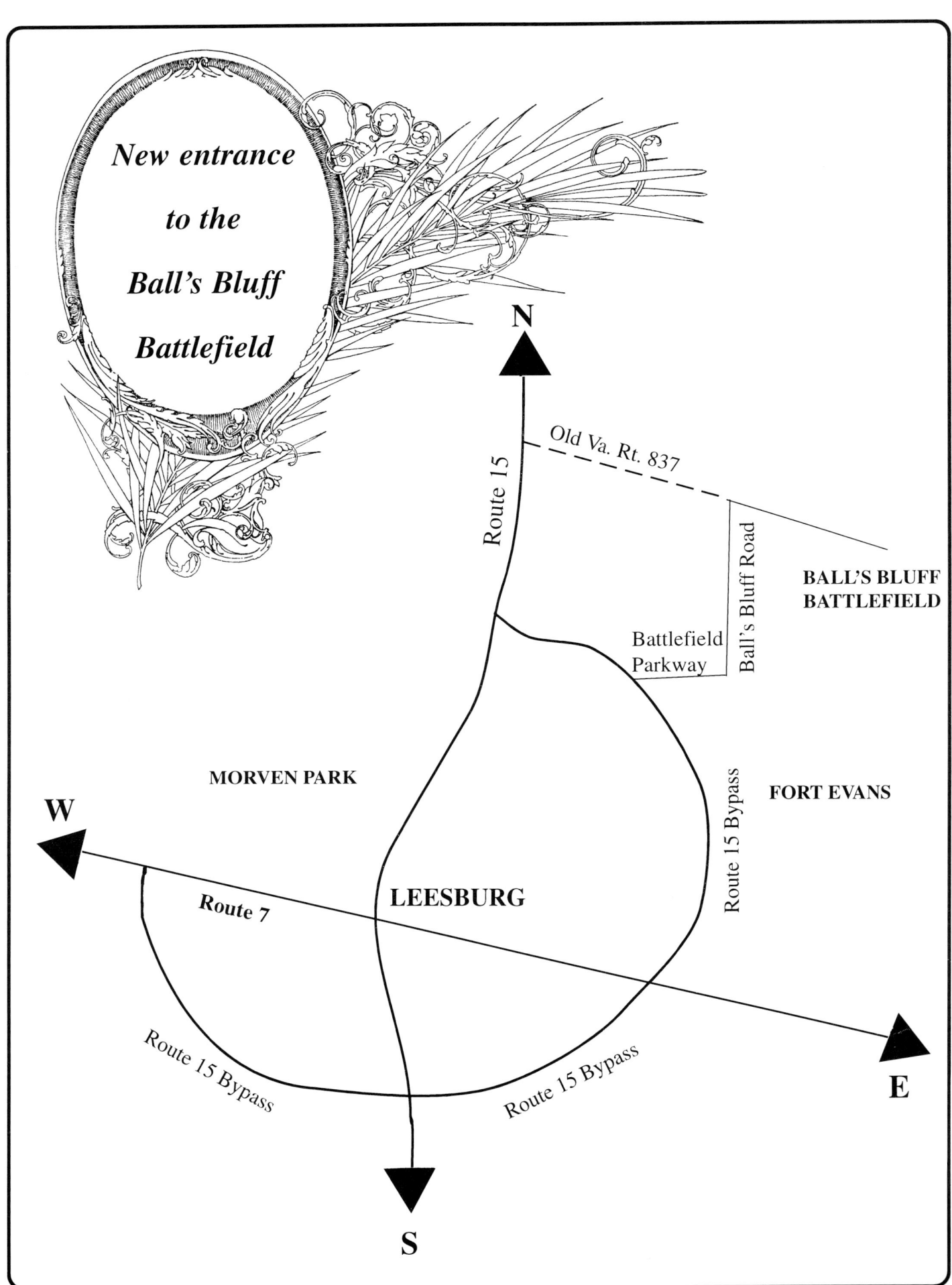

Unfortunately, major vandalism took place in December of 1994 with the desecration of the United States soldier's grave in the National Cemetery atop Ball's Bluff. The perpetrator of this heinous act was looking for a Pennsylvania belt buckle. Obviously such criminals deserve the total contempt of all citizens of the Republic.

By 1995 the United States Army had recognized the historical importance of Ball's Bluff as a location for Army staff rides. The US Army Reserve Components Computer Training Center at Fort Belvoir was the first there in January, and they were followed by the US Army Center of Military History of Washington, DC.

New Signs Planned for Ball's Bluff

The Northern Virginia Regional Park Authority is currently planning six more major interpretative sign boards to be placed at strategic locations on the battlefield. These will be:
(1) Confederate leaders (located at the parking lot),
(2) Union leaders (located on the upper river overlook),
(3) the Cemetery,
(4) Colonel/Senator Baker (located at his stone marker),
(5) Clinton Hatcher (located at the Clinton Hatcher Monument), and
(6) the attempted breakout to Edward's Ferry.

Further, small interpretative trail signs to be constructed are for the:
(1) 17th Mississippi Infantry,
(2) 18th Mississippi Infantry,
(3) 20th Massachusetts Infantry,
(4) 15th Massachusetts Infantry, and
(5) 8th Virginia Infantry; also,
(6) one for The Battle at Ball's Bluff.

Currently located on the battlefield are three bronze markers noting the contributions of Judge Hanum in preserving the battlefield, the Northern Virginia Regional Park Authority's establishment of the Ball's Bluff battlefield, and the National Historic Landmark status of Ball's Bluff battlefield. The Regional Park Authority plans to restore the bronze marker on the National Cemetery gate.

In addition, benches, visitor overlooks, a safety fence along the bluff, clearance of more trails and of the "Cleared Field," and a new visitor's brochure are under way as this newly revised edition of *Battle at Ball's Bluff* goes to press.

Kim Bernard Holien
March 1995

II

Pictorial Supplement

Left, Surgeon Justin Dwinelle, who served as assistant surgeon for the 1st California Regiment in mid-1861, then as surgeon for the 5th California and the 106th Pennsylvania Regiment as the war ground on. (The 106th Pennsylvania was known as the 5th California before the Battle of Ball's Bluff.) He was surgeon in charge of the Union 2nd Corps hospitals until the position was eliminated in April 1864.

Dwinelle was surgeon on General Baker's staff when Baker was killed at Ball's Bluff, and treated Lieutenant Colonel Wistar's arm during the battle.

This photograph was taken at the Brady Portrait Gallery in New York City circa 1861-'62 and appears courtesy descendant Scott M. Dwinelle. The family is still in posession of many papers pertaining to Surgeon Dwinelle's service records, and they are currently housed at The Virginia Historical Society in Richmond, Virginia.

Opposite, a professional cartographic rendition of the Battle of Ball's Bluff drawn by a Union soldier who fought there.

View of the Battleground at Ball's Bluff

Camp Benton. Edwards Ferry.
Head Quarters. 19th Regt. Mass Vol.
Friday. Oct. 25th 1861.
Dear Mother. Sisters & Brothers

...
all w...
the but dest is
right in good con...
who helped to ma...
Bertha Buckli...
Mrs Cheever f...
of us, tell them w...
are glad to be rem...
Charles no need
to ...ve. got enou...
had hardly time
Sunday. before
for battle. our c...
river opposite ...
the Regt stati...
the river from ...
12 O clock Sun...

Camp Benton. Maryland.
Head Quarters 19th Mass. Vol.
Wednesday. Oct. 30th
Dear Mother & Sisters.
we received your letter
last night and thought we
would write a few lines to you
to let you know how we are. glad you
received the money we sent you. will send you thirty
five or forty dollars in a about a fortnight. our pay
rolls are made out. I helped to make ours out. we are
glad Hannah has work and Andrew & Dave's
have Dave move up home this winter. it wants somebody there to look after things. we are going to send
money home this winter and what you dont want
you can keep to fix the house up next summer.
tell Dave to stay at home and look out for things
at home and we will send home money so he can fix
the house in the summer. the battle of Monday
Seems to throw a gloom over our troops about here.
our loss is mostly known now. it is considerable
in killed. wounded & prisoners especially among the
officers. Col. Lee formerly Superintendent
(of the 20th)

A soldier of the 19th Massachusetts describes Baker's death at Ball's Bluff

Camp Benton, Maryland.
Wednesday, Oct. 30

Dear Mother and Sisters,

We received your letter last night and thought we would write a few lines to you to let you know how we are. Glad you received the money we sent you. Will send you thirty-five or forty dollars in about a fortnight. Our pay rolls are made out. I helped to make ours out.

We are glad Hannah has work and Andrew and Dave. Have Dave move up home this winter. It wants someone there to look after things. We are going to send money home this winter and what you don't want you can keep to fit the house up next summer. Tell Dave to stay at home and look out for things and we will send home money so he can fix the house in the summer.

The battle of Monday seems to throw a gloom over our troops about here. Our loss is mostly known now. It is considerable in killed, wounded and prisoners, especially among the officers. Col. Lee of the 20th, formerly superintendent of the Boston and Providence railroad, is a prisoner and Col. Devans of the 15th is supposed to be dead. The death of Baker throws a gloom over all. I was in the boat that brought his body over to the island. The officers that came in the boat with his body did not wish his death to be known at once and said it was the body of a captain. I knew better as I was standing on a high ledge of rocks on the Virginia shore waiting for a load of wounded and saw him fall. Baltimore papers say he was helping to get a field piece into position and had his shoulder to the wheel of the gun carriage when he fell. That is not so. While the right flank of our troops seemed to be in some confusion owing to a severe fire from the enemy in that direction and while Col. Baker's attention was drawn to that quarter I saw an officer on a horse who appeared to be dressed in our uniform approach to within a few yards of our men and dismount and get behind a tree. Then he went within about a rod of where Baker was standing. I suppose our men took him for one of our own officers. Suddenly he stepped close to Baker and shot him with a revolver. The one who shot him was shot by one of our officers who stepped close to him and shot him through the head as he was taking Baker's sword.

The papers also state that we have thirty thousand men on the other side and that we hold Leesburg. We haven't a man in Leesburg nor a thousand on the Virginia side.

Altogether we had four hour's notice to leave the island Tuesday night. Jake and I were on guard night before last. We were together, he on one post and I on the other next to him. It was rather cold and we had a good fire that we sat by our two hours. We made coffee and had some biscuits and butter. We sat there two hours talking about old times at home. About Aunt Sallie's party that Jake and Augusta Scampleton went to without an invitation as Aunt Sallie said. Jake said he wished you could see us there that night and said he would draw a picture of us and send

"I knew better as I was standing on a high ledge of rocks on the Virginia shore waiting for a load of wounded and saw him fall."

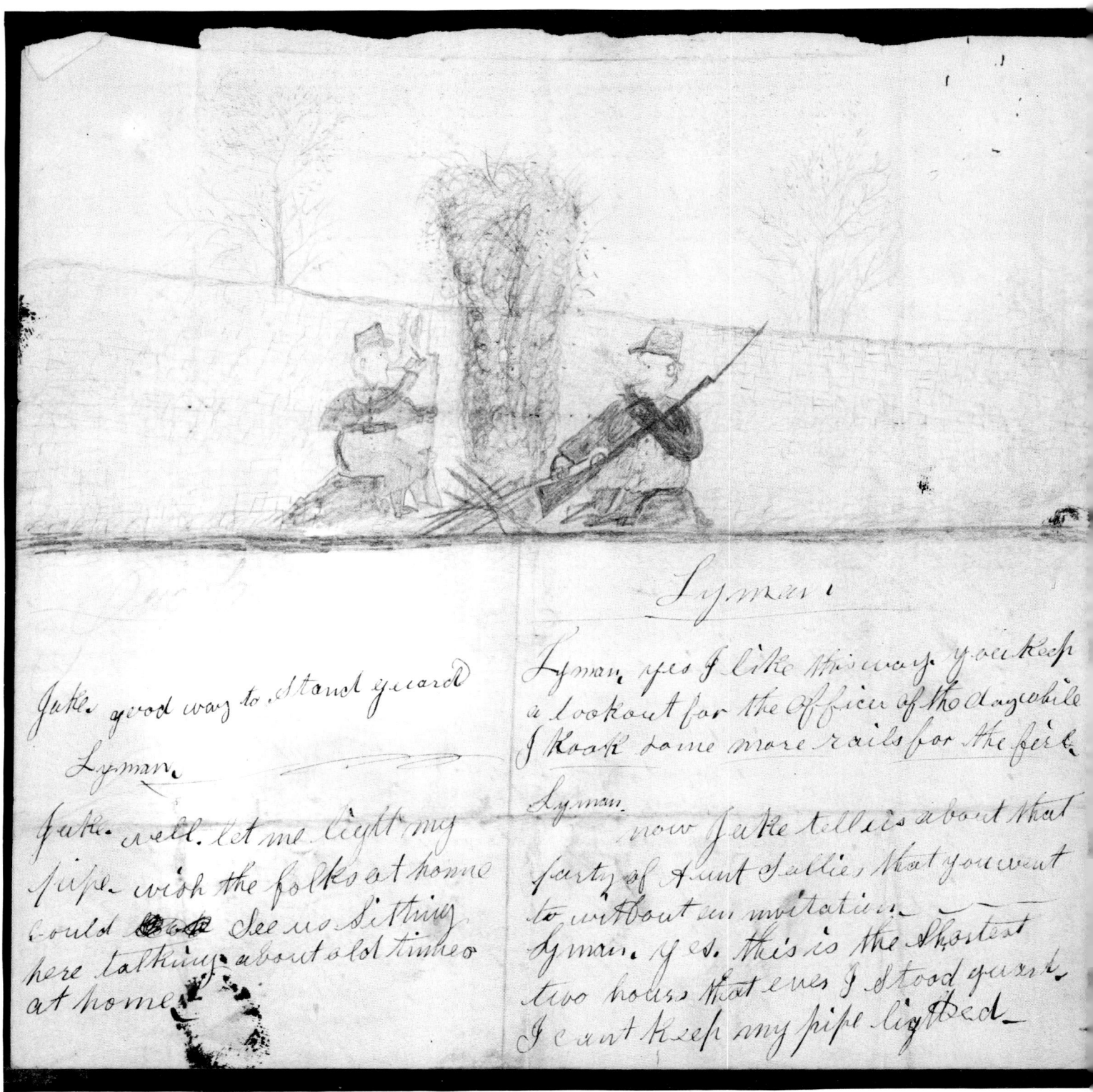

Lyman had his comrade-in-arms Jake show his artistic flair in this depiction of the two standing—or rather sitting—guard the week after the battle. In this light-hearted look, Jake's primary duties are to keep an eye out for the officer of the day and keep the fire going; Lyman's is to keep his pipe lit.

you. You can see us up against the wall, the fire between us. We are supposed to be smoking and telling yarns. Now, that black line across the paper is our beats that we have to walk. Mine is the right hand one and the other Jake's. How we walk our beats! That night we sat by the fire and did not walk the beats twice the whole two hours. I will bet you will say it looks just like us.

It is getting colder here now. Plenty of frost nights. We don't know yet where we shall make our winter quarters. Some say at Washington, some, here where we are. If we do stay here we are going to get an army stove for our tent. It will be so comfortable this winter to have a fire to sit by. We can get one for five dollars, about a dollar for each one in the tent.

There is not much hopes of fighting for the 19th just now. I have picked out the house in Leesburg that I am going to have for my winter quarters. Generals Scott, McClellen and myself don't give up all hopes yet of crossing the Potomac and staying in Virginia this winter.

Goodbye. Write us soon and tell us if Dave will move up there this winter.

Lyman

P.S. I think we will be paid next week up to the first of November.

Friday we are going to be inspected by the commanding general of our division, Stone. Yesterday when we were drawn up in line for dress parade which takes place every night at dark, Col. Hinks complimented Private Lyman Blackington for going across the river the night after the fight and for bringing over the ten men who would otherwise have been taken prisoners in ten minutes afterwards. The Col. almost flattered me by saying it was the bravest thing that has been done by any one of the 19th regiment yet. It was God's hand that saved me that night. I went the third time after a load and hunted around sometime after them. There is an old mill close to where I landed. I went to the door of it and made a noise to see if any of our men where hid in it. Our 2d Lieutenant called me back then. Ten minutes after that about thirty rebel cavalry came galloping up to the mill and searched the mill with lights to see if any of our men where in there. Lucky the Lieutenant called me back as he did, isn't it?

I had his revolver with me and had the gentlemen arrived before I left the mill they might have had the satisfaction of taking my dead body, but never would they have taken me alive. You may hear of my being killed any time, but never of my being taken prisoner alive if I can raise an arm to prevent it.

Goodbye,

Lyman

"It was god's hand that saved me that night . . . Lucky the Lieutenant called me back as he did, isn't it?."

About the author

Kim Bernard Holien has been a professional military historian specializing in the Civil War at the Center of Military History, Department of the Army, since 1979. As such, he served as the historian for the MacArthur and ANZUS (Treaty) Corridors in the Pentagon. From 1986 to 1989, he was the civilian Civil War hisorian for staff rides to various Civil War battlefields for the secretary of the army, the chief of staff of the army, and the army staff in the Pentagon. For these and many other historical projects, he received recognition from President Ronald Reagan; Secretary of Defense Casper Weinberger; Secretary of the Army John O. Marsh, Jr.; the chief of staff of the army; the commanding general, US Army Materiel Command; the chief of military history; the ambassador of Australia; and the Royal Norwegian Embassy.

Active in Civil War living history since 1961, Mr. Holien was an officer in the First North-South Brigade from 1974 to 1984 and narrated the 125th anniversary reenactments of the battles of Manassas, Ball's Bluff, Gettysburg, New Market, and Monocacy.

He is past president of both the Alexandria, Virginia, and District of Columbia Civil War Round Tables, a former director (1979-1981 and 1983-1984) of the board of the Northern Virginia Association of Historians, and a founder of the Friends of Fort Ward, for which he currently serves on the board of directors.

A descendant of both Union and Confederate soldiers, he is the recipient of the Sons of Confederate Veterans and Sons of Union Veterans Commander-in-Chief's Awards. Mr. Holien is listed in Outstanding Young Men of America (1981), Who's Who in the South and Southwest, and Who's Who in the World.

A recognized Civil War tour leader, he has given over a hundred presentations about the Civil War in the mid-Atlantic region. For his work on staff rides to the Gettysburg Battlefield, Mr. Holien received the US Army Civilian Achievement Award.

Works-in-progress include several volumes dealing with the War Between the States.